Stacey Marden

Stacey Marden

Letter Perfect

Letter Perfect

A Business Person's Guide to
More Effective Correspondence

Abraham Ellenbogen

COLLIER BOOKS
A Division of Macmillan Publishing Co., Inc.
New York

COLLIER MACMILLAN PUBLISHERS
London

Macmillan Publishing Co., Inc.
866 Third Avenue, New York, N.Y. 10022
Collier Macmillan Canada, Ltd.

Library of Congress Cataloging in Publication Data
Ellenbogen, Abraham.
    Letter perfect.
    Published in 1963 under title: The Collier quick and easy guide to business letter writing.
    1. Commercial correspondence. I. Title.
HF5726.E46 1978   651.7′5   78-17700
ISBN 0-02-079940-3

Letter Perfect is a revised and updated edition of *The Collier Quick and Easy Guide to Business Letter Writing.*

First Printing 1978

Printed in the United States of America

Contents

Foreword

Since the first edition of this book was written, the business office has seen a revolutionary change, mainly in the equipment used. As a result of the electronic wonders coming out of space technology, computers and typewriters with memories are now in common use for the automatic reproduction of information and correspondence. At the same time, the *relative* cost of telephone and telegraphic communications has come down. In keeping with the rapid pace of American business today, all of these developments have speeded business decisions and rhythms. As a result, there is a subtle change in the nature of business letters.

It is becoming more difficult for a business to reach all of its customers in person or by telephone or teletypewriter. Therefore, it is even more important that business correspondence convince the customer or prospective customer that the communication is personal and direct, not "canned."

And there is the continuing challenge to make all business letters selling letters. Whether they inform, question, convince, or present knowledge, they always represent you and your company and can be expertly composed to accomplish this purpose. You can do so with the aid of some simple rules and a little practice.

Reducing Letter Costs

Management consultants have been trying for decades to determine the cost of a single average letter. Since 1938 the figures have risen from 88 cents to over $4. This amount includes the time required to dictate and transcribe and allows for interruptions, fixed costs, costs of materials, mail procedures and postage, and filing and storing of carbon copies. In most of these many changes have occurred: dictators use recording equipment, photocopy machines make instant copies, electric typewriters have progressed, correction techniques have improved, storage and retrieval have changed, inserting and folding machines are more common, postage meters are in general use. The operation has become more technical and complex in a way.

Costs can be cut, however, by attention to the suggestions included in this book. Those who need to can improve their method of dictation and preparation for dictation. More skillful stenographers can be hired; their wages will be slightly higher, but their production will be greater and of better quality. If the office needs are broad enough, a word-processing center can be installed, thereby substantially increasing the flow and lowering the unit cost. Any or all of the modern equipment discussed in this book should be seriously considered: copy machines, automatic typewriters, typewriters with memory, duplicating machines, form letters and post cards, centralized files, computerized files, sealing and stamping machines, microfilming, mag card machines, good filing systems, teleprinters, direct lines, WATS line, and so on. Last, but most important, write only those letters which are necessary; whenever possible, substitute form replies, especially when the purpose is only to acknowledge, thank, or inform.

Letter Perfect

Chapter 1

The ABCD of Good Letter Writing

IN THE WRITING of letters, it is wise to address the correspondent as you would someone with whom you are having a long-distance telephone conversation. You cannot see him; he cannot see you. You address yourself directly to him. You do not ramble on, because the rates are high. You use your words sparingly and meaningfully. The ABCD of good letter writing is:

Accuracy. Be accurate in what you say in a business letter. Nothing annoys a customer more than to be written to about a bill already paid, an amount owed but incorrectly referred to, or an item placed in his account in error. An incorrect amount quoted in a letter can be very costly. If the sum in question is very low, the customer may hold you to it with a subsequent loss to you. If it is too high, it will undoubtedly lose you a customer. If it is an amount owed but incorrectly stated, the letter gives the offender a basis for a new delaying tactic. It is wisest, therefore, to check all facts before writing the letter, during the dictation, or—not quite as satisfactory—before it is mailed.

Not too long ago, we received a letter from a large department store indicating a large amount due on our charge account and noting, threateningly, that this was the third request. Our first reaction was to call that writer and give him a piece of our mind. The truth of the matter was a double error. First, our account had been quite inactive for years. Second, we owed not one red cent. When we had calmed down, we simply addressed a postal card to the writer of the letter and explained the obvious error. Not only did we receive an apology, but a small box of three cakes of "soft soap" to soothe a ruffled customer. We have been a regular customer since, with an active account. We always have wondered, however, whether this was a clever gimmick to make an inactive account into an active one! If it was, it worked on us.

Brevity. Can you recall a long lecture or speech that left you yawning? Well, don't do the same to your correspondent when writing him a letter. On the other hand, you must guard against becoming telegraphic in your style. The trick is just the right amount of dressing on the salad.

Remember, the reader is just as busy as the writer. Keep your message as brief as possible without leaving out any important details. Give him tasty mouthfuls, well seasoned. To do a good job and keep the letter brief, you must plan the response carefully:

Get out the file for this customer.
Read any pertinent material.
Check with any other department if necessary.
Make notes of findings directly on his letter.
Obtain any other facts needed—prices, shipping date, express charges, etc.
Verify all facts with any third party involved.

When all the facts are collected, answer the letter. You do all the research. Send him only the conclusions in a sensible, logical order. Imagine your correspondent reading your letter between interruptions. Is the message brief enough to remember?

You must remember the story of the devoted but frugal husband who wished to inform his wife in pre-airplane days that he was called away suddenly to London on business and would write her from there. By the time he composed the message, the boat was under way and the radiogram rates were rather high. He had never been known to be too free with his money, so he reread his message and began to look for words to eliminate:

SUDDENLY CALLED LONDON URGENT BUSINESS RETURN THREE WEEKS LARGE CONTRACT WONDERFUL DEAL LOVE JOHN

"Well," he said to himself, "she knows it was 'suddenly' or she'd have known of it. Cross that out. Naturally I was 'called' or I would not have been running off to London. Now 'London' she must find out about because she does not know where I am going. However, she will know where I went as soon as I send her my first letter and it will also give her my full mailing address. Cross that out too.

"It goes without saying that it was 'urgent business' or I would not have taken off so suddenly. I can't honestly say 'return three weeks' because I don't know for certain. That's out. Naturally, a 'large contract' is a 'wonderful deal'—any idiot knows that and my wife is so smart it would be insulting. She certainly knows by now that I love her very much. Never mind, operator. I'll write her."

Of course, we are not recommending that you be as brief as our frugal husband, but don't become wordy to no purpose at all.

Clarity. You can recall many talks delivered by an authority in a certain field, who, when he had finished, had succeeded in making nothing clear. If he went into too much detail, he may have lost you. If he skipped logical steps along the way, he may have lost you in that manner. In comparing notes with others during intermission or after it was all over, did you discover others were in the same boat with you? We can recall several professors at college whose remarks were, to a great extent, beyond their audiences, and to avoid embarrassment many people remarked after their lectures on the depth of their wisdom. There is also danger in knowing a subject too well and not being able to make explicit to the neophyte the essentials of what is said.

Before a letter is signed, the writer must read it to be very certain that it is clear and correct. Ordinarily, the letter was dictated several hours before. If at the time of signing it no longer sounds clear, it should be reworded or reconsidered before it is sent. If the letter is quite clear to the writer after the lapse of several hours, it will probably be clear to the reader.

Even though the letter is clear to you, if its importance is great, enlist the patience and understanding of a sympathetic colleague. Ask him to read it. He does not know the subject or purpose of the letter, and if it is clear to him, you can trust that the letter will probably be clear to the addressee, who does know the subject. Also, in the case of a letter complicated with technical detail, the same procedure is advisable. Avoid, if you can, placing a stenographer in a position in which she is to decide the clarity of a letter. When you have your own secretary, however, this is one of her routine duties. Clear communication with those with whom you do business is a must.

Dignity. The dignity of a letter has to do with its tone, its courtesy, and its sincerity. A dignified letter commands respect and reflects authenticity. The correspondent believes a dignified letter.

A message in language as simple as a friendly conversation will not only be clearer to the reader but will seem earnest as well. As long as the conversation is not permitted to become too colloquial, it will bring across to the correspondent some of the personality of the writer.

Nothing will lower the dignity of a letter more rapidly than a tone of forced sincerity. If the language used is unnatural to the writer, the reader will either sense it and be disappointed, or, when conversation actually does occur between them, a feeling of falseness will unconsciously overcome him. This is not the personality he became acquainted with in correspondence.

Occasionally, for purposes of a sales pitch, frivolity may be in order. Used properly, this can be refreshing. Avoid negatives in writing whenever possible. Negatives inform one about what *not* to do. However, in business letter writing, it is good psychology to suggest the positive—what *to* do. Effectively used, this positive attitude should lead to action, the primary goal of every business letter.

In making statements, keep in mind that the customer or correspondent cannot see you. It is therefore wise to give him the picture of a pleasant, cheerful, helpful writer:

It was nice to know that you enjoyed our . . .
The pleasure of knowing that we helped you . . .
Your kindness in answering so soon . . .
We are grateful to you for giving us an opportunity to bid . . .
Who could ask for anything more than a customer who is kind enough to . . .
Please accept with our best wishes this sample of . . .

Your letters should develop the same character that you actually have in person—without your faults. Keep away from the overused, shopworn phrases and aim for the ABCD, as well as freshness. Nobody enjoys a stereotyped letter. Keep the letter as short as possible, as simple as possible, and as directly sincere as possible. Don't "fill" a letter because it does not seem that it will occupy sufficient space on the typewritten page. Leave the customer with a reason for responding.

As you follow the development of this book, it would be advisable for you to keep in mind that the most important asset of a good correspondent is adaptability. Each learned area must be adapted to the immediate needs of the moment as the letter is

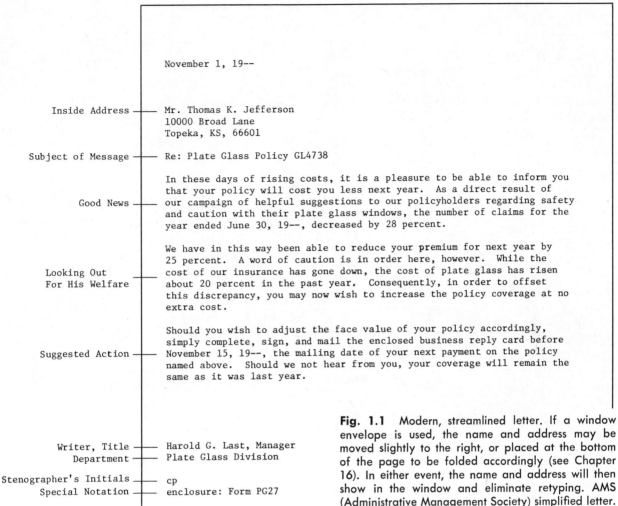

November 1, 19--

Inside Address ——— Mr. Thomas K. Jefferson
10000 Broad Lane
Topeka, KS, 66601

Subject of Message ——— Re: Plate Glass Policy GL4738

Good News ——— In these days of rising costs, it is a pleasure to be able to inform you
that your policy will cost you less next year. As a direct result of
our campaign of helpful suggestions to our policyholders regarding safety
and caution with their plate glass windows, the number of claims for the
year ended June 30, 19--, decreased by 28 percent.

Looking Out
For His Welfare ——— We have in this way been able to reduce your premium for next year by
25 percent. A word of caution is in order here, however. While the
cost of our insurance has gone down, the cost of plate glass has risen
about 20 percent in the past year. Consequently, in order to offset
this discrepancy, you may now wish to increase the policy coverage at no
extra cost.

Suggested Action ——— Should you wish to adjust the face value of your policy accordingly,
simply complete, sign, and mail the enclosed business reply card before
November 15, 19--, the mailing date of your next payment on the policy
named above. Should we not hear from you, your coverage will remain the
same as it was last year.

Writer, Title ——— Harold G. Last, Manager
Department ——— Plate Glass Division

Stenographer's Initials ——— cp
Special Notation ——— enclosure: Form PG27

Fig. 1.1 Modern, streamlined letter. If a window envelope is used, the name and address may be moved slightly to the right, or placed at the bottom of the page to be folded accordingly (see Chapter 16). In either event, the name and address will then show in the window and eliminate retyping. AMS (Administrative Management Society) simplified letter. Start this style slightly lower because of omission of salutation and closing.

being composed. If the letter is to be duplicated and sent to many people, it must be more carefully composed than usual and aimed at many people rather than a single reader.

In addition to traditional styles (Fig. 1.2), a letter style with no superfluous matter is gaining favor all the time (Fig. 1.1). It is not formal but it is businesslike, and its warmth is left to come from the message rather than from flowery salutations or closings.

How to Get Ready to Dictate

Before calling your stenographer to take dictation or making a recording to be transcribed, you must be prepared to dictate, to become conversational with your unseen correspondent. If you value your time as an executive and that of your stenographer or typist, you won't waste a minute of it.

As you read the morning's mail and decide which letters you will answer that day, obtain all necessary materials—price lists, catalogs, stock availability, account record, and anything else required from the file. Gather all papers together and make notations directly in the margin of the letter to be answered.

When you are ready, call your stenographer or dictate to your machine with the material before you as you talk. Only experience and attention to writing technique will develop the real skill required. How to begin, what is the message, how the ABCDs are followed, the importance of repetition, how to end, and many other considerations are taken into account by the skilled letter writer (see Chapter 18 for a full checklist).

Dictate as many letters at one sitting as possible. Indicate any special instructions at the outset—special delivery, certified, etc. If you are interrupted, do not depend on memory, have the letter read back to regain your trend of thought. Certain letters which are more important than others should be read back to you or played back by your machine as you sit back and listen. If you do use a dictating machine, follow precisely the instructions of the manufacturer for the best results.

If you are the one responsible for the improvement of correspondence at your office, and wish to save money, consider these steps for more effective business correspondence:

Use form letters and postal cards wherever applicable. It takes very little time to fill in necessary information on a form letter or card that is preprinted or duplicated.

Authorize each secretary to compose or choose her own responses to routine mail. Check until her good judgment is proved, then give her free rein.

If the company has a teleprinter, send as many messages to correspondents by this method as possible without overloading the operator. Your special Telex directory will list all companies which have the same equipment and may be reached directly. It is fast and allows for two-way telecommunication when needed.

Set specific cost standards for additional personal contact and encourage telephone responses within certain budgetary limitations.

Train yourself to compose good, short letters for more effective results. Eliminate excessive verbiage, but do not sound like a telegram or computer-produced message. Teach the same skill to the other executives or persons initiating correspondence. Because an executive's time is valuable and costly, require all of them to learn how to prepare for dictation and keep letters short. It will also save the secretary's time.

Letter Placement

The attractive placement on the page of a business letter can be planned to the exact line. All typists have been taught in school the method of placing a letter on the stationery based on the size of the message. The fixed parts—date, inside address, salutation, closing, typewritten signature, title, initials, etc.—have little effect on the placement. There are as many methods of determining this placement as there are authors of typewriting textbooks. With experience, the typist soon learns to set up a letter in the proper position on the sheet of paper without any conscious computation.

Confining ourselves to the traditional style of letter, we will describe several methods a typist can use to decide where to place the letter. All methods discussed have the following constants: paper guide placed at zero position*; traditional (block or semi-block) style; pica (10 letters to an inch) or elite (12 letters to an inch) type.

LETTER PLACEMENT: METHOD 1

A placement scale is a precalculated set of figures which help the typist to know how far down from the top of the paper to start a letter and what margins to use in order to have the letter attractively placed on the page. The number of words in the body of the letter must be known or estimated. This number determines the various points in the placement scales given below. For instance, in the first placement scale, a letter of 120 words would be started 17 lines down from the top of the letterhead paper with a 55-space line of typing, in single spacing. The 17-line figure is based on the fact that spacing between parts is fixed—date to inside address, 4 lines; address to salutation, 2 lines; salutation to first paragraph, 2 lines; etc. (See Fig. 1.2 for further details.) When it is desired to be more exact in placement, one line should be subtracted from the number of lines from the top of the page to the date line for every 35 words over the minimum. In addition, for an attention or subject line or for every two paragraphs over two, one line should be subtracted from the number given. Should the 120-word letter mentioned above have four paragraphs, for example, the letter should start the date 16 lines from the top instead of 17. Variations to allow for other inserts will come with experience.

When letters are to be typed on half-sheets of stationery, 5½″ × 8½″, which are generally used for short letters, it is necessary to determine which way the paper will be utilized—vertically (lengthwise) or horizontally (broadside). Used lengthwise, it provides an extremely short typing line. It is recommended that it be used horizontally so that the lines of typing are the same as on standard-size paper, and all arrangements on the page follow those similar to full-size 8½″ × 11″ paper.

It must be said, however, that the vertical page is a little more attractive. If you decide to use the

---

* For 8½″ × 11″ or 8½″ × 5½″ papers: Royal, Adler, Olympia, SCM—set paper guide on 0; use 42 center pica, 51 center elite. IBM (Model D), Remington—use 0 on paper table scale as *center* of paper. Adjust paper guide accordingly. IBM Selectric, Olivetti—center indicated on paper bail scale. When in doubt and for any size paper, insert paper, add number on scale at left to the number on scale at right, and divide total by two. That is the center point. Old-style method is to crease the paper in half lengthwise, insert, and note number at crease. That is the center point. For IBM Executive or proportional-spacing typewriters, use last procedure.

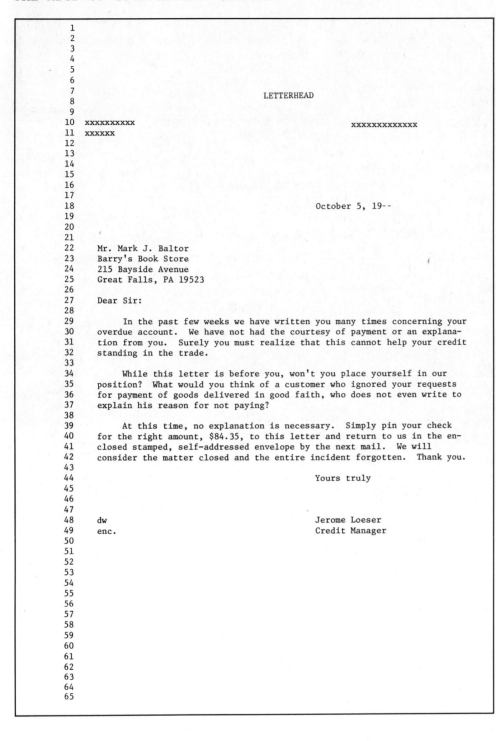

```
1
2
3
4
5
6
7                                    LETTERHEAD
8
9
10   xxxxxxxxxx                                   xxxxxxxxxxxxx
11   xxxxxx
12
13
14
15
16
17
18                                    October 5, 19--
19
20
21
22   Mr. Mark J. Baltor
23   Barry's Book Store
24   215 Bayside Avenue
25   Great Falls, PA 19523
26
27   Dear Sir:
28
29        In the past few weeks we have written you many times concerning your
30   overdue account.  We have not had the courtesy of payment or an explana-
31   tion from you.  Surely you must realize that this cannot help your credit
32   standing in the trade.
33
34        While this letter is before you, won't you place yourself in our
35   position?  What would you think of a customer who ignored your requests
36   for payment of goods delivered in good faith, who does not even write to
37   explain his reason for not paying?
38
39        At this time, no explanation is necessary.  Simply pin your check
40   for the right amount, $84.35, to this letter and return to us in the en-
41   closed stamped, self-addressed envelope by the next mail.  We will
42   consider the matter closed and the entire incident forgotten.  Thank you.
43
44                                    Yours truly
45
46
47
48   dw                                   Jerome Loeser
49   enc.                                 Credit Manager
50
51
52
53
54
55
56
57
58
59
60
61
62
63
64
65
```

Fig. 1.2 Placement outline of a traditional-style letter. The numbering of the lines helps to demonstrate the relative positioning and spacing on the page.

Number of words in letter	Date line from top		Length of line		Spacing
	Plain	Letterhead	Pica	Elite	
under 50	18	20	45 spaces	50 spaces	Double
50–100	18	20	45 spaces	50 spaces	Single
101–175	15	17	55 spaces	60 spaces	Single
176–250	12	14	65 spaces	70 spaces	Single
over 250	Two pages		55 spaces	60 spaces	Single

half-sheet vertically, the typist will need to measure the paper against the typing scale. She can then determine a standard set of margins to use and an attractive placement of the letters.

If monarch or executive stationery is to be used, the same procedure should be followed.

LETTER PLACEMENT: METHOD 2

The method shown above is an approximation method, with a fixed distance of 4 lines between the date line and the inside address. In the procedure below, the only difference is the spacing from the date to the inside address and the size of the typewritten line, which is half an inch shorter than above.

Letter length	Line length*	Date line from top	Lines from date to inside address
Short (under 100 wds)	4″	18	6
Medium (100–200)	5″	15	5
Long (200–300)	6″	12	4
Two-page (300 or over)	5″	15	5

* Represents elite type; if pica, increase each ½″.

Note: All single spacing as indicated.
Notice only slight variation in distance between date and inside address.
8½″ × 11″ paper only.
Date-line placement is from top edge of paper, whether on letterhead or blank paper.
For each two paragraphs over two, go down one line less from the top; likewise for each attention line, subject line, or other special notation requiring similar placement.

In short letters under 50 words, either the 5½″ × 8½″ paper may be used or a full sheet of 8½″ × 11″ paper with double spacing in body or message of the letter only. This serves to spread the letter over a greater area, to fill nearly as much space as a single-spaced letter with twice the number of words.

LETTER PLACEMENT: METHOD 3

In the preceding two methods the date line takes a specific position above the inside address. The third method places the date line 2 lines below the letterhead and adjusts for various letter sizes by moving the inside address up or down accordingly. All allowances for extra paragraphs, attention, sub-ject, etc. do not affect the date line but do move the distance to the inside address in the same fashion as the others.

Size of letter	Size of margin*	Spacing	Start inside address
Under 50 words	2″	Double	12 lines from date
50–100	2″	Single	10 lines from date
100–200	1½″	Single	8 lines from date
200–300	1″	Single	6 lines from date
over 300 (2 pages)	1½″	Single	8 lines from date

* Pica is 10 letters to the inch, elite 12 to the inch.

LETTER PLACEMENT: METHOD 4

There are several other methods of determining the placement of a letter on the stationery. A little too cumbersome to memorize is this one, known as the exact method. The exact method is for 8½″ × 11″ paper with a fixed position for the date—4 lines above the inside address. In all methods, you will notice, it is necessary to be able to estimate the number of words in the body of the letter.

No. of words in body	Spacing	Margins		Single spaces from top edge to date line
		Pica	Elite	
50	Double	20–65	25–75	15
75	Double	20–65	25–75	13
100	Double	15–70	20–80	13
125	Double	15–70	20–80	11
50	Single	25–60	30–70	19
75	Single	20–65	25–75	18
100	Single	20–65	25–75	17
125	Single	20–65	25–75	16
150	Single	20–65	25–75	15
175	Single	15–70	20–80	15
200	Single	15–70	20–80	14
225	Single	10–75	15–85	14
250	Single	10–75	15–85	13
275	Single	10–75	15–85	12
300 (2-page)	Single	15–70	20–80	14

An experienced typist will probably use none of the scales given. Estimation of margins and placement merely by eye is the mark of the accomplished stenographer or typist.

Chapter 2

Accepted Letter Styles and Forms

JUST AS A salesman's appearance affects his success, so does the appearance of a business letter. Let us consider how your letter will come to the attention of your correspondent. He may open the envelope himself and see the letter as it emerges; or, more likely, it will be opened by a clerk, sorted, and placed on his desk as one of a pile of letters. How will that letter compare with the others before him?

Stationery

The paper chosen for stationery must be suitable in several respects. Not only must it look attractive as paper, but it must also feel good between the fingers; it must take printing well for the best appearance of the letterhead, and it must take typing and erasing well.* The reaction of the recipient must be considered when making the selection. In a machine shop or heavy trucking business, a delicate letterhead and stationery might cause an unconsciously antagonistic response. A heavy, solid paper and bold letterhead in the lingerie business would be likewise out of place. Be governed by the advice of the printer and your own personal taste in this matter.

Your printer will be able to show you thirty to forty different papers suitable for letterhead stationery. Do not economize on stationery; the finest paper with the most elegantly engraved letterhead will not add appreciably to the cost of each sheet. Furthermore, the difference in cost between one and the other may not work out to more than a fraction of a cent per sheet. Careful selection of good typists and good stenographers, good erasers and erasable paper will save more stationery money than any other form of economy. Never order more stationery at one time than is needed for two years of normal

use, depending upon the permanence of the location and other factors. In this way, revisions or rearrangements may take place at regular intervals to give your stationery a fresh look. Should a change then be necessary, it will not be too costly to cut up the remaining stationery for scratch paper or alter the information with a rubber stamp for a short period of time.

COLOR

The use of colored paper should be considered also, but avoided when in doubt. Some of the most attractive letter papers use color judiciously. For instance, a pale buff paper with rich chocolate-brown printing was used by one firm, the Brown Company. All typewriters used brown-ink ribbons, as did the mimeograph machine. It was very effective. After five years, the office manager changed to white paper, retaining the brown ribbons and brown mimeograph ink, which was still very effective.

Multicolored letterheads should be considered very carefully before being used. It is possible for a very bright letterhead to detract from the appearance and effectiveness of the typewritten letter. Deckle edges or other such embellishments should also be avoided for business correspondence, although they do serve an excellent purpose for personal stationery and announcements. For dramatic effect, they might conceivably be used in the lingerie, perfume, cosmetics, or similar businesses.

The weight of the paper used is purely a matter of taste. For airmail stationery, the weight of the paper is very much worth considering because of the cost of foreign airmail. Foreign airmail costs about four times as much per half-ounce as regular first-class mail. If much business is being done abroad, it would be worth considering lightweight stationery and lightweight envelopes with red, white, and blue stripes for speedy airmail service.

---

* There are special bond typing papers chemically treated for easy erasing. The IBM Selectric II Correcting typewriter removes errors automatically. Corrections on proportional-spacing machines are more difficult due to split space bar and two-unit backspacer.

```
Mead, Crosby & Curtiss
Page 2
October 1, 19--


In view of the facts presented above, won't you be kind enough
to confer with your Board of Directors as to further action in
this case.  We shall expect to hear from you before August 15,
the legal expiration date.  Please keep in mind that there is a
matter worth a possible $80,000 which is implied in the con-
vertible feature of the bonds.

We trust you will make a decision in our favor and inform us to
that effect as soon as possible.

                              Yours sincerely



                              (Ms.) Charlene E. Hughes
                              Vice President


hm
cc:  Mr. Mead
     Mr. Binger
     Mr. Fried
```

```
Mead, Crosby & Curtis          -2-           October 1, 19--


In view of the facts presented above, won't you be kind enough
to confer with your Board of Directors as to further action in
this case.  We shall expect to hear from you before August 15,
the legal expiration date.  Please keep in mind that there is a
```

Fig. 2.1 The two-page letter.

PAPER SIZES

Stationery comes in standard sizes. The standard size for business stationery in the United States is 8½″ × 11″. Half-size stationery (5½″ × 8½″) is also common for short letters (under 50 words) and is generally used with a slightly smaller letterhead. It may be used lengthwise or broadside, as desired. For both sizes of paper mentioned above, the standard-size envelopes—business (commercial) or legal—may be used (see Chapter 16).

Paper is also made in an executive or baronial size (7¼″ × 10½″) and a government size (8″ × 10½″). Both require envelopes slightly different from the two mentioned above. The cost of paper this size is comparable to that of those above. Remember, paper may be purchased in any size desired, at a slightly higher cost to cover cutting.

LETTERHEAD

The letterhead on your stationery is a combination business suit and calling card. It governs the appearance of the letter and may give information vital to the business, such as its name, address, telephone number, cable address, names of officers, and the addresses of branches. Without cluttering the appearance, vital information should be provided to suit the needs of the customer. If the company has a trademark or other symbol, it is wise to place it prominently on the letterhead. If there are many such symbols, it might be advisable to place them in miniature at the bottom of the stationery in a proud row. Many concerns place them on the left side of the paper in a vertical row. Trademarks or distinctive symbols should appear on all the firm's stationery—bills, statements, postage-meter imprint, and so on. On the other hand, should the president of the corporation have his own executive stationery, this is best kept as simple as possible for greatest dignity. Plain block letters on good rag-bond paper is best for this purpose. Once again, your printer can show you many examples from which to choose.

Normally the letterhead is centered at the top of the paper. Occasionally, however, there is printed information at the bottom of the page as mentioned above or on either side in the margin. In some cases these items are added to the regular stationery for special occasions (such as a silver anniversary cele- bration and sale, a special clearance offered for a limited time, and the like). Many fraternal, profes- sional, and charitable organizations list in a side margin the names of the officers, members of com- mittees, honorary officers, or board of directors. The bottom of the page is sometimes used to give the addresses of branch factories or offices.

TWO-PAGE LETTER

Sometimes letters require more than one page for typing. For the first page of the letter, a regular letterhead sheet is used. For the second and subse- quent pages, the letterhead merely indicates the firm name in the same style of printing as the first page, as well as in the type, color, and weight of paper. When such a letter is typed, the typist indicates the name of the correspondent, the page number, and the date at the top of the new page (Fig. 2.1). A letter should never be typed so that the only material ap- pearing on the second page is the complimentary close, firm name, name, title, and identifying initials.

For the second-page carbon copy, use the reverse side of the first-page carbon copy. This will save space in the file and prevent accidental separation of the sheets. If carbon sets are used, separate sheets *must* be used.

Letter Form

In recent years, letter forms have been in a state of flux due to the usual pressures of business which have increased the typist's production in the office. For this reason, progressive office managers have adopted the letter styles which require the least manipulation by typists. Every indentation slows the typist. The elimination of them, naturally, increases her speed. Hence, the growing popularity of the block and pure block forms—ideally suited to pres- ent-day needs—over the semi-block. As in all change, older people in the business world are usually the ones to put up obstacles—not because they do not recognize the value or need for the change, but because it is simply human nature to resist change when traditional practice works well.

By the early 1960s block and semi-block styles were neck and neck, with the pure block gaining rapidly. The full-indented style has been relegated to the Smithsonian Institution along with closed punc- tuation. The hanging-indention style, also ripe for the Smithsonian, continues to be found in sales let- ters as an eye-catcher. Samples of the various forms of letters and interoffice memoranda are illustrated in Figs. 2.2 through 2.7, as well as in Figs. 2.10 through 2.15 at the end of the chapter.

```
                    Certified Mail
                    September 19, 19--


Mr. Edward J. Small
Burgess Tool Company
Kenosha, WI 53140

Dear Mr. Small:

We are willing to purchase the cutting tools you mentioned in
your telegram received this morning.  The unit price of $1.87½
is satisfactory to us and we are sending this note as confir-
mation.

Please remind those concerned that this order is based on a
completion date of March 1, 19--, or the entire order becomes
null and void.

                    Yours truly



8J                  Kevin J. Kerr
                    President
```

Fig. 2.2 Letter on 5½″ x 8½″ paper. Sam- ple of a short letter typed on 5½″ x 8½″ sta- tionery. It is typed in block style with mixed punctuation. Note the coding of the stenog- rapher's identifying initials sometimes used in confidential matters. It is common to center the date as well as to indicate directly before it that the letter is being sent by certified mail.

JAMAICA PLUMBING COMPANY

                                                      Special Delivery
                                                      November 4, 19--

Mr. Daniel Boone
Parsons Fish Store
114-15 Parsons Street
Flushing, NY 11355

Dear Mr. Boone

    One of our estimators examined some pipes in your store

which need replacement because of excessive rust. You asked

him to send his estimate for the job by return mail.

    This is to inform you that the entire job can be com-

pleted in three days at a cost not to exceed $100.

                          Sincerely

                          JAMAICA PLUMBING COMPANY

jd   George Simon
                          Manager

Fig. 2.3   Letter on 8½″ x 11″ paper. Sample of a short letter typed on regular 8½″ x 11″ paper in double spacing. It is typed in semi-block style (sometimes called modified block style). The punctuation is entirely open. Note reference to method of mailing.

DAKOTA ELECTRICAL SUPPLIES, INC.

        June 1, 19--

Mr. Thomas Ringlemier
The German Cafe
88 Broadway
Three Forks, NY 89834

Dear Sir:

It has been three months since we installed the electrical
wiring for the air conditioner in your restaurant and made
some other minor repairs. Since we have not heard from you,
we assume that you have had no cause for complaint about our
work. We are glad to note this.

We have a complaint, however, against your bookkeeper, who
has now ignored three notices from us concerning the balance
of your account due since May 1. Regretfully, therefore, we
must bring this matter to the attention of the proprietor
because our original price was based upon payment within 60
days from the time of completion of the work.

Won't you kindly inform your bookkeeper that our overdue
account needs settling immediately? It only amounts to
$127.50.

Yours truly

Clare Dakota
Treasurer

jp

Fig. 2.4   Pure block style letter. Note that all lines are flush with the left margin so that there is no need to indent at any time.

LAKE SUPERIOR HAULAGE

February 24, 19--

Superior Shipping Lines
777 N.E. Minnesota Avenue
Duluth, MN 55511

Subject: Confusion over Atlantia Shipment #4-257A

On August 1, shortly before 6:00 A.M., the SS Atlantia berthed at Dock 14, West
Shore, Duluth, Lake Superior. As soon as the customs agents had checked the
ship and authorized unloading, our men proceeded to follow the instructions   .
given them a week before arrival. They had three ten-ton trucks waiting to
load the cases of goods in question. So far so good.

The chief of our trucking crew asked a member of the ship's crew where the goods
we were to transport were located as they were all marked in Greek lettering.
This crew member, who spoke good English, assured our crew chief that the cases
he designated were the ones required and the unloading began. The number of cases
checked out exactly and the three loaded trucks left the dock area at 4:00 P.M.,
reported in to the dispatcher, Mr. Weiss, who assigned new drivers and helpers
so that the cases could be sent quickly to their destination as ordered by you.

Upon arrival at the Billings Company plant the next day, a foreman discovered
that the contents were not as ordered. By rapid movement of men and equipment,
we were able to return the cases to the dock, exchange for the correct ones, and
return to the Billings Company within 36 hours! We, of course, only charged for
one trucking shipment.

If I can answer any further questions you may have about this incident, do not
hesitate to call me collect.

Charles Dorn
Vice President

Fig. 2.5 Pure block, AMS simplified letter. This letter is typed in pure block, streamlined form recommended by the Administrative Management Society and the National Secretaries Association. Note the businesslike appearance and absence of unnecessary elements.

New York Metropolitan Insurance Co.
INTEROFFICE MEMORANDUM

June 15, 19--   Marshall Funder, Cashier

Employee Benefits   Hale J. Driscol, Treasurer

Suspend all adjudications of employee benefits until July 1.
On that date you will receive completely revised employee
benefits handbook which will go into effect on that date
and which will contain answers to all pending questions.

Should there be any emergency problems, refer them directly
to me.

gz
cc: all managers

AVOID VERBAL ORDERS
PUT IT IN WRITING

Fig. 2.6 Interoffice memorandum expressly printed for firm. Printed on 5½" x 8½" stationery. It will be distributed by the company's interdepartmental mail system. To managers outside the company's central office it will be sent by regular U.S. mail.

INTEROFFICE MEMORANDUM

TO: Gerald Q. Deanno   Subject: Home Mortgage 116118A
        General Manager

FROM: Francis S. Butler   Date: June 15, 19--
        Mortgage Department

      You requested an outline of the situation concerning the above
mortgage. The following account is accurate to the best of my knowledge.
There is a gap of two weeks during my vacation. For that period, I have
attached a statement from Harold Caster, who handled the matter during
that time.

      On January 5, 19--, the gentleman in question came to my office to

      In my opinion, this account is quite clear and complete.

or
enc: Statement by
      Harold Caster

Fig. 2.7 Interoffice memorandum This form can be obtained from any good stationery supply house or commercial stationery printer. It is available in several sizes, preprinted.

```
                                     -------------------- Pivoted Date


            Inside   --------------------
            address  --------------------------
                     ------, -- -----


                     ------------:  ------------ Attention line

  Salutation  ------------

                     ------------:  ------------ Subject line


            ------------------------------------------------------
            ------------------------------------------------------
            -------------------.

 Body       ------------------------------------------------------
 or         ------------------------------------------------------
 message    ------------------------------------------------------
 of         ------------------------------------------------------
 letter     ------------------------.


            ------------------------------------------------------
            ------------------------------------------------------
            -----------------.

                                              ------------------ Complimentary Close
                                              ------------------ Firm name



  Identifying initials  --:--                 ---------------- Typewritten signature
           Enclosure  ----                    ---------------- Title or department
     Carbon copies to  --:  ----------
                            ----------
                            ----------
```

Fig. 2.8 A diagram of a business letter with most of the possible parts. The style of this letter is traditional block, with all the formal letter parts included. The punctuation is open.

Parts of a Letter

DATE LINE

The *date* identifies the currency of the letter. It is typed at the right margin in the block and semi-block forms, at the left margin in the pure block. In some offices the date is centered (Fig. 2.9a), in others it is aligned with the complimentary close (Fig. 2.9b), in still others it is pivoted with the right margin (Fig. 2.9c). In the vast majority of offices, the date appears as month, day, and then year (Fig. 2.9d). For special effect, some offices type the date on three successive lines in carefully planned patterns (Fig. 2.9e). In a small but growing minority, and in foreign correspondence, you will find the type used by our military forces and many other government agencies—day, month, year (Fig. 2.9f). In some offices the set-position date line is used. Regardless of the letter margins, the date position is standardized as at 50 (pica) or 60 (elite).

INSIDE ADDRESS

The *inside address* is placed directly below the date at the left margin in any style of letter unless the letter is to be sent in a window envelope, when it will be slightly shifted to the right. (Even then it is possible to use the regular position if the window is situated to accommodate it.) The inside address should never consist of fewer than 3 lines and can contain as many as 6 lines.

Some examples of inside addresses:

Ms. Dallas Gordon
Rapid City
South Dakota 57702

(Three lines, no street address.)

Mrs. Richard Foster
1212 Bedford Avenue
Atlanta, GA* 30339

(Three lines with street address.)

---

* Official two-letter abbreviations for states, requested by the U.S. Postal Service, are typed both letters capitals, no punctuation, two or three blank spaces before the ZIP Code (see Chapter 14).

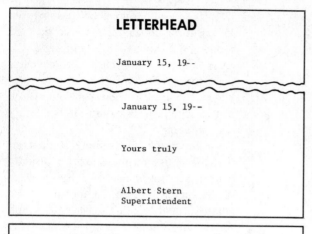

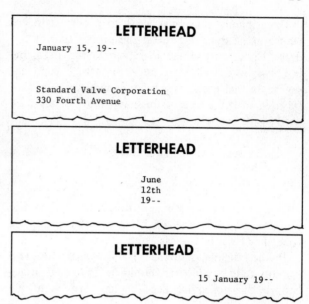

Fig. 2.9 Date line: (a) centered date (centered below letterhead); (b) aligned date (both date and close begin at center); (c) pivoted date (even with right margin); (d) pure block (flush with left margin); (e) three-line (varied to suit the length of name of month); (f) government or European (day, month, year).

Mr. Walter Schochenmaier
Todd's Department Store
111 State Street
Salt Lake City, UT 84120

(Person's name, company name, and complete address, 4 lines.)

Mr. Charles W. Harper
Assistant Superintendent
Empire State Building Corp.
345 Fifth Avenue
New York, NY 10016

(Person's name, full title, company name, complete address, on 5 lines.)

Atelier Fabergé Frisonne
35 Cote de Nege
Montreal, Quebec H3H 1H9 CANADA

(Full name and address most important on foreign mail.)

While the full addresses may seem cumbersome, in fact they are not. The more information given in the address, the surer you can be that the letter will be delivered promptly to the correct place.

SALUTATION

A *salutation* has been traditional in letters since Roman times, as has the closing. Fig. 2.5 is a streamlined modern letter which does not employ either device. However, custom will undoubtedly retain them for many years to come. When the salutation is used, it should be followed by a colon or no punctuation at all. When the colon is used, it is customary, but not mandatory, to use a comma after the closing. This is called mixed punctuation.

When addressing a letter to an individual, it is customary to use:

    Dear Madam
    Dear Sir:
    Dear Mr. Smathers:
    Dear Ms. Peterson

For a personal business relationship:

    Dear Harry:

When addressing a letter to a firm, it is customary to use:

    Gentlemen:
    Dear Sirs

As soon as the name of the person with whom you will correspond at any company becomes known to you, use it directly in the address of the letter; the salutation, of course, will change accordingly.

Occasionally, for special purposes (usually for sales letters or circulars), the following salutations might be used:

    Dear Customer:
    Dear Neighbor
    Dear Electric Razor User:
    Fellow Commuter:

Occasionally one must write to a correspondent whose name does not reveal the proper title of address. Either only initials are given, or the first name is not indicative of the gender, or there is sufficient doubt. In that event, it is recommended that no title be used in the inside address and the full name be used in the salutation:

>Dear Jean Fredericks
>Dear Hua Mei Lai
>Dear L. C. Stewart

In case a known female correspondent does not indicate whether Miss or Mrs. is to be used, the trend has been to use Ms.

Public officials, diplomats, foreign dignitaries, and ranking religious leaders should be addressed in appropriate formal style. (See Chapter 9 for examples.)

THE BODY OF THE LETTER

The most important section of the letter—its reason for being—is the *message* or *body*. In business letter writing there are a few rules regarding the appearance of the body of the letter which should be followed:

1 Avoid divided words at the end of a typewritten line as much as possible.

2 Divide words (if you have to) strictly according to the syllables in the dictionary, following this simple rule: Never separate two letters or less from the remainder of the word either at the beginning or the end of the line.

3 *Whenever possible*, without spoiling the appearance of the letter, keep the elements of a name, date, or figures which occur in the body of a letter *on one line* for greater ease in reading.

Don't	Do
Mr. Carl Thompson	Mr. Carl Thompson
January 2, 19—	January 2, 19—
$1,447,— 218.49	$1,447,218.49
28 yards, 2 feet, 7 inches	28 yards, 2 feet, 7 inches
35.3 millimeters	35.3 millimeters (or 35.3 mm.)

Occasionally, if absolutely necessary to avoid a freakishly long line, such items may be divided as shown above.

4 *Never* use part of a word as the last complete line in a paragraph.

5 Keep the right margin as even as possible for the best appearance of the finished product. Of course, it is unusual for a letter to end with all lines exactly even at the right margin.

6 Unless the letter is merely a note of one or two sentences, it should rarely be only one paragraph.

7 Keep paragraphs fairly short. Remember that the entire business letter is usually concerned with one subject. By the rules of freshman English composition, this would probably call for one paragraph for the entire letter. But in business correspondence, any change in reference calls for a new paragraph. For instance, if we write to a customer (*a*) calling attention to good past relations, (*b*) reminding him of a small amount due on his account, and (*c*) asking him to use the enclosed envelope to remit or explain the delay, we have three good paragraphs right there.

8 Avoid the use of quotation marks and underlining as much as possible. In the case of titles of articles or publications, use solid capitals instead. They are more effective, neater, and faster for the typist to handle. When the article and publication appear in the same sentence, it is advisable to use solid capitals for the name of the publication only.

9 The whole letter, of which the body is the largest part, should always be placed on the page so that the border or margin is about equal in size on all sides except for the bottom margin, which may be a little larger.

10 When numbers occur in the body of a letter, a good general rule is to spell out numbers up to twenty. From that point on numbers get a little involved with the hyphenated spelling and should be avoided. Round numbers, such as thirty, forty, eighty, etc., may always be spelled out. Numbers which are part of catalog, stock, model, or file designations should be typed in digits; do *not* spell out. All money and percentage numbers must use digits, written with the appropriate sign. Fractional numbers should be uniform; don't combine ½ and 3/4 in the same letter. If fractions other than the ones on the typewriter keyboard are to be used in one letter, use the diagonal for *all* (e.g., 7/8, 1/4).

11 Use a short opening paragraph and a short closing paragraph whenever possible. The opening paragraph should be introductory in nature. The closing paragraph should be a call to action of some kind—come to see the new model on display, send a check to cover this amount, return the enclosed card for a free sample, make an appointment with our representative now, etc.

12 The highest standards for accuracy must be upheld. Letters must be proofread carefully and all errors, typographical and other, corrected before mailing. With the use of erasers, correction papers, correction fluids, or devices on the IBM Selectric II correcting typewriters, corrections must be as invisible as possible. Erasable bond papers merely require a soft pencil-type eraser to correct errors. Tremendous improvement in typewriter ribbons has also enhanced the appearance of letters. It pays to use the best. If a smudge on the paper resists erasing, smear with the chalked side of correction paper or with a piece of soft chalk. Typing and correction on the IBM executive and proportional-spacing typewriters require special training and skill. Letters are spaced according to their size. For instance, the letters a, k, and z and all numbers are three units wide; the letters m and w and all capital letters are four units; capitals M and W are five units; while l, i, (,), ;, and : are two units. The backspacer returns the carriage two units at a time. The space bar is split for two or three units. To aid the typist, the machine has a pop-up printing point indicator to locate the exact center of the space for the correction.

13 The letter must not sound indefinite. Remember that the desire for action being conveyed cannot be activated by indecisive words. Give the correspondent a definite, reasonable course of action and leave the door open for an alternate proposal.

COMPLIMENTARY CLOSE

The *complimentary close* is another bequest from olden times. In Spanish correspondence, letters used to end with "your humble servant who kisses your hands and feet and begs to remain" or words to that effect. These forms die slowly. Until such time as you feel you can eliminate the complimentary close entirely, you have your choice of the following forms:

```
Yours truly        ⎫
Yours very truly   ⎬  formal, businesslike
Very truly yours   ⎭

Sincerely          ⎫
Yours sincerely    ⎪
Sincerely yours    ⎬  less formal
Very sincerely yours ⎪
Yours very sincerely ⎭

Cordially          ⎫
Yours cordially    ⎪
Cordially yours    ⎬  less formal,
Yours very cordially ⎪  friendly
Very cordially yours ⎭

Yours respectfully ⎫
Respectfully yours ⎪  formal,
Yours very respectfully ⎬  to a superior
Very respectfully yours ⎭
```

Let simplicity be the rule. The first form in each group is the best and least pretentious. The writer of the letter should always indicate the complimentary close to the stenographer, who may not know which is the most appropriate.

In sales letters, it is sometimes effective to use unusual complimentary closes, such as "Gratefully yours," "Expectantly," "At your service," and so on. Only the first letter of the first word is capitalized.

In the more traditional style, the firm name is typed after the complimentary close in a variety of ways. Most modern letter writers, however, omit this entirely, since the same information already appears in the letterhead. Examples:

```
          Yours very truly,

          EXCELSIOR PACKING COMPANY

          John J. McCoy, Manager
          Purchasing Department


          Yours very truly,

          EXCELSIOR PACKING COMPANY

          Purchasing Department
```

(Recommended)

```
          Yours very truly

          John J. McCoy, Manager
          Purchasing Department
```

ATTENTION OR SUBJECT (REFERENCE) LINE

One of the most time-consuming tasks in the office is the sorting and correct dispatching of mail to the department or official for whom it is intended. Mail which must be read to determine its recipient will take the longest to sort and deliver after its arrival. To expedite delivery of your letter within the offices of your correspondent, you may do three things.

First, you may direct a letter to the attention of a specific individual, using either his name or his title or both. Note that either "attention:" or "attention of" (no colon) may be used and that the attention line may be centered or, if pure block form is used, aligned with the left margin.

```
The Gordon Company
222 Broadway
New York, NY 10018

Attention of Mr. James Blake

Gentlemen*
```

```
The Gordon Company
222 Broadway
New York, NY 10018


      Attention:   Sales Manager


Gentlemen:
```

```
  (Recommended form)
Mrs. Jane Blake
Sales Manager
The Gordon Company
222 Broadway
New York, NY 10018

Dear Mrs. Blake:
```

Attention lines should not, however, be used often. If the letter is for the man's attention, address it to him, or if you do not know his name you may correctly address the letter to him by title only.

When you do not know the appropriate name, title, or department, you may expedite delivery of your mail by using a subject or reference line—a title to the message contained in the body of the letter, and the more specific, the better. This is a good method, because you have solved the incoming-mail clerk's problem. As the mail is opened and stacked, the mail clerk has to read through rapidly to determine the

---

person or department which can most properly answer the letter. If the letter is addressed to a specific person, it is immediately directed to him. If the letter is directed to a specific department, it is also quickly dispatched. If there is no hint as to the recipient of the letter, it must necessarily be set aside for reading and further sorting.

```
Peck Communications, Inc.
2345 Commonstate Street
Bala Cynwyd, PA 19004

Gentlemen:

      Subject:   S3 Intercom
```

```
Peck Communications, Inc.
2345 Commonstate Street
Bala Cynwyd, PA 19004

Gentlemen:            Re:  S3 Intercom
```

Note that either "subject" or "re" may be used. Some firms indicate in the upper right-hand corner of the letterhead a code to be indicated in the response:

LETTERHEAD

```
                           When answering
                           refer to: VM23
```

If the respondent places this reference number or code in the same place when answering, the mail clerk who understands the code can quickly send the correspondence along. More examples of this type of identification follow:

```
Gentlemen:

Subject:  March 8 shipment GL84 Casein
```

```
Gentlemen:            Reference No. 357KG
```

```
                        June 8, 19--
                        Re:  File WT476

Peck Communications, Inc.
```

SIGNATURE

The signature at the end of the letter should be correct. For a man, there is no problem; it is simply a matter of deciding how he likes his name to appear. The writer of the letter will make the final decision as to the form he likes best, his correct title, and the usage of his name; for example:

---

* The salutation is "Gentlemen" because the letter is addressed to the firm, not the person.

[signature: John Lee Sullivan]

[signature: John L. Sullivan]

[signature: J. Lee Sullivan]

It is quite acceptable for the typewritten signature to give the name in full and for the writer to sign with his first and middle initials only, a practice that is quite common among writers who have rather long names. Merely to initial a letter above the typewritten signature is not considered good taste.

Yours truly

[signature: J. L. Sullivan]

John Lee Sullivan
Controller–Auditor

For women, however, some simple rules should be followed. An unmarried woman, or one who uses her maiden name for business purposes, merely signs her name; the typewritten signature may indicate the marital status if she wishes.

Yours truly

[signature: Mary Smith]

(Miss) Mary Smith
Ticket Agent

A married, divorced, or widowed woman would also use this method except on legal documents, when it is desirable that she indicate her legal name but sign her own name.

For legal purposes:

[signature: Mary L. Smith]

Mrs. George J. Smith

For business purposes:

[signature: Mary L. Smith]

(Ms.) Mary L. Smith
Treasurer–Secretary

There are two other types of signature. One is the indication after the signature that the individual whose typewritten signature appears at the end of the letter did not actually sign for himself. This can occur when the writer is out of town, otherwise unavailable, or authorizes such signing.

Very truly yours

[signature: John L. Sullivan CMJ]

John L. Sullivan
Purchasing Manager

The other instance occurs when the secretary is responding for her employer. The difference here is that the secretary takes full responsibility for the letter, showing quite clearly that she composed it and signed it herself.

Yours truly

[signature: Harriet Green]

Secretary to Mr. Sullivan

It is customary in all letters to leave three blank lines, within which the writer has ample space for his signature. The name, then, appears on the fourth line from the complimentary close when no firm name is typed, as in the examples above.

IDENTIFYING INITIALS

The initials of the writer, followed by those of the stenographer or typist, appear at the margin, to the left of the typewritten signature in the traditional style letter. These initials may be written in many different ways, utilizing capital letters (upper case) and small letters (lower case), or a combination. A good typist or stenographer learns quickly to use the initials to balance the placement of the letter on the page. If the letter is completed and well placed on the page, the identifying initials are placed on the same line as the typewritten signature. Should the letter happen to end a little too high on the page, the initials are typed two lines below the typewritten signature or title, whichever comes last.

JDW:SK	Joseph D. Warren Project Director
JDW:bw	Joseph D. Warren Project Director
jdw/sk	Joseph D. Warren Project Director
bw	Joseph D. Warren Project Director
Joseph D. Warren/8	Project Director

When the letter ends too high on the page:

```
                              Joseph D. Warren
                              Project Director

bw
enc. (2)
```

It is well for the writer to consider, however, when his stenographer or typist types his letters that his initials are certainly superfluous when his typewritten signature appears at the end of the letter. In such cases, it is faster and more sensible to give only the identifying initials of the stenographer or typist or the code number or designation assigned that person, as in the last two examples. The latter is done in situations in which a secretary's identification through her initials might subject her to undue pressure from outside interested persons.

TYPEWRITTEN FIRM NAME

By the same token, the repetition of the firm name at the end of the letter is also superfluous; the information appears in the printed letterhead. True, the carbon copies will not contain the name of the firm if it is omitted on the original. This can be easily remedied by either rubber stamp or printed identification. Omit the firm name in typing when mailing carbon copies, and indicate the name by a simple rubber stamp. Since carbon copies are mainly read internally, it will be rarer to need to copy them for outside readers.

SPECIAL NOTATIONS

Other notations may appear following the identifying initials for the purpose of record, clarity, and notification to the outgoing-mail clerk of the correct contents of the envelope. When the stenographer handles the outgoing mail herself, she often does not consider it worth the time to indicate what the enclosure is. Even so, no one's memory is perfect and the skilled secretary will make all such notations to avoid errors of omission. It is also quite possible that more than one notation may appear after the identifying initials (jb). The abbreviation "cc:" indicates the persons to whom carbon copies of this letter were forwarded.

```
                              Charles H. Stahls
                              Plant Manager

jb
enclosure:  check
cc:  Mr. W. A. Carey
     Ms. S. B. Buck
```

Enclosures may be indicated in many ways. When they are self-explanatory from the text of the letter, many secretaries merely indicate the fact that there is one. Others, more exacting, never fail to indicate either the number of enclosures or their nature.

```
jb                 JB
enc.               Enc.

jb                 jb              gr
enc. (1)           Enclosure       enclosures (3)

jb                 jb              gr
enclosure          encl.           encl. (3)

jb                 jb              GR
Enc.               Enc:  Check     Enc:  check
                                         card
                                         envelope

jb                 jb
enc: check         Enclosure:  Check

jb                 jb
Enc. (1)           enclosure:  check
```

An alert, skillful stenographer or secretary will indicate after the initials the fact that something has *not* been enclosed. For instance, in a letter which contains reference to a catalog or sample, the stenographer may indicate under the identifying initials "Catalog sent separately" or "Sample sent parcel post" to set the reader's mind at ease should he expect to find the item in the same envelope. This procedure, however, has taken a new turn with the use of the combination envelope. This is a large manila envelope suitable for mailing a sample or catalog (see Chapter 16). On its face is a smaller window envelope which will hold a first-class letter. This eliminates the possibility of the two becoming separated in transit.

Postscripts are to be avoided in business correspondence, except for seeking dramatic effect in the sales letter. In the regular business letter, it is wiser to retype the entire letter than to include a postscript. It may be a little bit insulting to the customer who feels that you have failed to think through carefully enough what you have to say to him and therefore had to tack an extra point on at the end of the page.

HIGH POINT FURNITURE CO.

November 18, 19--

Winslow, Boyd & Jones
175 Eastbourne Parkway
Providence, RI 02919

Gentlemen

The sketch of the desks and chairs you forwarded to us yesterday
is now in the hands of our furniture designers. They have already begun work on planning and estimating the construction
details. Thank you for sending it so promptly.

Within a week we should be able to offer you the price and
delivery estimates for the furniture in a variety of finishes.
These figures will be computed to compete favorably with any
other similar quality manufacture. Please keep in mind that the
chairs and desks will be made to last. We are glad you so wisely
included details of your decor. It will help greatly in saving
time.

Our regional salesman suggested that you might wish to see a
similar custom order which we completed last month for another
business office in your area. He has already ascertained that
you would be most welcome there to see the charm and serviceability of our desks and chairs add to this modern office. Should
you desire this opportunity, please communicate with me at once.

Sincerely

(Ms.) * Carol Powers
Executive Vice President

mq

Fig. 2.10 Pure block style, block date,
open punctuation.

November 18, 19--

Winslow, Boyd & Jones
    175 Eastbourne Parkway
        Providence, RI 02919

Gentlemen:

    The sketch of the desks and chairs you forwarded to us
yesterday is now in the hands of our furniture designers. They
have already begun work on planning and estimating the construction details. Thank you for sending it so promptly.

    Within a week we should be able to offer you the price and
delivery estimates for the furniture in a variety of finishes.
These figures will be computed to compete favorably with any
other similar quality manufacture. Please keep in mind that the
chairs and desks will be made to last. We are glad you so wisely
included details of your decor. It will help greatly in saving
time.

    Our regional salesman suggested that you might wish to see a
similar custom order which we completed last month for another
business office in your area. He has already ascertained that you
would be most welcome there to see the charm and serviceability
our desks and chairs add to this modern office. Should you desire
this opportunity, please communicate with me at once.

                    Sincerely,

                    HIGH POINT FURNITURE CO.

                    Carl W. Powers
                    Executive
                    Vice President

Fig. 2.11 Indented style, pivoted date,
mixed punctuation. Archaic.

* Carol is an example of the type of name which is not clearly male
or female. The title in parentheses is considerate of the correspondent.

HIGH POINT FURNITURE CO.

November 18, 19--

Winslow, Boyd & Jones
175 Eastbourne Parkway
Providence, RI 02919

Gentlemen:

The sketch of the desks and chairs you forwarded to us yesterday
    is now in the hands of our furniture designers. They have
    already begun work on planning and estimating the construc-
    tion details. Thank you for sending it so promptly.

Within a week we should be able to offer you the price and delivery
    estimates for the furniture in a variety of finishes. These
    figures will be computed to compete favorably with any other
    similar quality manufacture. Please keep in mind that the
    chairs and desks will be made to last. We are glad you so
    wisely included details of your decor. It will help greatly
    in saving time.

Our regional salesman suggested that you might wish to see a
    similar custom order which we completed last month for an-
    other business office in your area. He has already ascertained
    that you would be most welcome there to see the charm and
    serviceability our desks and chairs add to this modern office.
    Should you desire this opportunity, please communicate with me
    at once.

                         Sincerely,

CWP/MQ   Ms. Carol Powers
                                 Executive Vice President

Fig. 2.12 Hanging paragraph, or inverted indent, style, centered date,
mixed punctuation.

HIGH POINT FURNITURE CO.

November 18, 19--

Winslow, Boyd & Jones
175 Eastbourne Parkway
Providence, RI 02919

Gentlemen

    The sketch of the desks and chairs you forwarded to us
yesterday is now in the hands of our furniture designers. They
have already begun work on planning and estimating the construction details. Thank you for sending it so promptly.

    Within a week we should be able to offer you the price and
delivery estimates for the furniture in a variety of finishes.
These figures will be computed to compete favorably with any
other similar quality manufacture. Please keep in mind that the
desks and chairs will be made to last. We are glad you wisely
included details of your decor. It will help greatly in saving
time.

    Our regional salesman suggested that you might wish to see
a similar custom order which we completed last month for another
business office in your area. He has already ascertained that
you would be welcome there to see the charm and serviceability
our desks and chairs add to this modern office. Should you
desire this opportunity, please communicate with me at once.

                    Sincerely

                    HIGH POINT FURNITURE CO.

CWP/MQ   Ms. Carol Powers
                            Executive Vice President

Fig. 2.13 Semi-block style, pivoted
date, open punctuation.

HIGH POINT FURNITURE CO.

November 18, 19--

Winslow, Boyd & Jones
175 Eastbourne Parkway
Providence, RI 02919

Gentlemen:

The sketch of the desks and chairs you forwarded to us yesterday
is now in the hands of our furniture designers. They have already started work on planning and estimating the construction
details. Thank you for sending it to us so promptly.

Within a week we should be able to offer you the price and
delivery estimates for the furniture in a variety of finishes.
These figures will be computed to compete favorably with any
other similar quality manufacture. Please keep in mind that the
desks and chairs will be made to last. We are glad you wisely
included details of your decor. It will help greatly in saving
time.

Our regional salesman suggested that you might wish to see a
similar custom order which we completed last month for another
business office in your area. He has already ascertained that
you would be most welcome there to see the charm and serviceability our desks and chairs add to this modern office. Should
you desire this opportunity, please communicate with me at once.

Sincerely,

Ms. Carol Powers
Executive Vice-President

CWP/mq
cc: Charles Renault
    Harrison Thomas

Fig. 2.14 Block style, pivoted date, mixed punctuation.

Chapter 3

Letters Requesting Information

IN THE COURSE of a business day there are many occasions to write for information or to answer communications requesting information. Some of these are quite routine, but some are confidential. The confidential nature of any letter should be given due regard. As a matter of fact, the most routine letter should be treated in a certain amount of confidence. If the correspondence is treated in this manner, it will be filed promptly away from prying eyes. An efficient, businesslike system of filing correspondence as soon as possible is best for all purposes. The faster it is stored, the easier it should be to locate, and the less chance there will be for unnecessary or unauthorized reading.

Prospective Employee

It is common practice to verify the claims of a prospective employee as to past experience and character reference. Other firms will write to you for this purpose and you will write to them. There is a psychological factor involved here that must be considered when writing or answering such inquiries.

When writing to others, make the form of request so simple to complete that they will not delay answering. Including a stamped, self-addressed envelope will aid in speeding the response. (Make it a practice yourself to answer these requests within forty-eight hours; it is good policy and makes an excellent impression on the recipient.) The copy of the reply should be kept in the personnel file which is considered a confidential one, restricted to authorized personnel only. For rank-and-file employees the form may be duplicated, with space provided for the date, name and address, and name of prospect involved.

If the inquiry is concerned with an applicant for an executive or junior executive position, either a form-type letter or an individually prepared letter may be used. The individually prepared letter may, however, follow the format of the form letter below. Any added items may be inserted. In the case of a

Inquiry Form Letter for Employee

Frank Manufacturing Company
100 Girrard Street
Tuscaloosa, AL 36003

Subject: Personnel Record of Amy Person

Miss Person has applied to us for employment as a stenographer in our purchasing department. She has referred us to you for a testimonial of recent similar experience.

Would you be kind enough to supply us with the information requested concerning Miss Person?

Dates of employment with you_____to_____
Title of last position held_____
Did the position involve some supervisory decisions?
                                             Yes_____No_____
Title of position when first employed_____
Any intermediary job titles held (1)_____
                                        (2)_____
Got along with fellow employees.....
                    Well_____Average_____Poorly_____
Got along with supervisor(s).......
                    Well_____Average_____Poorly_____
Attendance record was.............
                    Good_____Average_____Poor_____
Employee's reliability was..........
                    Good_____Average_____Poor_____
Quality of work performed was......
                    Good_____Average_____Poor_____
Would you rehire this person if needed? Yes___No___
Stated reason for leaving_____
If discharged, reason_____
Other comments:

Your answers in the spaces provided will be greatly appreciated. All facts or opinions given will be held in the strictest confidence. An envelope is enclosed for your convenience in replying.

purchasing manager, for instance, you might wish to know a little more about the area of his responsibility in a previous job.

Present Employee

If the candidate for a position is hired pending replies from former employers, it is only fair to inform him of it. It is his prerogative not to begin employment on such an indefinite basis. When the vacancy needs to be filled urgently, it may be necessary to hire before a reply can possibly be obtained. The references subsequently received should still be placed in the employee's personnel jacket or folder. These files should be available only to trusted, authorized personnel. The confidential nature of personnel folders cannot be overemphasized. The contents of these files should not be grist for the office gossip mill.

The form letter given here, or a similar one, will serve its purpose well for an applicant who is awaiting a call to work or whom you have taken on pending references. Some firms request present employees who wish to be considered for promotion to compose a résumé and letter of application as though they were answering a classified advertisement. They should receive the same consideration as, if not more than, a new prospect. Some business firms have a centrally located bulletin board on which announcements of vacancies are posted for a specified period of time for the consideration of present employees before the vacancy is thrown on the open market. The practice is an excellent morale booster. Coupled with an incentive reimbursement educational program, it brings surprisingly rich returns on the investment. In the case of present employees, the reference from a superior may be obtained orally in a matter of minutes or in writing within a very short time. The same form may be employed for this information.

In other business houses, employees requesting raises in pay are requested to write an analysis of their duties and a covering letter making formal request for that increase.

TO: Mr. Irving Cohen, Controller   Date: 2/6/——
FROM: Robert Brockman
SUBJECT: Wage Increase

The attached analysis details my duties as assistant chief circulation manager under the supervision of Mr. Jay Daniel. Several points indicate the reasons for the request for salary increase:

1) It will be noted that the number of hours required for supervisory duties since my last report has risen by 28 percent.
2) Decision-making activities have almost doubled with the tremendous rise in circulation figures and the consequent increase in burden upon the circulation department.
3) The number of clock hours has gone up 20 percent since the last report.
4) The circulation manager has received a 10 percent increase in salary in the light of his increased burdens.
5) Six months have elapsed since my last review of salary by you.

In view of these facts, may I respectfully request that an increase of 10 percent be granted to me.

Submitted in accordance with company policy for approval and transmission to the personnel director.

enc.   Assistant Circulation Manager

Employee Credit Inquiries

With the tremendous growth of installment purchasing in this country, there has naturally been a sharp increase in inquiries concerning the wages of employees who have requested credit rating to make such purchases. Since it is general policy to determine ability to pay before permitting any sizable purchase, the earnings of the prospective customer must be ascertained. The type of form letter used by many such organizations is shown in Fig. 3.1. It is necessary to answer them promptly so that no permanent employee may be unduly inconvenienced.

The inquiry illustrated could be handled most expeditiously by the employee responsible by merely writing in the answers by hand. Then, in order to have a copy for the file, make a photocopy of the entire letter, send the photocopy, and file the original in the employee's personnel folder. By this method the personnel clerk or executive responsible for replying to these inquiries could just complete the few blank spaces and pass the rest of the task on to a photocopy clerk and a file clerk, who in some organizations may very well be the same person.

Personal Inquiries

There are inquiries which get into the "ticklish" area because they are so personal and confidential. In these instances, a procedure should be employed to guarantee continued privacy. There are at least 3 types of occasions on which confidential inquiries arrive and must be answered very discreetly. In each case the subject of the correspondence should have informed management, but there is so much embarrassment involved in these situations that most times he does not. It is understandable.

Employee A is the subject of an inquiry from a psychiatric clinic or physician attempting to determine the ability to pay in deciding the professional

```
                                                          November 25, 19--



          Prompt Service Company
          27-15 Northern Boulevard
          Long Island City, NY 11101

          Gentlemen:

          SUBJECT: Mary Longden, Employee

          The above-named individual has applied to us for credit approval on the
          purchase of a washer-dryer on our monthly payment plan.  As this purchase
          amounts to $315.50, we desire certain information before approving credit
          for this customer.  In order to advise the customer of her ability to meet
          the obligation, it is necessary for us to know the extent of her income.

          We are sorry to have to trouble you for the information, but as there is
          no other way to obtain this very essential data, please bear with us.
          The answers to just four simple questions are necessary.

                 1)  Weekly salary_____

                 2)  Length of service as of this week____months

                 3)  Home address_____

                     _____

                 4)  Is there any cause for possible
                     termination of employment at this time?____


                                      _____
                                         Signature and title

          We wish to thank you for your patience and kindness in supplying this
          information so promptly.  A stamped, self-addressed envelope is enclosed
          for your reply.

          Gratefully



          Jon David, Credit Manager

          ss
          enc.
```

Fig. 3.1   Form letter for credit inquiry.

fee based on means. It is generally a routine request concerning wages and general behavior on the job, but the employee deserves the utmost protection against publicity. In some personnel departments the personnel director himself handles these and similar requests. He has one secretary who handles all responses and the carbon copy is placed in a sealed envelope and filed in the personnel jacket. On the outside of the envelope is the notation *Not to be opened under any circumstances without written approval of the personnel director.* This is an excellent practice. One firm has a system in which the personnel director has a special and separate file in which all confidential correspondence is deposited. It is locked at all times and only he has the key.

Employee B is the subject of a court inquiry into the record of an ex-convict. Rehabilitated, hardworking people who have paid their debt for their errors certainly deserve every consideration to keep their secret. The withholding of this knowledge from others is desirable for all concerned, especially since most people see too much television and have vivid imaginations. Inquiries are most likely to come when such an employee is still on parole. They are routine. In one such case, the personnel director personally typed the reply and personally placed the carbon copy in his confidential file and locked it away. This treatment is admirable and laudable.

Employee C is the subject of an inquiry in the case of the support of a child in which paternity has been proved. The courts will check at regular intervals to determine whether or not the support amount is a burden on the man paying it. After a request by the man to reduce the amount or a request by the woman to increase it, such an inquiry is a matter of routine. This information comes to the attention of the employer only because he holds the key as to the employee's ability to pay and the employer should keep the confidence.

In all of these cases and any others of a similar

extremely personal nature, it is best not to sit in judgment; leave that to the authorities. Respect the confidence and do not allow it to influence that employee's opportunity for advancement.

Service Inquiries

For companies which produce a manufactured item there is always a type of service inquiry that requires great patience and understanding in answering. For instance:

17 Elm Street
Sioux Falls, SD 57101
March 8, 19––

Apox Manufacturing Company
275 West 47 Street
New York, NY 10016

Gentlemen

In January I bought one of your Vel-Tux storm jackets at Jason's Department Store. Here it is only six weeks later and the zipper doesn't work any more. I can't say that I am pleased with your product for which I paid $69.95!

I certainly expect you to do something about it. Shall I send the jacket back? I hope not. It was 16° here this morning.

Yours angrily

Joseph Greenley

There are two types of response to appease this customer's anger and turn it into good will. Responses will depend on company policy. Both are quite effective.

Response A

SPECIAL DELIVERY
March 11, 19––

Mr. Joseph Greenley
17 Elm Street
Sioux Falls, SD 57101

Dear Mr. Greenley

Please accept our deepest apology for the difficulty you have had with the zipper on your jacket. We are em-barrassed. We took such care to choose the best zipper manufacturer in the East to make our zippers for us. We have advised him of your complaint, and he is most anxious to examine the zipper in question.

Because the weather is so cold and we know you cannot do without your jacket at this time, we prevailed upon the zipper manufacturer to make good even at this distance. It will mean that you will only be without your jacket long enough to have a brand new fastener sewed in. We hope you will agree that this is fair.

This morning, by special delivery, a new zipper to replace your defective one was mailed. The new zipper will be sewed in for you at no cost if you will go to Harry's Tailor Shop, 417 South Main Street, Sioux Falls. The tailor has been paid for his services. Do *not* pay him.

Once again, we are sorry you had an unpleasant experience with our Vel-Tux product. We trust that this adjustment will be satisfactory to you.

Sincerely yours

Jerome Sweder
Vice President

jd

Response B

SPECIAL DELIVERY
March 11, 19––

Mr. Joseph Greenley
17 Elm Street
Sioux Falls, SD 57101

Dear Mr. Greenley

Our face is red. Your letter is the first one of its kind we have ever received. The zipper manufacturer who supplies us is speechless.

So, without further ado, let us explain what we have done for you. We have wired Jason's Department Store to accept your jacket in exchange for a brand-new one. They will ship the jacket back so that our zipper manufacturer may see the damaged fastener.

Present this letter to Mr. Harvey, the manager of the men's sporting goods department, and he will immediately authorize the exchange. There is no charge. We hope this is agreeable to you.

Regretfully yours

Jerome Sweder
Vice President

Another type of service inquiry is much more difficult to handle because the writer does not offer enough information to identify the product for advice to be rendered. Here are examples of the handling of one such instance in a couple of ways.

A letter is received from a customer indicating that the duplicating machine he purchased has been working well, but for the past few days has not been feeding paper properly. The model, size, and age are not given, nor is the identification of electrical or manual operation.

When the customer is located in an urban area where trained servicemen are readily available, this type of answer would serve:

SPECIAL DELIVERY
August 8, 19––

Mr. Paul Zalon
521 Howard Avenue
Topeka, KS 66605

Dear Sir:

We were sorry to hear of your difficulty with our duplicating machine. We shall see to it that this matter is cleared up at once.

Walden Office Machine Service in nearby Rutledge is sending one of their factory-trained servicemen to see your machine. If there is merely an adjustment to be made, there will be no charge and we are glad to have been able to help.

However, should there be a defective part, and should your machine have passed its 90-day guarantee period, we shall have to charge for the part to be replaced and the labor to install it. We have requested Walden to charge us for transportation costs in any event.

We know you will agree that this is a fair arrangement.

Sincerely,

Norma Rosenberg
Digehex Sales Manager

ek

In the event that the customer is in a more remote rural area to which a visit by a serviceman would mean an entire day's time, another tack can be taken to keep the customer mollified. The first letter should request full information and offer immediate advice. If this fails to satisfy the customer, a follow-up with

detailed assistance can be given. Sometimes a salesman passing through or a service organization to whom you have been of assistance in the past may be willing to repay the favor. Assuming that the customer needs one set of advice, this letter might be sufficient:

CERTIFIED MAIL

Mr. John Henderson
RFD #7 North
Wallace, AZ 72619

Dear Sir

We regret very much the fact that you have been inconvenienced by a defect in the feeding of paper in our machine. However, we believe it merely needs a simple adjustment. Would you be kind enough to follow these suggestions.

On the face of the paper bed upon which the completed copy falls is a set of instructions for adjusting all parts of the machine. Item #7 refers to a small pressure gauge on the top rear left of the machine. Inadvertently, some person may have turned this. In the center is a metal rod with rings inscribed on it. Check to see that this is set on the third ring on the rod as it faces you from the front where you normally stand to turn the handle.

Should that fail, we have enclosed a set of "Instructions for Operating" on which we have marked in red ink a small paragraph. Using some paper which is marked or of little value, follow these instructions carefully.

We are certain that either of these instructions will solve your problem. In case they do not, please let us have the model number, serial number, date of purchase, and indicate electric or manual model. We shall then arrange to have some qualified person take care of the matter. Please keep in touch.

Sincerely

Louis G. Martin
Service Consultant

zw
enc: Instructions for Operating

General Trade Information

For this type of inquiry, it is best to follow a set, complete procedure. This is the type of letter which asks whether or not you manufacture a certain type of product, how much it costs, and where it may be purchased in the writer's area. If advertising is purchased, you can expect such inquiries to arrive. When the follow-up method is employed, the prepared set is mailed and a salesman may call soon after.

A typical set that may be prepared for use in responding to an inquiry through advertising could consist of a copy of the advertisement, some further printed material illustrating other products, a form letter thanking the writer for his interest, and a business reply card for requesting a demonstration or a visit by a sales representative. These sets, prepared in advance, are mailed immediately to each respondent while the matter is still fresh in his mind. Having the sets ready must be planned as part of the advertising program; doing this permits it to become a routine clerical task which any clerk may perform. When the advertisement refers to products sold at retail, a list of dealers in the vicinity of the writer should be included. If this last procedure is employed, send a note to the nearest dealer with the name and address of the prospect.

Association or Club Membership

When an organization solicits members, it is necessary to reply to all inquiries. Many businessmen join organizations, belong to organizations, hold office in organizations, sponsor and otherwise support organizations. Courtesy dictates that in whatever capacity you act on behalf of such an organization the writer must be given very promptly the response to which he is entitled. Your response will then reach the writer while his interest is high.

Suppose you are the secretary of an association of office managers for a given area. An inquiry reaches you from an interested writer. You are the secretary of the association. You should send a brochure, a short personal letter, and an application form. The brochure should outline the purpose, activities, publications, and benefits of membership. The letter should thank him for his interest and invite him to attend a meeting as your guest to meet some of the members. The application blank should be a simple form, to make replying as easy as possible. The cost of membership should be clearly stated. The exact time, date, and topic of the next meeting should be prominent.

Dear Mr. Nathanson:

Your recent inquiry into the membership benefits of the Westchester Office Managers Society arrived today. We are sending you an immediate response so that you may take advantage of our various activities at once.

Next Wednesday evening our regular monthly meeting will be held at Chan's Restaurant at the Westchester Shopping Center in White Plains. This shopping center is easily accessible by either the Cross County Parkway or Route 123.

As is our custom, we shall dine at 7 p.m., after which our meeting will take place. At this particular meeting we shall have as our guest speaker the President of Remington Grand, whose topic will be "Data Processing for the Smaller Office." Won't you join us for dinner and this most interesting talk?

Enclosed are an application blank, our brochure, and an outline of our proposed activities for the remainder of this fiscal year. Won't you complete the application form, and, together with your check for $15, send it to me with word that you will be my guest for dinner? I shall look forward to meeting you and introducing you all around.

Cordially,

tl   Richard di Castro
enc. (3)   Secretary

P.S. If you would like more information, please call me at 555–3300, Extension 43; or 555–3343 direct.

Employment Inquiries

Enterprising applicants will write seeking employment or information as to the qualifications necessary to be employed in some specific capacity with your firm. For rank-and-file jobs, sufficient response is a form letter inviting the applicant to consult the personnel department during interview hours, thanking him for his interest, and indicating the constant need for skilled help with ambition and fresh views.

Dear Miss Laser

Our personnel department is always on the lookout for skilled stenographers. We are glad to have received your inquiry about the chances of employment with us at Central Products.

The personnel department will be most happy to inform you of the opportunities here if you will come in for an interview between 1:00 and 4:00 p.m. any business day. No appointment is necessary. Due to the ever-changing needs in an organization of our size, we cannot let you know of any specific opportunities until we have had a chance to determine the extent of your skills.

Thank you for your interest. We look forward to making your acquaintance.

Yours truly

Margaret Delehanty
Personnel Director

gg

When inquiries arrive from prospective employees who offer a specific skill or profession needed by the company, it is wise to answer with more definite promise than that given above. At times of critical need, this more inviting response is called for. Suppose there is a particular shortage of mechanical engineers in your company and an inquiry is received from a recent graduate of an engineering college who is seeking employment. A letter such as the following might be an appropriate reply:

Dear Mr. Cocoros

We are glad you wrote us regarding a position in the engineering department of Central Products.

If you would be kind enough to call our personnel department any afternoon between 1:00 and 4:00 p.m. and ask for me, I shall be glad to arrange an interview at a time which is mutually convenient. It would be rather lengthy to outline for you the qualifications necessary for employment in our engineering department because, as you can understand, we have opportunities for many different types of engineers.

Please get in touch with me as soon as you can and bring with you a complete résumé of your education, training, and experience. If the hours mentioned above are inconvenient, call me at 555–4242 (Ext. 458) so that we may determine a more suitable hour.

I look forward to making your acquaintance.

Yours truly

Alexander Fecher
Chief Engineer

ch
enc

P.S. To save you time when you visit us, I have taken the liberty of enclosing an application form.

Throughout this chapter we have used the term "form letter" rather loosely. A form letter may be reproduced with appropriate blank spaces that will be completed before mailing. On the other hand, a predetermined, preconceived letter which can be adapted by a competent person to suit the exact situation serves the same purpose. Both are great time-savers. Appropriately numbered or coded, they may be referred to simply as PF123 or GK789. In this way, at the bottom of the applicant's inquiry a notation may be made: "11/29/—— TY48 sent. JBW." No carbon of your reply is required. The form letters are on file.

If the need for this type of reply is frequent, it may be necessary to investigate other avenues of reproduction by the use of automatic typewriters. An automatic typewriter is one for which the use of punched cards, punched tape, or magnetic tape is necessary. Newer devices such as the IBM typewriter with memory or the MC/ST (mag card) or MT/ST (mag tape) also serve the same function, as well as computer-produced notations (Fig. 3.2). Only experienced people can detect the difference between a letter prepared on an automatic typewriter and one which was typed individually on an electric typewriter. Both machines are electrified, and both are simple to operate. The advantage of the automatic typewriter is that after typing in the date and the inside address manually, the machine may then be used to produce the form letter, letter-perfect. This applies only when all such letters are to be fairly identical except for programmed stops at which the name or an amount is to be typed in by the operator. (See Chapter 15.)

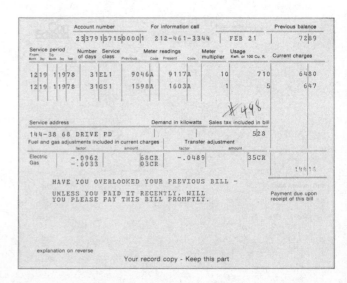

Fig. 3.2 Computer-produced comments on an invoice. (Courtesy of Consolidated Edison of New York)

Chapter 4

Credit and Collection

Credit

IN COLONIAL DAYS, business was conducted locally by barter. As more products became available by import, more money was needed, but little was available. As a result, credit was granted until the buyer received payments from his sources; then payment was made.

As more cities and merchants developed, credit grew and it became necessary to determine who could be trusted until payment was forthcoming. Character and earning capacity became the most important factors in credit judgment. All other customers paid cash as money came into regular circulation and banking became more common. Banks, in turn, issued letters of credit stating that the holder of the letter had a certain amount on deposit at that bank. However, by and large, vendors gave credit to those whose character and occupation they knew.

These days the vast majority of business is conducted on the basis of credit. More people are able to buy on credit because they can easily obtain credit cards backed by banks that benefit by charging interest for the period of the indebtedness.

This credit explosion has been made possible by the phenomenal speed and simplicity of the computers which are programmed to assimilate and regurgitate the information for each subscriber. For their own protection and because credit determination was becoming increasingly difficult, many dealers, manufacturers, wholesalers, or other groups formed associations which set up central clearing houses, where they had access to information obtained for them by specialists. Storing the voluminous information in a computer with a retrieval system, electronically operated, makes any data available in milliseconds.

Just as the credit associations grew from this, so did the credit departments of many business firms. The volume of business on a credit basis forced many to give the responsibility of keeping track of such matters into the hands of a specialist who became known generally as a credit manager. He was usually concerned also with the problem of collection when payment was not forthcoming in the agreed time. Since he had granted the credit risk in the first place, it was assumed that he should also be responsible for the collection when his judgment proved wrong. In some companies with large numbers of accounts receivable, these two functions are separated, so that there is a credit manager and a collection manager. In either case, they work closely and carefully with the executive in charge of keeping the accounts-receivable records.

It is clear then that the credit manager is responsible for determining the extent of the credit risk for each customer based on any sources of information at his command. In effect, he is saying that in his opinion the amount he decides on is the limit for which this customer should be expected to repay comfortably from current and expected resources and revenues. The amount is usually based on formulas, facts, records, other credit information, and experience in making credit determinations. Unfortunately, when the credit manager's estimate of ability is wrong, it becomes necessary to go to the collection procedures of the law or its appropriate agency.

Credit Rating

When a customer first writes in or is brought in through the efforts of a salesman, it is the credit manager's task to determine the extent of credit to be granted. The salesman himself will be asked to submit certain information, observable during his visit. Sometimes the executives of the new organization were known when they worked for another organization. Their reputations for integrity will be known. Integrity is probably the most vital factor in credit determination.

Generally, the credit department will attempt to investigate promptly in order not to delay the purchaser. Dun & Bradstreet's credit ratings will be consulted. Other organizations common in many industries may supply information of the same nature. Manufacturers' associations sometimes have a system of obtaining such information on short notice. Research in the records of the credit department's own company might reveal previous experience with this customer under another name or before previous financial reverses. Such information would tend to make the credit manager more wary.

In many cases when credit information is not readily available, the company will ask the customer to pay cash until the investigation is completed and they are able to judge the credit limit. If the customer is obviously able to pay, the credit manager will make a tentative credit evaluation until full data are received.

For a well-known product or service, the request to open an account may come by mail. This request is not to be confused with a direct request for cash for various uses. (The latter type of inquiry would go directly to a bank or loan company and would be repayable in monthly or lump-sum payment.) We refer here to a business account which becomes an account receivable on someone's bookkeeping record of transactions. Below are several different types:

Gentlemen:

Re: Charge Account

It has been obvious to me lately that I could save myself a great deal of trouble and effort if I had a charge account at your store. In recent months I have been purchasing more frequently.

Would you be kind enough to send me all necessary information and forms to enable me to open a full charge account at once.

Yours truly,

Mrs. Sylvia Slobin

Gentlemen

Your salesman called on us several months ago but at the time we did not sell electrical appliances. Since that time we have established a small department for the convenience of our customers.

In the last issue of HOUSEHOLD PRODUCTS we noticed your advertisement of 110 volt, ½ h.p. air conditioners which require no installation. Would you be kind enough to ask your salesman to return with full details on this type of appliance.

While we await his call, please be good enough to determine our credit rating so that we may know the extent of our purchase. We deal with

NORTHERN ELECTRIC COMPANY
210 Crowell Street
Abilene, KS 67410

and the

GENERAL MERCHANDISING CORPORATION
1600 West Temple Street
Boston, MA 02151

We bank at

FIRST CHASE CHEMICAL BANK
Wabash Building
Cleveland, OH 44144

Yours truly

Vincent Connors
Merchandising Manager

Gentlemen:

Re: Credit Rating

For the past six months or so we have been doing business with you on a cash basis. You will certainly agree that this has gone a long way in aiding us to prove our good faith and financial ability.

We are quite gratified by the response of our local customers and the future looks promising. On the basis of this expected improvement in business and our past credit record, would you now consider extending us credit on an open account? Your approval of this request will permit us to broaden our scope.

We wish to supply you with these three references:

A) Mercantile Products, 444 Crail Street, Chicago, IL 60609
B) Sinister Frocks, 876 Fifth Avenue, Brooklyn, NY 11208
C) Bachelor Products, 234 Angel Street, Macon, GA 31206

We bank at the Falls Trust Company in this city. Mr. James R. Butler handles our account there.

May we have your decision as soon as possible.

Sincerely,

Michael J. Furey
President

ae

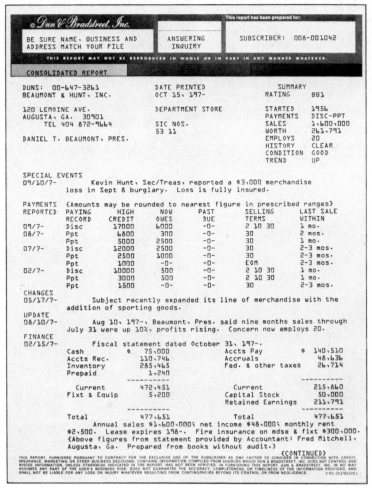

Fig. 4.1 Sample Dun & Bradstreet credit report, first page. (Courtesy of Dun & Bradstreet, Inc.)

Credit Inquiry to References

In addition to this type of inquiry will come those which the salesmen bring in routinely. The sources of knowledge, both personal and business, must be investigated by letter. We will not presume to tell the credit manager how to determine the amount of the credit rating, but a thorough investigation will prevent embarrassment and unjust decisions all around. Those companies which belong to their industry's service organization will discover that it is most helpful. Dun & Bradstreet's service (Fig. 4.1) or a bank will supply other information in most cases. A few more careful concerns will contact the local Chamber of Commerce, trade service organization, or the local Better Business Bureau. Because there is a period of quiet between the collapse of a business and its actual demise, local sources of information are the most reliable and helpful.

To establish the correct credit rating, inquiries to all concerned must go out at once. For this purpose a form letter is most helpful and expeditious. This is one area in which there is no danger of injuring anyone's sensibilities by sending a prepared form letter. It is necessary to have one for the customer himself and another for the bank and other business houses with which he deals. If it is also customary to follow up with the Chamber of Commerce, Better Business Bureau, and so on, a third letter will be needed. In all cases, a follow-up post card should be used to encourage a more prompt response.

One of the greatest time-savers is to have the salesman obtain the name of the bank and the names and addresses of three companies with which the customer has done business for at least one year. This permits writing to them directly, immediately upon receipt of the salesman's order. Of course, if they are rated in Dun & Bradstreet or other trade association listing, you can be more leisurely about verifying their financial standing. If not, form letters (Figs. 4.2, 4.3, 4.4) will be needed. When you are acquainted with other businessmen in town, it is possible to obtain confidential replies when good relations exist between you.

The day the credit-inquiry letter is mailed, a notation must be made to that effect. In a given number of days a follow-up card should be sent to hasten the receipt of the reply. Carbon copies of form letters need not be made. A notation of the form-letter code number is all that is necessary.

To the customer:

                                               January 4, 19––

Gentlemen:

About a week ago we sent you a request for certain credit information to facilitate the opening of a credit account for you.

Your prompt attention to this matter will enable us to comply with your wishes. If you have already sent your reply, please ignore this reminder.

                        Yours truly,

td   Credit Manager
cb5   Central Products Corporation

To the bank and suppliers:

                                               January 4, 19––

Gentlemen   Re: Credit Inquiry

About a week ago we sent you a credit inquiry for

– –

As this customer is in need of the goods ordered and we require the information you can supply, won't you send your response soon? Thank you.

                        Yours truly

td   Credit Manager
cb6   Central Products Corporation

Occasionally, when a person is just beginning a business venture, he has no business references. He may still attempt to obtain credit for purchases on open account by supplying good personal references. It is necessary to approach such an individual on a personal rather than a business level, and the letter should reflect this difference.

Dear Mr. Balser

This week we received an order from a young man who has just started in business for himself. After five years' experience in the repair of typewriters, he has decided to open his own repair, rental, and sales shop. His name is William J. Lynch.

He has requested that we send him typewriters and adding machines on a consignment basis. Before we can do so, we must establish his trustworthiness and his expectation of success in his present venture.

Would you be kind enough to tell us what you can to aid us in deciding? We know you have had no business dealings with Mr. Lynch, but you have known him well for many years. Anything you can tell us as to his honesty, industry, and reliability would be greatly appreciated.

Yours truly

George Hutner
Credit Manager

dm
enc: reply envelope

Credit Limitation

When all the facts are in and it has been decided to grant credit, and how much, the customer should be informed immediately. The following is a form letter which one company sends when the first order on an open account has been received and shipped and the terms have already been set up:

Your first order, given to our representative, Mr. ––––, is greatly appreciated.

It will be shipped to you on open account terms as explained in the enclosed schedule.

It is a privilege to have you as a customer, and we shall look forward to having many opportunities to be of service to you.

                        Cordially,

CCB:sta   Credit Department
Enc.

The letter below is more personal in tone, though it may still be used as a form letter:

Dear Mr. Olshaker:

We are pleased to inform you that all your credit references and your bank have replied to our inquiries. We are now able to let you know our decision concerning the credit limitation of your account.

In view of the facts received, we shall allow you a credit limit of $100. This means that, within the terms offered to you of 2/10 EOM, you may purchase up to this amount as your total indebtedness at any one given time. We believe you will find this a liberal allowance. Naturally, the amount you may purchase over this limit for cash is unlimited. All our services are included.

We trust that you will make full use of this account and that you will find every satisfaction in our products. We look forward to a long and profitable relationship.

Yours truly,

Jerry Berglund
Credit Manager

fj

On other occasions it may be advisable to increase or decrease the credit limit for a given customer according to his record established with you. This is a decision for the credit manager, who should review ratings every six months as a regular practice. Here is a form letter warning a customer of the overextension of his credit:

"Easy credit can be convenient but . . . if it is used to excess, it can be harmful."

We like our good charge account customers; so much so that we wish to protect their credit standing.

Although your recent purchases have increased your account balance, your payments have not increased accordingly. The amount of credit which we can allow on your account is determined by the amount of your monthly payments.

With our many years of experience in handling customer accounts we feel that we can be of some assistance to you, and thereby prevent future credit problems.

```
Gentlemen

We are very pleased with your vote of confidence.  We want you to know
that we appreciate your order for our products given to our representa-
tive, John Schubis.

To aid you in establishing your credit rating with us rapidly, would you
be kind enough to answer these questions, and return this form letter to
us as quickly as you can.  It will facilitate future handling of your
account here.

Are you rated in any standard credit listing?_____

Name(s) of credit service(s)_____

    _____

Bank(s) with which you do business

_____|_____
_____|_____

Three suppliers with whom you have done business for more than one year:

        Name          Street Address      City, State, Zip
_____|_____|_____
_____|_____|_____
_____|_____|_____

In round figures, would you give us the total amount of annual sales of
your business for the last three years:

19__ $_____    19__ $_____    19__ $_____

How long have you been located at your present site?_____

How long have you been doing business under this name?_____

We would appreciate your prompt reply.  All answers will be considered
strictly confidential.

Yours truly

Conrad J. Saphier
Credit Manager

Name and title of officer completing form_____

Note:  We have attached another copy of this letter so that you may
       retain a copy for your files.
```

Fig. 4.2   Credit inquiry letter to the customer.

```
Gentlemen:

The XYZ Company, 274 West Broad Street, your city, has applied to us for
an open credit account.  They have given us your name as the bank in which
they deposit their funds.  In order to aid us in determining their credit
rating, we shall need certain information.

How long has their account been in your bank? _____

Is the bank balance fairly steady? _____

If not, is it subject to drastic fluctuations? _____

Would you consider their account with you a normal one? _____

Have they ever overdrawn their account? _____

Have they ever borrowed funds from your bank? _____

Have you ever denied them a loan?  Why? _____

Do you consider the management satisfactory? _____

Any other comments you wish to make which would aid us in deciding
the extent of credit?
_____
_____

Needless to say, all remarks made will be kept in strictest confidence.
If we can ever be of service to you in return, please do not hesitate
to call on us.

Yours truly



Lester Myers
Credit Manager

sl
enc:  reply envelope
```

Fig. 4.3 Credit inquiry letter to the bank.

Please call our office before you make your next charge purchase so that we may assist you in restoring your account to good standing.

We appreciate your patronage and look forward to a long and happy association with you for many years to come.

Very sincerely yours,

J. B. Lefkowitz*
Credit Sales Manager

JBL:da
140L

___

Another letter dealing with overextension of credit is more explicit though polite:

Gentlemen

For the past three years you have purchased our products within the $250 credit limitation we set on your

account. We now feel, however, that the time has come to review this amount.

Occasionally it has been necessary for you to seek extensions of time in which to satisfy your indebtedness to us. We believe that you will be better served if your limitation is set at $150, subject to review in six months. There will be no decrease in our desire or effort to satisfy your needs to the best of our ability. We know that you understand the necessity for this action.

Sincerely

Doris Culver
Credit Assistant

___

Sometimes the review of a customer's credit rating calls for an extension of his credit:

Gentlemen

We hope that in our association over the past five years you have found our products and services satisfactory.

* When typing a name with initials only, remember to treat each as a word; therefore, space between them.

We have been glad to help you satisfy the needs of your growing number of customers.

During this period you have always lived up to your indebtedness to us and, in addition, have taken advantage many times of our liberal discount policy. It is, therefore, very pleasant to inform you that we have decided to increase your credit limitation with us from $500 to $750.

You can look forward, then, to further satisfactory service with our constantly improving products on a larger scale than heretofore. Thank you for your past patronage. We appreciate it.

Sincerely

Herbert A. Groening
Assistant Credit Manager

vc

Suspension of Credit

It is sometimes necessary to notify a customer that because of his poor credit performance you can no longer sell him your products on open account. You could merely send a note of a few sentences and let it go at that. However, there is gratitude for past business, there is courtesy, and there is compassion. Whether or not you give the customer a fully detailed explanation is a matter of choice. Usually it is better not to.

It has been said that it is not the kindest act to ask a dying man the answers to riddles. You know the customer is having financial difficulties; don't berate him for it. Give him the simple message he has been expecting and sign off graciously.

Dear Mr. Damm

We have been pleased to be one of your suppliers over the past six years. You know much better than we

```
To the suppliers:

Gentlemen

Re:  XYZ Company, 274 West Broad Street, Chicago, IL 60608

As we all must with new accounts, we call upon you for certain information
regarding the customer above.  They have applied to us for an open credit
account.  The company states that they have done business with you for
over a year and have referred us to you.

Would you kindly inform us:

How does this customer pay bills?

        a. Takes advantage of discount by paying in 30 days_____
        b. Pays bills on time but does not take discount_____
        c. Pays at the end of the full credit period_____
        d. Sometimes pays after the credit period_____
        e. Has occasionally been quite late in payment_____
        f. Other:

Exactly what credit terms do you extend them?_____

How long have you done business with them?_____

What part of that period has been on open credit account?_____

Do you consider them a desirable customer?_____

At present, is there a balance past due on their account?_____

Any other pertinent data you would care to furnish:

_____

_____

_____

All answers will be treated with the utmost confidence.  If we can ever be
of similar service to you, please call on us.

Yours truly


Nicholas Burliuk
Credit Manager

mc
enc:  reply envelope
```

Fig. 4.4 Credit inquiry letter to the customer's suppliers.

that the cancellation of the proposed housing project in your area injured your expected gross income extensively. We believe you know also that in spite of this unfortunate event our credit manager recommended that we continue your orders on open account on regular terms.

Since it has been necessary to extend the date for payment on the last four payments of modest sums, our credit manager has now recommended that we alter your credit standing. Please be kind enough to make all future purchases for cash with the usual cash discount. We would appreciate also the promptest possible settlement of your last purchase on open account which is now two weeks overdue.

In the meantime, you know that we understand the nature of your financial reverses and you have our full sympathy. Our regular services and advice are at your beck and call. Please do not hesitate to call on us.

You have our sincere wishes for improved business soon.

Sincerely

James Landes
Credit Department

hb

Perhaps as a result of the semi-annual credit review, your credit sources inform you that XYZ Products is in shaky condition at a time when you still extend to them a credit limit of $100. It is only fair to notify them immediately of your decision to change the limit so that no further indebtedness will be incurred under the old understanding. True, it is similar to throwing salt in the wound, but the injured party should not be surprised by a turn for the worse. Business is business. This move is not personal. Only a wonder drug can cure the situation—money. If it is forthcoming, there is no difficulty whatsoever in reappraising the customer's credit limitation.

Gentlemen:

In our semi-annual credit review by our auditor, it has been noted that your last few payments have been quite slow although complete. We appreciate the difficulty with which these payments were made.

At his recommendation, therefore, we must inform you that on your receipt of this letter, we have reduced your credit rating. Future purchase orders should be accompanied by your check in full for the amount, less the usual cash discount.

Nevertheless, we want you to know that we appreciate your patronage and hope that you will find it possible to continue as one of our valued customers and old friends.

Sincerely,

Florence Weitz
Assistant Credit Manager

ae

Refusal of Credit

Not all prospective customers can be granted credit. In many instances customers are accepted on a cash basis subject to the satisfactory submission of credit references. A new customer who has no credit listing should be clearly informed of general policy to sell for cash until the credit investigation is completed.

Gentlemen

We are very grateful to you for the order placed with our salesman, Charles Wagner. You can expect to take your place along with our hundreds of satisfied customers who have found it profitable to carry our goods.

You can take advantage of our cash discount by forwarding your check for your order, less the cash discount. As soon as we receive it, we shall ship the goods to you with our recommendations for display. All display materials are furnished at no extra cost.

In this way, without delay to you, we shall be able to ship the goods at once, while we complete the credit investigation. We know you will understand the necessity for this procedure and hope that this is the beginning of a long and profitable relationship.

Yours truly

Actually, this letter has refused a credit rating to the customer, but no reference is made to this fact. The positive approach is used, indicating the usual services and the discount advantage of a cash purchase. Another way of treating the same refusal might be in the rewording of only the second paragraph of the above letter.

We are at once shipping the goods ordered. Please be kind enough to give our truckman a check for the full amount of your purchase less the usual 5 percent cash discount. He will also deliver free display materials which have been prepared by our experts to aid our customers in presenting our products most favorably to the public. All display materials, national advertising, and sales promotional advice are without charge to you.

The following letter refusing credit is more direct, perhaps because the company which sends it is a large established one, with thousands of outlets.

Thank you for your patience while we have been making our credit investigation for your account.

Unfortunately, the information we have obtained is not adequate for us to arrange credit accommodations for you at this time. We shall, of course, be happy to review your account at a later time, if you wish, and we hope that better terms may then be provided.

In the meantime, however, when orders are placed, will you please be sure to enclose your payment for them to prevent shipping delays?

Cordially,

GTS:bcc   Credit Department

Consignment Credit

The transfer of goods from the manufacturer to the consumer frequently involves a middleman. Such middlemen as wholesalers, distributors, brokers, and jobbers are essentially the same except for the methods of purchase they employ. They are the links in the chain between the manufacturer and the consumer. The manufacturer produces large quantities; the wholesaler or distributor purchases a small portion of this production; the retailer buys from the manufacturer (large quantities) or from the wholesaler (smaller quantities) or from the jobber (very small units) to resell to customers one item at a time. The broker is usually a link between the manufacturer and the retailer. He differs only in that he buys nothing directly himself, but acts as the intermediary or salesman for the transaction.

Some wholesalers who are convinced a product is sure-fire will sell it to the retailer on consignment to help convince him of its salability. A consignment purchase is not paid for until it is actually sold; the retailer takes no risk and may return the goods according to the original agreement. For the wholesaler to indulge in consignment sales, the product must be fairly stable because if not, by the time it is returned it would be out of date, out of season, or depreciated in value. Consignment might be an arrangement such as this one:

Gentlemen

The goods were shipped this morning as we promised in our letter. . . .

We agree to accept the return of any unsold scarfs in this shipment within sixty days of their receipt by you. In order to keep all records clear and definite, please complete the lower portion of the form which accompanies the shipment. Send it to us at once and keep the carbon copy for your records. The cost of all scarfs from this shipment not returned by the end of the sixty days shall be payable by March 15. The returned scarfs will not be charged to you at all. The cost of freight for the entire shipment should be included in the final payment.

We know you will find these scarfs to be all that we said they were. . . .

It is necessary in consignment sales to be as clear as possible in all stipulations to prevent later claims. Most companies who engage in such practices have a consignment-sale contract which must be signed by the retailer. In it he guarantees the safety and condition of the goods while they are on his premises. All other considerations should be spelled out in the agreement.

Extended Payments

Apart from customers who deliberately purchased on the installment or multiple-payment plan, occasions arise which necessitate resorting to an extended payment to aid customers who have encountered ill fortune—fire, theft, community disaster, or other mishap. This service to a customer is cheap even if it must be financed by you. The customer's good will is retained, his business is retained, and normally he should become a regular customer once again. Of course, during the period of the payments, the credit limit must be adhered to. All purchases above that figure, including the sum of the unpaid installments, must be for cash.

Gentlemen

We learned with deep regret of the damage to your store as a result of a flash fire. Our sympathy to you in this calamity. We should like to assist you in restoring order to your wrecked premises.

Your account with us shows a balance due to us of $314.87. We realize that requiring full payment at this time would be disastrous to you and unreasonable of us. May we, therefore, propose this plan which may help you, in a small way, to restore full commerce to your excellent establishment once again.

We shall postpone for three months all payments by you on the balance owed. At that time, we shall expect to receive the first of ten equal monthly payments from you on the 15th of each month, commencing September 15 of this year. No interest charge will be added.

In the meantime, all purchases needed by you in order to resume business at your store may be made on a half cash, half credit basis. The first of these, when repairs have been completed, we shall approve on a consignment basis, but all others as stated, may be made under these special terms, until such time as the old indebtedness mentioned above is fully repaid. At that time, all things being normal, we shall revert to a full credit account.

We trust you will find this arrangement satisfactory. Please call on us for any assistance we may render in your return to normalcy.

Sincerely

John Thomas Daniels
Credit Manager

gh

Under other circumstances of normal business conditions, the same type of offer may be made, but not often so liberally. In the above example the insurance received by the customer will help balance things again. In the instance below, only improved business management, good fortune, and the business cycle will help.

Gentlemen

We were so sorry to learn from your recent letter that unemployment conditions in your sector have hit your volume of trade, and, naturally, your revenues. We wish to be as cooperative as possible under these circumstances.

We can offer you a plan of extended payments to discharge your debt to us of $274.80. You may remit on the 10th of each month 10 percent of this amount until it is erased. We trust that this is satisfactory.

In the meantime, we know you understand that all purchases made by you under this arrangement must be by sight draft. This is a satisfactory arrangement, we believe; don't you?

If there is any further way in which we can assist, call on us. Our most sincere wishes for improved business conditions in the immediate future.

Sincerely

Leon Ginsburg
Credit Manager

gg

The most common type of extended payment is the simple extension of time for the completion of the payment. For instance, at the request of the customer, an extension of thirty days is given on the due date. This is a flat time extension at the end of which the total sum is due.

Sources of Credit Information

On the national scale, credit information may be obtained from Dun & Bradstreet's Credit Service Bureau and many others. In the New York City area, for the children's and ladies' apparel industries alone, besides Dun & Bradstreet, there are:

> Children's Wear Credit Guild
> Credit Exchange
> Women's Apparel Board of Trade
> National Credit Clearing House
> National Knitted Outerwear Association.

Unofficial sources of information are:

> Salesman calling on the customer
> Other merchants supplied in the area
> Business associates in the area (truckers, etc.)
> Bank branches in the area
> Registered professional investigators
> Local Better Business Bureaus
> Friends in the area.

For the greatest credit success, the credit department should function as a coordinating liaison—credit ratings for customers of the sales department and collection agent for the accounts-receivable department. We have outlined a large portion of the credit area. Now to the less pleasant and more arduous task of collection.

Collection

Almost 90 percent of all accounts receivable pay their invoices by the day they are due or within a very reasonable time thereafter. The other 10 percent or so have to be tickled a little to remind them of their indebtedness. In a very small percentage of cases, the matter may go so far as to be handled by a lawyer. It is the aim of all companies never to allow the matter to reach that last and inevitably distasteful stage.

Some business concerns have gone to much pain to prevent the legal collection or the collection agency arrangement. In order to arouse action, some have used the repetition of the statement *Past Due Please Remit*. Others use gummed stickers with the same message. Still others use "tricks" such as cartoons, rubber bands, new pennies, or small plastic objects. One department store sends a miniature statement in a small envelope with the caption "Just a small statement—so small you have probably overlooked it." Another uses a series of four cartoons with a space in which the amount is filled in. The first one is a drawing of a man with an oversized finger with a string tied to it to which is attached a small tag on which the amount is printed. Underneath are the words "Please remember us."

Following these reminders, or without these reminders, most business firms use a series of letters carefully worked out to encourage a response. Each series is labeled by code number and entered on the customer's record so that it will not be repeated. Other firms change the series periodically to avoid repetition. If discovered, it may destroy the seemingly "personal" touch. The most common order of approach is mild, hurt and disappointed, strong, and finally threatening. One nationally known controls-system manufacturer uses no series at all, but employs instead a single form letter worded quite strongly and indicating action unless a response is received in ten days. One such set of letters might be formulated as those given below. They are in the order in which they would be employed.

First Letter

Gentlemen

We note with surprise that there is a balance of $118.37 in your account which was due about six weeks ago. This amount covers purchases made in January, and, therefore, was due on February 15. It is now the beginning of April.

Since the amount is so small, we know it is merely an oversight on the part of your bookkeeper. We know there is nothing wrong with the merchandise delivered or we certainly would have heard about it from you by now.

Your settlement of this matter as promptly as possible would be appreciated. We enclose a self-addressed, stamped envelope for your convenience.

Very truly yours

Ludlow Thiel
Credit Manager

hy
enc.

Second Letter

Gentlemen

We are disappointed that our statements and letter to you have brought no reply.

In January, as a good business friend, you sent us your order for our nationally advertised, fine quality merchandise. We appreciated your order and your faith in our products, and showed it by shipping the goods at once. From the receipt of our trucker we learned that the goods were received in good condition three days later. That's good service.

You must have a problem to ignore our requests for payment for so long; and you have let us down by not even allowing us to help you. Perhaps we could arrange equal, reasonable payments; perhaps we could take some of the goods back and credit you for part of the value; perhaps we could help you in some other way.

Won't you call me when you receive this letter to discuss the matter? Call me collect at 555–7700; we will do our best to help you.

Yours truly

Third Letter

Gentlemen

If you were drowning and I held out my hand to you, wouldn't you grasp it? Or would you turn your back and continue to go under? Surely you must know that you have been ignoring our offers of assistance. In our last communication we offered to work out your debt in any way you wished. But you did not respond.

Your indebtedness to us for January purchases is now four months past due. Our auditor will permit no further delay in payment from you, because we have had to pay our suppliers on time. In order to do so, we had to borrow money at the usual interest. Our auditor has requested us to inform you of payment past due this last time by certified mail.

Therefore, unless we hear from you by return mail informing us of your intentions in this matter, we shall have no choice but to turn this account over to our attorney in your county, Henry Lichtig. He has been instructed to institute action against you if he does not hear from us by June 15.

Won't you act now and save yourself the additional expense and annoyance of a lawyer's fee and court costs?

Yours truly

Ludlow Thiel
Credit Manager

hy
cc: Henry Lichtig

The *fourth letter* would be a direct communication from the attorney in the local county, containing notification that action had been instituted in the local county courts to collect the amount due.

These letters can be spaced two to three weeks apart. The action and strength of appeal is quite clear. Some business firms believe in using humor in the first request, mild persuasion in the second, and so on up to a fifth and last "threatening" letter.

When customers who have poor payment records send their checks in on time or very shortly after due date, some companies use a simple post card to thank them. It also permits another sales pitch.

April 5, 19--

Gentlemen:

Your check in payment of past purchases was received today. Thank you for your cooperation in this matter.

In a short time our salesman will be showing you our latest model KG281 KOPY-R. It is a major step forward in design and operation. Just imagine! No special, expensive paper required. Copy on any paper. Ask him to demonstrate for you.

Yours truly,

Kopy-R Corporation
Sales Manager

eto7

Other companies use a sales slant in all collection letters in the belief that no opportunities should be overlooked to plug the product. Department stores are particularly adept at this and may approach an overdue account this way:

Dear Mrs. Booth

In the whirl of the holiday season, it is easy to forget about such a small matter as your charge account balance for October for $26.48. We would appreciate a check for this amount in order to close this item in your account.

We also wanted you to know that our Starlit Room plans to show the latest creations from Paris. Undoubtedly you will enjoy this preview of anticipated Spring fashions. Won't you come? It's on Thursday, December 18, at 3:00. The Starlit Room is on the 7th floor at the Broadway side of the building.

Oh yes, we have enclosed a stamped, self-addressed envelope for your convenience in mailing your check for $26.48 and also for requesting a ticket of admission to the fashion show.

Yours truly

Theresa J. McNamara
Credit Department

zo
enc.

Within the past few years all sorts of personal appeals have been made in collection letters—keeping your good credit reputation intact, not losing the convenience of charging purchases, preventing action which will disclose financial difficulties to others, etc. An alert salesman can help suggest the best approach to a customer or point out personal or other difficulties for the guidance of the credit manager. As previously mentioned, fire, flood, widespread unemployment, personal illness, may be contributory factors. Once it is confirmed, the letter offering financial cooperation is a tremendous good-will tool.

Some manufacturers have found it profitable to send a specially trained representative to help the customer with display advertising, selling techniques, and any other area which will improve the firm generally or specifically. Of course, if there is an improvement in business, the customer is going to show his gratitude by increased patronage.

In some instances, credit managers have written to customers informing them that they may still take the discount if they pay by the end of the month. This is unfair to customers who pay on time, and slightly dishonest. Besides, a 2 percent discount will hardly be a serious part of the reason you are not receiving payment. Still others will use the mailgram appeal to settle an overdue account on the theory that the urgency of the mailgram may stimulate them to action far sooner than a letter will.

SYRACUSE, SEPTEMBER 18, 19--

LMN VARIETY STORES
125 BRONX ROAD
BUFFALO, NEW YORK

URGENT RECEIVE $56.85 OVERDUE YOUR ACCOUNT. AUDI-TOR PRESSING FOR LEGAL ACTION BY SEPTEMBER 28. PLEASE ACT NOW.

CHARLES G. STAHLS
CREDIT MANAGER
PDQ MANUFACTURING CORP.

When the delinquent is located within a dollar telephone area, the appeal is made directly by telephone by someone unknown to the customer, telling him that the account is being turned over to a collection agency. Many firms use the salesman for that account to "tip him off."

For the most effective credit and collection system, a policy of complete cooperation between the sales, accounts receivable, and credit departments is an unbeatable combination.

Chapter 5

Sales Letters

IN CHAPTER 1, you learned the ABCD of good letter writing. Just to emphasize the elements of good letter writing, here is a quick review:

Accuracy. Be most accurate in what you say in a business letter. The contents of a business letter over the signature of an officer of a firm is a legal offer to the addressee. Before writing, check the date of reference, amount to be stated, length of time for delivery, availability of stock, and any other pertinent data. Notify any third party who should be aware of your statement by sending him an extra carbon copy of the letter.

Brevity. Do not be terse, but do not be so prolix as to be boring. Vary the length of your sentences for pace or rhythmic interest. Use simple but businesslike phrases in a natural and shortwinded manner. Stick to the point. Don't become wordy to force the letter to fill a page. Far better, use short stationery. If the message is well worded, it will say a great deal in very few words.

Clarity. Explain the matter in a direct, clear manner. Obey the golden rule—be as clear to your reader as you would like your reader to be to you. Avoid indefinite words such as *about, nearly, almost.* Also avoid negative expressions whenever possible. Address your correspondent in the positive as much as you can.

Dignity. Maintain an air of courtesy and sincerity throughout all correspondence. Never talk down to your reader. Assume that you are dealing with a courteous, intelligent, informed, progressive businessman like yourself even if occasionally the correspondent has not shown these qualities. Be businesslike but pleasant, as you would in a face-to-face conversation which was interrupting urgent duties.

In usual sales letters the ABCD should be followed. However, a letter which is intended to be duplicated and mailed to a large list may need a novel approach to encourage reading. Let's examine the normal sales letter first—the letter which is generally a result of an inquiry, a salesman's request, or a lead from a business friend. After that we can pick up some pointers on the circular or duplicated letter for large-scale mailing.

Prospective Customers

The individualized approach to prospective customers must be tailor-made or it is worthless. All known facts should be considered in writing this kind of letter. Get a mental picture now and follow it through. An advertisement you have placed in a trade journal is answered by a request for literature and standard information. Before answering—and the answer must be very prompt, while the original interest lasts—all the facts must be known: customer's probable volume of business, location, prognosis for growth, quality of management, discount policy, and financial condition. Suppose we learn that the prospect can only use a minimum quantity of merchandise, has excellent management, is in good condition financially for its size, has good credit rating, is surrounded by new and proposed housing, and has just completed a hundred-car parking lot. Suppose these are the tidbits you have been able to gather in twenty-four hours. You might write this way:

Gentlemen

Thank you for writing to us regarding our products. As you know, they are advertised on a national basis, and STANDARD has become a household word.

Your excellent establishment is known to us. We have heard many complimentary things about its management and constant growth. As a matter of fact, we understand that only last month you completed a parking lot for about 100 cars. May we wish you continued good fortune.

It is, therefore, a real pleasure to enclose our latest price list which gives in detail all facts, prices, advertising aids, and shipping data. We know that STANDARD products meet your needs. We shall be more than glad to introduce them to your customers by a special initial offer. With the aid of a trained demonstrator from our staff, we could set up a special display at reduced price as a store attraction for the new products for a few days.

Our representative in your area, Louis Karmiohl, will be glad to explain and discuss our special introductory offer plan. He will call on you on Thursday of next week. We trust you will seriously consider his interesting proposal.

Sincerely

Aaron Toder
Sales Manager

vm
enc.

A carbon copy of this letter should be sent at once to the salesman so that he may plan his visit. A well-informed salesman is a successful salesman. The situation outlined above is a simple, pleasant one. Notice that the sales manager is offering to take over completely the most difficult part of the work for the customer, the introduction of a new product into his store. With such a helpful proposal as a beginning, the customer will envisage a future with a great deal of assistance from this manufacturer. You have made a good first impression.

Suppose that the knowledge you are able to cull about another prospective customer is derogatory. You learn that it is a small, one-man store; pays slowly but fully; is so crowded that your goods will not be displayed properly; the building is scheduled to come down in about a year to make way for an office building; most merchandise is sold at discount. The picture is distinctly not one of a modern, progressive establishment. Yet, you are in business to sell your products to anyone who can use them. You might write this way:

Dear Mr. Grant:

Thank you so much for your inquiry. STANDARD products are known and sold nationally. Your customers will get products scientifically tested in our laboratories.

We are happy to enclose our catalog which lists prices, descriptions, advertising aids, and shipping data. At the back of the catalog you will find an order form.

Read the catalog carefully and if you can use any of our products, list them fully on the order form, attach your check, and the goods will be delivered promptly. Or you might prefer to pay the truckman when he delivers.

If you have any difficulty determining your needs, please drop us a card or call us and our representative will be glad to make a personal visit. Ask him about the special, reduced rates where floor space is given for display.

Yours truly,

In the first letter, we are being as helpful and complimentary as possible. In the second we are polite, clear, helpful, and businesslike on a cash basis. The customer knows just where he stands.

New Customers

When orders come in from new customers via salesmen or by direct contact, let the customer know that you do not take it for granted that they are doing business with you. The letter acknowledging the order and thanking them should be sincere and, if possible, should notify them of something they will receive. Address the letter directly to the person who authorized the order.

Dear Mr. Bank

Your order was received from our salesman, Thomas Dente, and is very much appreciated. Although it is a trial order for only $45, we know it will be the beginning of a continuing and prospering relationship. Please let us (or Mr. Dente) know if there is anything we can possibly do to help you.

In December we sent all our customers some tokens of our appreciation of their patronage. We see no reason why you should not have them because you joined our growing family of progressive and up-to-the-minute customers a little late.

We have therefore instructed our mailing department to send you one of our beautiful desk-organizer sets complete with compartments for clips, rubber bands, and writing implements. It is very attractively presented in black and red plastic and was designed for beauty and utility by the famous Rawy Lünde. We know you will enjoy looking at it and using it.

May this be the first of many orders to help you in the expansion of your business.

Sincerely

This type of introduction starts the relationship off on a basis of good feeling. Everyone enjoys getting something for nothing. In addition, it never hurts to have your firm's name visible on the items usually given. Some business firms even go so far as to include some simple, useful item with the statement each month. Others include a colorful leaflet illustrating, describing, and pricing certain products. It is not costly and has been proved to bring results.

In certain businesses it is considered most important to acknowledge the receipt of an order immediately. In that event, it is best to have ready a simple post card that can be completed in a matter of seconds. There is something reassuring to a customer in receiving an acknowledgment that his order has been received instead of silence until the bill or shipment arrives (Fig. 5.1).

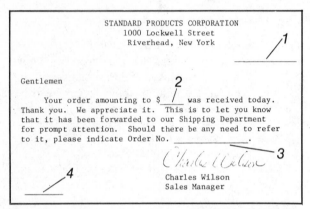

Fig. 5.1 Acknowledgment of order received.

For first orders from new customers, another wording (Fig. 5.2) might be advisable, but the same kind of post card should be sent as given above.

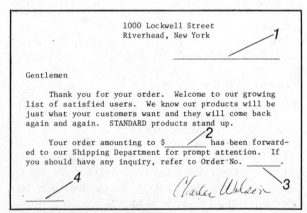

Fig. 5.2 Acknowledgment of initial order received from new customer.

Notice that these cards require the entry of (1) date, (2) amount, (3) order number, (4) initials of the clerk, and (5) sometimes customer's order

number (Fig. 5.4). It is only a matter of seconds. If these are not made up in excessive quantities, they can be changed readily according to need. Many firms use a preprinted set of forms: the top item is the post card which is mailed, and the next card (separated by perforations) is the instruction card for the Shipping Department, to which other forms are attached. A miniaturized letter is used instead of a post card when it is sent simultaneously with other materials (Fig. 5.3).

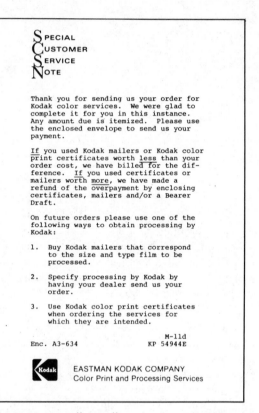

Fig. 5.3 A 4¼″ x 6¼″ enclosure with returned material. (Courtesy of Eastman Kodak Company)

Old Customers

Regular customers must never be allowed to think that you are taking them for granted, especially when you are in a highly competitive field. Their orders should be acknowledged as soon as received, even when they have been taken directly by a sales representative. The anticipation of the acknowledgment, and the understanding by the salesman that the customer expects it, hastens the forwarding of orders without delay. Otherwise there is no stimulus to get orders in rapidly. Many salesmen keep orders until they return from a sales trip, in spite of instructions to the contrary. An acknowledgment (Fig. 5.4) to a regular customer can indicate your appreciation.

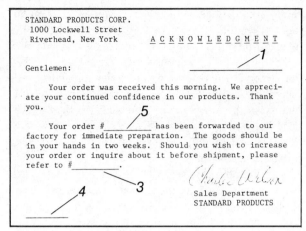

Fig. 5.4 Acknowledgment of order from regular customer.

Writer's Attitude

With the same care used in selecting your sales representative, you must select the best way to approach your customer. Every letter must build good will and make a good appearance, just like a salesman. Indeed, the ideal sales plan is a careful combination of personal and printed appeals. Just as your business serves many people, so must your letters. If you know personally the customer to whom you are writing, either by contact or by telephone conversation, you are likely to write him a more natural and better letter.

Before writing a sales letter, ask yourself these questions:

Has the salesman already seen the customer?
Has the customer seen the product?
Is the product known to the customer by reputation?
Was the customer favorably impressed with the product?
Does the product suit his needs?
In what ways is it superior to competitor's?
Is the price competitive?
What are the outstanding features of the product?
Why should the customer buy this product in preference to others?
Should the customer have seen our advertising— Where? Why? When?

You have certainly seen other types of checklists used in advertising: Does Car *X* have 4-wheel brakes? No. Car *Y*? No. Car *Z*? No. Hudson? *YES.* Prepare a checklist for all the features of your product and your letter will write itself. The product's most unusual feature is the one to stress. If there is none, you have discovered a vital weakness in your product.

The purpose of all sales and advertising work is to do four things:

1 Attract customers
2 Activate prospects to buy
3 Keep present customers satisfied
4 Increase sales to all.

These aims must be achieved without spending so much money doing so that you price your product above all others and out of competition.

Every sales letter attempts to bring about a completed transaction. The best way to achieve this is by enclosing a prepaid post card or envelope for the reader's reply. The number of those readers who have replied who will become customers then depends upon the alacrity with which you act to capitalize on their interest.

Sometimes the first sales letter invites the reader to write for a free booklet or illustrated leaflet. The mailing of this material gives the writer another opportunity to remind the reader of his original interest, present more facts, and indicate the name of the nearest dealer or the name of the representative who will call for an appointment. Whenever such letters are sent, the dealer or salesman should be notified so that he can make prompt follow-up.

The reader who did not respond at all should get a follow-up letter indicating new facts and making some interesting offer. Once again, a return card or return envelope should be enclosed. Because the reaction the first time was not positive, this follow-up should be as simple as possible. If a few check marks in the right place and a signature can do the job, keep it that way. No one is too busy for that. Never mention in the follow-up letter that the reader has not responded previously lest you recall to his mind his reasons for not reacting the first time.

Some business houses send a regular selling letter followed within a week by a special offer, trial offer, or free-trial-period offer. This allows the prospect little time to react to the reasons for not answering the first time. If he is curious at all, he will check off the items, sign, and send it back.

When this "paper salesman" reaches the potential customer, it must stand on its own to interest him enough to respond. For this reason, a letter intended to sell must feel good, look good, and sound good. Good stationery should be used. An attractive letterhead and a carefully typed letter for an individual or an automatically typed letter when a group is being canvassed adds to persuasiveness. Finally, the letter should sound good as the prospective customer reads it. Remember, he's busy; he's in a hurry; and we want to hit his mind with key items which will produce a favorable reaction. In order to prevent a negative reaction to a sales letter, remember these points:

1 Don't misspell the prospect's name.
2 Be certain the address is correct.
3 Don't allow even a smudge on paper or envelope.
4 Don't rubber-stamp the signature.
5 Don't talk down to the prospect.
6 Unless there is a general recession, don't joke about the poor condition of business.
7 Don't oversimplify the message or become pedantic.
8 Don't waste time by needless repetition.

One way of checking the effectiveness of an important letter is to write it out, leave it overnight, and come back to it in the morning.

Keep in mind that nothing is so positive as a written message. An oral message always leaves room for doubt as to clarity or meaning and cannot be pointed to in cold type later. Not so the written statement. Think, write, and proofread carefully.

It is interesting to note that it is far easier to obtain a response for a leaflet, sample, or visit of a representative than it is to make an immediate direct sale. It has been reliably reported that a 1 percent response to a direct sales pitch is customary. A good follow-up can only produce another 3 to 5 percent. However, we know of instances in which a 30 percent response was obtained, resulting in tremendous quantity sales.

Emotional Appeals

Madison Avenue has learned to use certain psychological factors in sales campaigns. They appeal to love or sex, pride, duty, profit or gain, self-indulgence, self-preservation, and class distinction. There is another school which still believes that the "hard sell," stressing the merits of the product, leads to the fewest disappointments and the most enduring clientele. The feeling is that once the emotional appeal is made, the customer begins to judge the product on its merits alone. The ideal, then, is to use an emotional appeal to get the prospect interested. The superiority of the product then makes him glad he bought it after the emotional appeal has worn off or been forgotten.

Series Letters

There are two basic types of approaches used when a series is planned. One approach will stress a different appeal in each successive letter. A boat manufacturer might use a series of letters based on class distinction, self-preservation, mechanical excellence, self-indulgence, and economy in successive letters—one letter devoted to each. A furrier might use styling, class distinction, comparative price or value, quality, and exotic type of skins. This is the concentrated-appeal approach; the writer hopes that one of these appeals will strike a responsive chord in a prospective customer.

A variation of the series letter is that in which each letter contains all of the features of the product's appeal, stressing one slightly more than the others. This is meant for the reader who likes to see all the outstanding features listed. Sometimes these letters do not succeed in selling the product discussed in the correspondence, but become leads into another sale which would have been impossible had the customer not responded to the first message.

Although these letters form a series, each should be able to stand on its own. At the end of each letter it might also be wise to offer the prospective customer a different method of response each time—the first might enclose a card; the second, a stamped, self-addressed envelope; the next, an invitation to call or wire the advertiser collect. You could also use various letter styles to increase the individuality of each letter. Experience and sound judgment will determine the variations necessary.

When the series is completed and planned, it should be bound in a folder for each executive in the company who may then know and follow the sales campaign.

Timing of Letters

The only features of a sales campaign left to stress are the address of the prospect and the timing of the letter. In almost all cases the name of the person in charge is available. A letter addressed directly to him will reach him quickly. Second best is to address the letter to the executive by title alone. The least desirable is to address it to the company without designating the executive for whom it is intended. You leave yourself at the mercy of the incoming-mail clerk and subsequently some secretary who may not wish to be bothered with the letter.

The time to send your letter must be carefully planned. In a seasonal business, the dates of mailing are vital. In season, no one can give adequate attention to advertising which imposes demands on the reader. In nonseasonal businesses the determination of the lull periods is much more difficult. Likewise the interval between letters is difficult to determine. The average is about a week to seven business days.

Sales letters should not be mailed on Fridays because they arrive in the heap of mail from the weekend accumulation. Arrival in the middle of the week is best, so a Monday or Tuesday mailing is advisable, depending upon the distance the letters must travel.

To sum up, the greater the effort in the planning stage and the broader the scope of the actual finished product, the better will be the result. During the writing process the writer must constantly be able to place himself in the position of the recipient of the letter. It is the ability to be objective and personal at the same time that counts. The writer must present the product to the customer as the customer sees it. He must get the reader's undivided attention, keep his interest, create a desire for the product or service, and stimulate him to action.

Circular Letters

There is no question that a personal letter will bring far better results than a circular letter. Whether personal or circular, the letter with a first paragraph which pinpoints a real need or problem of the consumer will produce the best results. If you can stop him, even for an instant, you have his attention.

You can then hold his interest by giving him facts on his level, not yours. The facts that satisfy *his* utilization of your product are sufficient. A technical point here and there for variety is good for the "authentic" touch. It proves to the reader you are not talking down to him. Occasionally, with prospects who have proved difficult to budge, a trick first paragraph, a cartoon, a photograph, or a small plastic

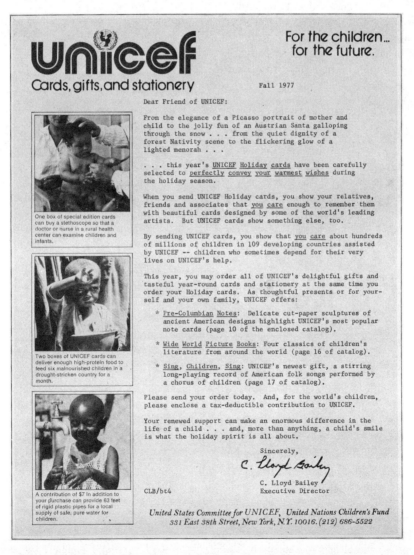

Fig. 5.5 Circular sales letter with general salutation. (Courtesy of U.S. Committee for UNICEF)

object at the beginning will prove successful. Avoid it generally, however, as too risky.

In most successful letters, there is a noticeably logical transition from one point to another, as a natural sequence.

In the central or presentational section, the kernel is evident, bare, clear. This portion of the message is like the store window in a very elegant jewelry shop which has a black frame around the window and on a black velvet display stand under a spotlight there is a diamond brooch with a tiny price tag—$15,000. This display is startling in its effect—much more so than a jewelry-store window showing hundreds of items in a glistening confusion. Even a window with a few items individually set and priced in the store's full range is effective. Similarly, the body of a sales letter must be direct and uncluttered.

Occasionally, a quote from the testimonial of a well-known person, when this is available, can make a good impression. For a product that is not sold to the retail consumer, a statement from other offices, factories, or laboratories should be used.

The conclusion of the letter must suggest urgency. This, you hope, will stimulate the reader to action if he is at all interested. If he is left with a choice, he most likely will not reply. "We hope to hear from you soon." "It will please us to receive a reply from you." These endings are too mild and hopeful. The reader must be made aware that delay will cause disappointment or loss. "My mail clerk informs me copies are going so rapidly that we can not promise to have one for you unless you respond at once on the enclosed postage-free reply card." "Our supply of samples is limited, so please return the enclosed card promptly before we exhaust our allotment." "Orders for this sensational hand-finished worsted suit will be on a 'first come, first served' basis. So hurry to avoid unnecessary disappointment or limitation of color or size selection."

An unusual style or format in a business letter will win it a second glance. A cartoon could be placed at the top of the letter; topical headings in bold type could precede each paragraph; the handle or inverted paragraph style might be used; a coupon could be cut off the bottom for the receipt of a free or low-priced product.

To get a true picture of the effectiveness of any particular letter campaign, careful records must be kept. Careful planning and good judgment by those responsible for such a campaign should be rewarded. An effective letter should be varied and used again. If the results show even a slight decline, a new approach should be formulated. Sales letters should be used as supplements to the efforts of salesmen. They have an advantage over the salesman in being in writing and leaving no room for doubt or misunderstanding.

Lost Customers

Customers from whom you have not heard for a long period or whose orders have become quite small must be wooed back. The proper approach depends upon the quality of the intelligence information available. One fact about such a customer, culled from your salesman or from another source, may go a long way. Such facts might be an interest in sports, horses, or dogs; in the theater, art, or music; or in the stock market. Here is a letter of this type which obtained good results. Note that such a letter cannot be a form letter if it is really to reach the customer.

Dear Mr. Wexler

I noticed in this morning's newspaper that the playoffs in the college basketball games start in two weeks. This reminded me that it is always nice to attend with someone who enjoys good basketball. Won't you join me when you come to the city on your buying tour? Please let me know promptly so that I may arrange for tickets.

A business service to which I subscribe informs me that there has been a mild recession in your area but that business is improving slightly as spring approaches. This explains, no doubt, why we have not seen you around our newly redecorated showroom. I suppose you have had your share of reduced revenue. I am sorry to hear about it.

In order to take the opportunity to replace out-of-season merchandise with the latest styles, stop in when you are in the city so that we may make some offers and suggestions. May I expect you in about two weeks?

Sincerely

Joseph Warren
Sales Manager

Dear Mrs. Storelli

We are deeply ashamed that Tracy's efficiency, of which we boast, has failed us and that your firm was the victim. Your shipment went to Lakewood, New Jersey, instead of Lakewood, Ohio. No one caught the mistake until the package was returned today.

We wish to make amends for our blunder. Is there something we can do to erase this blemish on our otherwise perfect record? We sincerely hope we did not interfere with any special sale or disrupt your regular supply of merchandise so that you, in turn, had to disappoint some of your old customers.

Please call me or write me at once to tell me what Tracy's can do to restore our previous good relations.

Most sincerely

Edward Garramone
Sales Manager

Not all promises of services to a customer should be put in writing. A telephone call and an agreement to supply what is needed is better because a written, signed offer is sometimes a source of later embarrassment. We all know that customers of many companies expect certain special services which are rarely placed in writing. When they come in on buying tours to the big city, they are offered theater tickets, trucking service, limousine service, research information, night-club entertainment, plane reservations, and other indirect inducements. Some companies even go so far as to send gifts on the birth of a baby, wedding gifts, and other gratuitous indications of friendship. The acceptance of any of these items places the relationship on a quasi-personal basis. It is never a certainty thereafter whether the purchases made are on the merits of the product or the gratitude of the recipient. The practice is an accepted American business method which has created a great deal of heated controversy in many quarters. This is strictly a matter of business ethics. A small number of companies do not even mind putting these offers in writing in business correspondence. Others have been known to discharge employees who even suggested such a procedure.

Long-Established Accounts

When a relationship with a customer has been established over a long period of time and has grown with the development of the customer, an occasion might be found to write a letter of thanks for continued confidence. Such a letter should not attempt to sell anything directly but should only offer warm good will and appreciation. Yet, as we have said above, all letters should sell your company at all times. One firm we know used this combination of thanks and a special offer.

Dear Mr. Menikoff

It is gratifying to us that for twenty-two years we have been able to satisfy your needs for the products we manufacture. As you and your excellent staff know, we have never taken that patronage for granted. It has been the result of mutual respect and understanding. During the war years you understood our difficulties with limited materials. We understood your need for goods to sell. We believe we adjusted to each other's limitations to build a lasting relationship. We just want to say thank you.

To show that we really mean what we say, we wish you to take advantage of a special offer by which we can show our gratitude. You know that we never offer any special discounts or "deals." But, for this spring order, we propose this arrangement. Please let me know at once if you would be interested in taking advantage of this unique offer.

We shall make available to you a special discount on our products for a one-week sale. At the end of the sale, if you will itemize for us all products sold during this week, we shall reimburse you for 25% of the cost price. As soon as we receive your reply, we shall mail you the sales agreement to sign, an outline of our advertising facilities, and an advertising-cost-sharing plan. If you wish to save time, call me at 555–4400, Area Code 212.

Sincerely

Herbert Balish
Sales Manager

It is inevitable that from time to time a new salesman is assigned to an old customer. The customer may be used to the previous salesman. It is only fair to pave the way as much as possible for your new representative. A letter informing customers of the change lends status and dignity to the replacement. The letter also removes from him the need to walk in "cold." He is expected. He will probably be welcome.

Gentlemen:

It is with much sorrow that we inform you of the death of Arnold Baker who represented us in your territory for twenty-seven years. We know that this distinguished member of our industry leaves many friends in his territory who will miss his kindness, desire to serve, and knowledge of plastics and merchandising.

Mr. Irving Reich
Purchasing Manager
Certain Products
125 Geary Street
San Francisco, CA 95409

Dear Mr. Reich

As you can easily see by all the strings, I'll be tied up for a
while. I tried to make like a young fellow on skis. The travel
folder did not recommend that I examine my birth certificate before going. So, here I am at 42 with two (count 'em!) broken
legs. I suppose I should be glad I wasn't a 42-year old centipede.

Since I have full use of my arms, hands, and brain, and the hospital has given permission for me to have a telephone by my bedside,
I thought I'd keep in touch. They may be able to keep me down
with weights and pulleys, but they can't count me out.

With your kind permission and indulgence, therefore, I shall be
calling on you for a while via telephone. Your usual courteous
and considerate reception will permit me to continue to serve you.
I know you will understand and forgive this unusual approach under the circumstances.

Sincerely

Irwin Glick
Sales Representative
Shoor Plastics, Inc.

Fig. 5.6 Imaginative sales letter written to suit special circumstances.

While it will be impossible to replace him completely, we must send another representative to serve your area. Milton Zinar is a personable, capable man with eighteen years of experience in the field of plastics. He will be calling on you soon to become acquainted. We know he can count on your usual courteous reception.

Sincerely,

Audrey MacLean
President

Although this is a bit unusual, one salesman used a short, simple letter to inform his customers that he would not be calling on them in person. This unusual approach placed him in a position to carry on his affairs by telephone without offending. On a ski-ing weekend he broke both legs and had to remain in casts and traction for weeks. Before the plaster of Paris had set, he had his photograph taken and a letter (Fig. 5.6) sent at once to all his customers and a few prospective ones. In the upper right-hand corner of the letter was a picture of the salesman in bed with his legs up and pulleys and strings going in all directions. Each letter was addressed to the purchasing manager.

Good Letter Writers

Some companies realize the importance of the skill of those who dictate letters emanating from their establishment and have developed special departments which train in and inform on good letter-writing techniques. Other companies have even gone so far as to issue bibliographies on the subject and have made them required reading. For those who com-plained of their lack of speed in reading, reading-improvement courses were found and paid for by the corporation. One of the most active companies in the area of business letter-writing is the Prudential Insurance Company of America. In their Public Relations and Advertising Department there is a section called the Correspondence Improvement Section. This section trains, reviews, and issues bulletins on business letter-writing improvements. We quote from one of their smaller ones to illustrate.

Are You Using Expressions That Are—

1 Superfluous
   a Old-fashioned and Shopworn
       Expressions such as *above-mentioned, advise, the writer,* and *kindly* date your letters. Instead, say *this, let us know, me, please.*
   b Literary and Flowery
       Use short, conversational words for quick, clear understanding; for example, *try* in place of *endeavor, find out* instead of *ascertain,* etc.
   c Wordy
       Make each word count. The same meaning can be expressed in fewer words.
   d Legalistic
       In lieu of, thereon, herewith is, on behalf of have a legal flavor and are better expressed by *instead of, on it, is, for.*
   e Repetitious
       Reread your letters to be sure you haven't said the same thing more than once.
2 Too long
       Short sentences are easier to read and understand. Avoid expressing too many thoughts in one sentence.
3 Telegraphic
       Don't omit the articles *a, an, the* and the pronouns *I* and *we.*
4 Awkward or Ambiguous
       Arrange your thoughts in logical order. Be sure the reader knows who or what you mean.
5 Too Full of *We* or *I*
       Aim the letter at the reader. Use more *you* and less *we* or *I,* especially in successive paragraphs.
6 Too Formal
       Use the reader's name. It attracts his attention and helps put him in a receptive mood.
7 Weakening Your Openings
       Place policy details in the subject. Reserve your opening for a courtesy or for attention-getting good news.
8 Negative
       Accentuate the positive. Avoid negative words such as *regret, unfortunately,* etc.
9 Likely to Imply Criticism
       No one likes to be told *you neglected, you overlooked, you failed, you claim,* etc.
10 Unfriendly
       Make your letter more friendly. Adding the courtesy of a *please* or *thank you* is often all that is needed.

(Reproduced by courtesy of
THE PRUDENTIAL INSURANCE COMPANY OF AMERICA)

Chapter 6

Direct-Mail Sales Letters

THIS CHAPTER DEALS with the direct approach to a customer by mail to try to get him to purchase a product or service. Many people consider this to be the province of "mail order" companies only. This is not true. It is merely a phase of all merchandising engaged in by all companies that do any kind of mail advertising. There is hardly an adult in this country who has not at one time or another been solicited by mail to purchase, subscribe to, or use a product or service. What adult in this country has not received coupons offering discounts on the price of soap, margarine, magazines, or other commodities? This is direct-mail selling.

Every business may avail itself of this method of merchandising. With some patience, originality, creativity, and effort, it can be a most productive procedure. It does not require a large investment of time or funds until it becomes large enough to warrant full attention. When that happens, the income should be adequate to pay for clerical service. Both individuals and business firms engaging in this branch of merchandising would do well to keep exact and accurate records to determine the profitability of direct-mail selling. As in any well-managed business, it is necessary to know if a department carries itself or runs at a deficit. Except for the service department of an equipment manufacturer, it is essential to be aware of the allotment of cost to any department in order to determine fees and charges. Service and repair departments, while they should be run at cost or a slight profit, usually fall into the red; it is an occupational disease. Yet a company often cannot exist without such departments.

Just as there is a definite technique for selling to a customer face to face, there is also a technique for selling by direct mail. The basic problem of a salesman is getting the prospect to listen seriously. The same is true in direct-mail selling. Once a prospective customer reads the pamphlets you have mailed, you stand a chance of selling to him. Every company, to be sure, does some form of direct-mail selling. Here are some methods commonly used:

Duplicated sales letters making an offer

Calendars sent each December and desk appointment calendars with the company name imprinted

Blotters enclosed with each invoice bearing an advertising message

Individual advertisements enclosed with each statement or letter

Mailing ball-point pens as giveaways with the firm name, address, and sales message imprinted

Periodic mailings offering a different product each time

Reprints of magazine articles praising products, mailed to all customers or prospects

Business reply cards sent to keep mailing list up to date: a short simple questionnaire

Special free-trial or limited-time offers

Testimonials from famous people about one or more of the products

Notices of price reduction due to unprecedented demand for product or service

Announcements of display of merchandise or of awards and prizes won at a convention, national show, or international competition

Samples, when feasible, of the product

Reminders that no order has been received and stock must be running low

Latest catalogs or price lists

Offers of aid by research and development departments for special products

Offers to produce merchandise for customer under his own label as a service

Occasional releases offering tips to customers on methods of obtaining better service from the product and prolonging its life and usefulness

Special trade-in offers for purchase of new models

Illustrated folders offering equipment or services with specific details, prices, accompanied by business reply card or envelope

"You have been chosen" in your area to head a discount group or club, special benefits to you

And many, many others.

National Geographic Society

WASHINGTON, D.C.   20036

BOOK SERVICE DIVISION

Dear Member,

Today, as we prepared to mail you the enclosed brochure and letter describing Visiting Our Past, something occurred to me. There are several very important things about National Geographic books that we often forget to point out to you.

1. THESE BOOKS ARE CREATED FOR YOU -- AS A BENEFIT of your membership in the Society.

2. THEY ARE PRICED FAR LOWER THAN COMPARABLE VOLUMES SOLD TO THE PUBLIC IN BOOKSTORES -- usually by at least 50% -- and often much more!

3. THEY ARE PUBLISHED ONLY AFTER A MEMBER SURVEY indicates that they are titles you want.

4. THEY UTILIZE THE TALENT AND EXPERTISE OF NATIONAL GEOGRAPHIC STAFF PHOTOGRAPHERS AND WRITERS.

5. THEY REFLECT THE SAME ATTENTION TO QUALITY AND DETAIL THAT MAKES NATIONAL GEOGRAPHIC MAGAZINE SO SUPERB.

Visiting Our Past -- the book we are offering you today -- meets these standards and passes these tests with flying colors!

Here in the third-floor Book Service Division at National Geographic, we are really excited about this new volume. With all our experience in the publishing field, we can tell when we've got a best-seller on our hands -- and this is one for sure!

So reserve your copy on the enclosed order form today. Get ready to enjoy a wonderful new way to look at America today ... and yesterday. And -- happy "traveling!"

Yours truly,

Jules Billard

Jules Billard, Editor-in-Chief
Book Service Division

Fig. 6.1 Special service of a magazine published for members at special rates which is not a purchase plan system. (Courtesy of National Geographic Society)

Ease of Replying

In direct-mail selling, it is most essential that the method of response be rapid and extremely simple. A busy executive (the one you need to reach) appreciates efficiency. You will notice in all the examples given some method of response was included.

Any of the large envelope companies would be more than happy to work out for and with you some special form that would suit your special needs. These are becoming so common that printers are now able to compose them for you and prepare them on regular stock. Some of the leaders in this area are Transo Envelope, United States Envelope, Reply-O-Letter, Hammermill Paper.

Clarity of Specifications

In the forms used, whatever their nature, there must be complete clarity. The only way to satisfy a mail-order customer is to send him just what he wants. Specifications must be simple, clear, and understandable to avoid returns, lengthy correspondence, adjustments, or dissatisfied customers. Business by recommendation runs high in this form of business.

Fig. 6.2A Combination renewal notice and letter indicating an inducement to do so, usually used after original renewal notice brought no response. (Courtesy of *New York Magazine*)

Fig. 6.2B Special offer to credit-card holders which may be charged directly by mail. Items usually not available elsewhere and are good value. (Courtesy of Shell Oil Co., Credit Card Division)

If there are sizes and colors involved, a checklist with a box next to each is best.

Size:			Color:		
(Check one)	10 ☐		(Check one)	White	☐
	11 ☐			Blue	☐
	12 ☐			Green	☐
	13 ☐			Red	☐
	14 ☐			Brown	☐

Care in composing forms cannot be too great. In the next combination for the same information there is chance of error.

Size:	10	11	12	13	14
Color:	White	Blue	Green	Red	Brown

In completing this form the customer who is in a hurry may easily check the wrong place. The ideal form is designed to prevent errors. For the same reason, when space is required between columns it is advisable to use leaders (a row of dots) to prevent errors. An examination at your printer of work done for other companies will supply more ideas.

Item	Amount
Screws, #8, round-head, metal . . .	_____
Washer, #4, flat-edge	_____
Bolts, #1, smooth, round	_____
Nuts, #8, sink-head, beveled edge	_____

Compose a few samples and try them out for ease, clarity, and usage. Then, if the first run is kept to a small number, any bugs may be ironed out without unduly raising original cost. Further revisions will become obvious as the offerings expand or contract and clerical difficulties arise.

Mail Paraphernalia

When a sample mailing is prepared, use all precautions to prevent it from becoming what is termed "junk mail." Junk mail is characterized first of all by stuffing envelopes needlessly. The contents should be essentials only—message, order form, and means of returning expeditiously.

One of the largest automobile insurers in the country has devised an ingenious method of obtaining the answers to vital questions from its customers. It is ingenious because it is all accomplished with the use of one card, yet confidential information is obtained in safety. The questionnaire arrives with the questions to be answered by the customer. When the questions have been answered, the question portion is torn off and only the answers remain, meaningless to anyone but the company. The reply takes only a moment; the card has been addressed by an addressing machine and the name plate also contains the policy number and other coded information.

Chapter 7

Social and Miscellaneous Correspondence

APART FROM THE correspondence described in previous chapters, there are various other types of letters. Some are letters of a social-business nature and others are not strictly commercial in purpose. These include announcements, invitations, messages of congratulation, sympathy notes, and charity appeals. Some of these are illustrated in the following pages.

Invitations

It is said that success breeds success. Announcing new quarters and inviting customers has a good-will effect whether they attend or not (Fig. 7.1). Customers want to know that the business they bring is not taken for granted, and they are by this means made to feel that others have confidence in your products, too.

An invitation is more effective if it is directed to an individual than if it is in the form of a circular. A personal invitation is unusual in business and attracts attention. Another effective type of invita-

tion is one that is used in the introduction of a new line, new model, or new service. Fig. 7.1 can be produced easily in quantity on MagCard equipment.

Gentlemen

Reserve the date—October 12—for our coming-out party. Yes, our NEW models come out of hiding on that day. Years of research have produced this revolutionary copying machine. This is the last word in electronic copy equipment.

We collected all your suggestions over a ten-year period, and gave them to our engineers and chemists. "Why can't we—?" we inquired of them. Three months ago they answered, "We can!" The exciting result is available. This is a no chemicals, no waiting, no technician, no preparation machine. Place the material to be copied on a piece of our KOPPY paper and insert in the machine. In five seconds, a perfect copy of anything printed, written, or rubber stamped is produced. Amazing?

Come and see it in operation, on October 12, in our newly remodeled showrooms, 9 a.m. to 9 p.m. Refreshments served all day. Just tell your taxi driver to take you to Washington Drive and Main Street. Then, follow the crowd! We look forward to seeing you.

Sincerely

Irene Patai
Sales Manager

```
        H O U S E W A R M I N G

     New Showroom and Offices


              *   *   *


           XYZ CORPORATION
          485 Madison Avenue
           Topeka, KS 66606


              *   *   *


     You are cordially requested to
   attend the festivities to celebrate
   the opening of our new headquarters.

   March 8, 19--            3 to 6 P.M.
   Admission restricted to customers
```

Fig. 7.1   Invitation to customer to visit new quarters.

Occasionally, of course, it will be necessary to make specific and direct invitations. There will also be a need to accept or decline invitations. The first example that follows requires no reply if you do not plan to attend. The next invitation should be answered, and an example of an acceptance and of a refusal are given.

Dear Member:

On the first of each month it is our custom to hold our general membership meeting. The meeting scheduled for Friday, December 3, is one you will not wish to miss. It is an event worth circling on your calendar as a *must*.

The meeting will take place at 7 p.m. at Joy Wee Restaurant, at 28 East Bradley, in their Shanghai Room. In keeping with this special occasion, the manager, Mr. Wing, has consented to serve his regular $8.75 dinner for $5. Imagine! The famous Hong Kong Dinner for five dollars!

More surprises! Our guest speaker is a man known to the nation for his daring and keen insight into American affairs. Yes, retired Admiral Gene Ross has consented to address us. I know you won't want to miss him. He is always stimulating and incisive.

Last, but far from least, the management of this fine restaurant has prepared a special batch of fortune cookies for us. Three of them will contain fortunes indeed. One contains a gift certificate for a free weekend in the Virgin Islands, all expenses paid. The second prize is a free rental of a Ford, Chevrolet, or Plymouth for one month, excluding gas. The last wonderful surprise is a small tape recorder which runs on batteries.

Can we count on you? Send the enclosed reply card at once as there are only accommodations for 150 in the Shanghai Room. Help us to end the year with a bang.

Fraternally

Hal Simpson
President

Dear Mr. Kanner

You do not know me, but I have heard about you from mutual friends with whom I was discussing business letters. Of course, your outstanding book is familiar to all of us at the Torrington Office Managers Association. All our members are directly concerned with the improvement of the quality and the reduction of the cost of daily business letters.

For this reason, and because we know you are in a position to give us much excellent advice on this topic, we have voted to ask if you would consider addressing our members on Friday evening, February 17, 19––. We would be most grateful to you if you would consider this invitation and attempt to work us into your crowded schedule.

As soon as I receive your acceptance, I will send you full details. Would you be kind enough to include with your acceptance an autobiographical outline so that I may introduce you properly to the members? Please say you'll come!

Sincerely

Amodeo Garanes
President

hh

Dear Mr. Garanes

Thank you so much for your invitation to address the Torrington Office Managers Association meeting on February 17, 19––. It is an honor to be asked to speak to such a fine group of executives.

Enclosed are a few details of my career which you may use in your introductory remarks. I shall arrive about half an hour early for your briefing.

If the meeting requires my presence at dinner, I feel I must mention my allergy to any form of seafood. I do hope that my peculiarity does not upset your arrangements.

Sincerely

Lawrence Kanner

ja
enclosure

Dear Mr. Garanes:

I was most flattered and pleased to hear that your members wished to hear me speak. You were also kind enough to give me two months' notice.

It is unfortunate that I am already committed for February 17. On February 1 I shall leave for Istanbul, Turkey, as a representative of the United States Department of State. The Turkish government wishes to set up a style and correspondence manual for government officials and executives. I have agreed to offer my services.

I am therefore sorry to have to refuse your kind invitation. I hope I may have the pleasure of being invited again after my return next June.

Sincerely,

Lawrence Kanner

ja

Newspapers and trade periodicals carry news of promotions, mergers, innovations, deaths, and other events which affect business life. Many executives who wish to keep in touch with prominent people in their own or allied fields of endeavor do so by reading or inserting such news items in publications and through their trade associations. A variety of circumstances might prompt the letters that follow.

Congratulations

Dear Mr. Warner

To the man who taught me all I know, at long last has come recognition for excellence. Congratulations!

I was so glad to read in today's newspaper that you were elected president of the Fuller Advertising Company.

They chose the right man. Best wishes.

Cordially

Rod McAlister

wo

Sympathy

Dear Carl

It was a great shock to us all at United to hear of your sudden loss. We all knew and loved your wife, who was our kind and gracious hostess on so many happy occasions.

We would like to convey with deep sincerity the sorrow with which all of us here received the news. Please accept our heartfelt condolences.

Most sincerely

Murray G. Rice

Illness

Dear Mrs. Friedman

When I called your office to place an order today, I learned that you were out because of illness. My secretary called the hospital immediately and was informed that you are "resting comfortably."

This is good news and I hope you will soon be your perky, efficient self again. But do not come back too quickly, as we want to make sure you are quite fit with a long, healthy career ahead of you.

Miss Renieris chose a book we both believe you'll enjoy. It was mailed to you this morning. We wish you a speedy recovery!

Sincerely

Richard Bongiorno

Resignations

Dear Jerry:

The last time I passed your office the fur was flying and work was proceeding in its usual efficient way. Now, I hear, you are going to give it all up to bask in the sunshine at warm Fort Lee on the shores of the Gulf of Pico. I believe it will take three men to replace you at Roberts!

After forty-three years of devoted and effective service, you do indeed deserve a pleasant retirement. We hope you enjoy every minute of it. We will be sorry to lose you.

Please let me know any time you are in this neighborhood again. I shall be delighted if you and your wife will visit us.

Cordially,

Harry Powers
President

Births

Dear Mr. Leff

My secretary remarked the last time you called on us that you had a faraway look in your eye. Now we know the reason!

Please accept our congratulations on the birth of your first child. May he bear your name proudly and bring you much joy.

Very sincerely

Milton Zinar

Charity Appeals

Dear Mr. Sessler

It is a pleasure to respond to your appeal for funds for the Arthritis and Rheumatism Foundation. I know of the great efforts that are being made to raise funds for research.

Please accept the enclosed check for $100 from this company to your great cause. We are happy that we are able to help.

Sincerely

F. Townsend
Assistant to the President

Wedding Anniversaries

Dear Mr. Saphier

I understand that next Sunday you and your wife will celebrate the fiftieth anniversary of your wedding. Please accept my own congratulations, as well as those of the staff of the United Company.

It has always been a pleasure for us to do business with you. We have appreciated your constant kindnesses. We would now like you to accept as a gift from us a Zenith World Traveler portable radio. We hope it will serve you for many pleasurable hours on your round-the-world second honeymoon.

Good luck!

Sincerely

Nathan Baltor
Controller

Errors

Gentlemen:

In this morning's mail we received an order sent by your company and intended for the Carlson Radio Company. It was obviously sent to us in error as we are the Carlson Transport Company.

We have forwarded the order to them.

Yours truly,

Marie Buonomo
Order Department

Gentlemen

Your check for $435.27 came in this morning's mail. We were very glad to receive it in full settlement of your account.

Inadvertently, however, the check was not signed. We are enclosing it so that you may sign and return it to us.

Yours truly

Gloria Ubertini
Head Bookkeeper

Courtesy Notes

Harrison Brothers Garage
742 Taconic Road
Rockland, N.Y. 12138

Gentlemen

You can imagine my mental state two nights ago while driving south on the Taconic Parkway when my motor suddenly stopped. It was about 1:30 a.m.!

A passing motorist called the AAA office in the area for me. The emergency operator at the AAA contacted a garage near my stalled car. In 20 minutes a tow truck arrived. Ten minutes later my car was in the garage. The mechanic had already been summoned and he arrived within minutes after we did.

The end of this tale is unbelievable. In a few minutes the source of trouble was located and repaired. My bill was $4.85! And, I was on my way in 50 minutes at such a late hour of the night!

All I can do is say "thank you" a thousand times to tell you how grateful my wife and I are for what you did. I don't know what I would have done without a kind motorist, the dependable AAA, and an honest, sympathetic garage crew. I am deeply grateful.

Most sincerely

Robert Jay Burton

ei

copy: Emergency Division
       Automobile Association of America
       Westchester County Office
       White Plains, N.Y. 10601

Chapter 8

Introduction, Reference, Recommendation

LETTERS OF INTRODUCTION, reference, and recommendation are often written in business. Their value is inestimable.

Letters of Introduction

When a business or personal acquaintance of long standing needs to see someone you know well, a letter of introduction from you will give him entree. He is no longer a stranger, but the certified acquaintance of a friend. In composing such a letter, therefore, the writer should attempt to give only as much information as is strictly necessary; its subject will be able to fill this out at the subsequent interview.

A young man, a friend of your son, asks for a letter of introduction to a business firm. You know that he is admirably suited for employment in this kind of business. In addition, you consider him a well-mannered, intelligent, alert, and serious-minded young adult. He requests the letter because you happen to know the executive in charge of the department in which he seeks employment. The competition is keen, but he feels that the job will go to the candidate with an advantage, such as a personal introduction. You agree and offer to write the letter, making it clear that the letter may work against him as an instance of the exertion of undue influence. He is willing to take the risk.

Dear Harry

John Ward is a friend of my son. In the course of four years, we have become friends also.

I am writing to ask you, as a favor to me, to consider seriously John's application to work in your company as a cost accountant. Although I am aware that he has little experience, I believe that his capacity for hard work, his integrity, and his intelligence will be an asset to any company that employs him.

His professional qualifications speak for themselves. I should merely like to see John have the chance that he deserves. I hope that you will see him.

Cordially

Wallace T. Smith

ru

You will notice that the letter above is really a combination reference and introduction. Here is a colder letter which is solely an introduction.

Dear Harley:

This will introduce the bearer, Thomas J. Farley, who is a young businessman in Santa Fe. He is the owner-manager of a men's wear shop on Main Street.

He is considering opening a branch in Albuquerque in the same line. As I know of no one who has a better knowledge of Albuquerque and vicinity than you, I have taken the liberty of giving him your name.

I shall take it as a personal favor if you will assist Tom in any way you can. It would please me to return the favor sometime in the future. Will you be my guest at lunch next time you are in Santa Fe?

Cordially,

John J. B. Cooper

This letter does not in any way praise or recommend the man being introduced. It is placed on the basis of a personal favor only. It is sincere, yet there is an air of cool business about it, although it ends with a personal touch. Here is another style for a letter of introduction.

Dear Jarvis

A look at the calendar just reminded me that it has been two years since our fishing trip. Can you get away for another this fall in Wisconsin? Please let me know.

The gentleman presenting this letter, Glenn E. Rockey, is a friend of twenty years' standing who has need of some help. He owned and managed the local dairy company until last week. It was a successful and growing operation. He is known and admired by our entire community.

A sudden health problem in his family that required immediate attention has taken him to Phoenix, where he has no friend or confidant. I told him that there is no one I trust more or consider a better friend in that area than you. I wonder if he could impose on you for some advice? Glenn will explain the details himself.

I know I can count on you to be as helpful as possible. I will certainly appreciate it.

Cordially

Raleigh G. Peck

ty

In some cities, businessmen send each other prospective customers in this way with the understanding of sharing the revenue. When a man makes a drastic move of home and business, he wishes to be directed to a trustworthy person who will help him to establish a new home and business. This is done widely by lawyers, real estate agents, doctors, insurance agents, and accountants, on a reciprocal basis.

References and Recommendations

By definition, reference and recommendation cannot be separated. Again sincerity is important. A reference is generally a statement of favorable qualities over a broad area and is the response supplied by a person or a business firm to a request from a new or prospective employer. A recommendation, or testimonial, is usually a letter given to an employee in person for the same purpose.

Reference inquiries usually come in the form of a prepared list of questions to which answers are sought. In Chapter 3 an example of a simple form is outlined. Some requests can be rather long and involved. It is wise to use the personnel record when responding in order to be accurate. When there is no information available, this should be stated; a blank

space may be taken as an evasion. Inquiries for reference can range from job qualities to subversive activities to home difficulties. Many companies will not hire an employee until they receive the completed form; a dilatory answer may hold up someone's employment opportunity. The writer is aware that the applicant expects a favorable reply because you have been given as reference.

Reference inquiries are concerned with character as well as past business record. An applicant for a character reference will naturally choose as a reference someone who, he feels, looks upon him favorably. In all courtesy, permission to use someone's name as a reference should be obtained in advance. Business references are requests for an opinion of the work and character from a place where he or she has previously been employed. Generally, a business reference requests information of the employee's duties, wages, length of service, attendance record, reason for leaving, relationship with equals and superiors, honesty, reliability, and health.

Occasionally, in about three out of twenty-five inquiries, the request will bear no form or checklist. "Your reply will, of course, be treated with the strictest confidence" is a standard promise.

Gentlemen

Margaret Holmes is a young lady we employed directly from high school in June 19--, as a stenographer. For three months she worked in our stenographers' pool. Her supervisor rated her as "good" in work and personality during that period.

She was promoted to secretary to the assistant purchase manager from the pool. While on this job she attended evening school to increase her skill in secretarial studies under our subsidized plan. When her superior was promoted to general manager he took this 19-year-old young lady with him as his secretary, a fine tribute to her ability. For a year and a half she took courses and became one of our best secretaries.

Immediately after her marriage she notified us she was moving to California with her husband where she is evidently seeking employment with you. We would be willing to employ her again should she return.

Sincerely

Irving Glauberman
Personnel Director

There are some interesting omissions in this letter. Not one comment was made regarding the personality of this employee or her relationship with others. Yet, she is praised very highly for her work. It is possible to read between the lines that she is a good secretary, but did not endear herself to others. The most important sentence is the last one and the fact that she left of her own free will because of marriage. That last statement may give the new employer cause to reflect. How long can they count on her services before she leaves to have a child?

Letters of recommendation are usually given upon request by a departing employee who is in good favor and who is moving to a new area or wishes to seek other employment. The knowledge that the letter is not given in confidence may change its entire tone. It is desirable to tell an employee upon departure whether he may use his immediate superior as a reference.

To Whom It May Concern:

William A. Carey was employed here for six years and two months, most recently in the capacity of assistant head teller. He started here as a graduate of a business school, 19 years of age, and advanced to his recent position by the age of 23.

Mr. Carey is leaving here of his own volition because he feels that he has advanced as far as possible under our employment plan. Since the positions to which he would be eligible for promotion are held by relatively young men and our bank is small, he has decided to seek occupation in a larger organization elsewhere.

We are sorry to see him go as he has shown himself to be resourceful, ambitious, pleasant, and capable. We recommend him with enthusiasm.

Yours truly,

Albert Alberts
Personnel Director

Sometimes it is necessary to address a letter of recommendation to an individual or company. In that event, it resembles the letter of reference, except that it specifies business competence.

Dear Mrs. Weitz

Charles Lamb informs me that your firm has offered him a position as credit manager when he leaves us.

I have known Charles since he came to us four years ago. He began work in the mail room while continuing his schooling in the evenings. He progressed through the general clerical department, the accounts receivable department to the credit department over a period of two years. For almost two years now he has been an able assistant to our credit manager.

Charles should do well for you as he is friendly, warm, ambitious, and intelligent. On the occasions when it was necessary to confer about troublesome accounts, he showed mature judgment beyond his years. He should be an asset to your firm.

Sincerely

Bernard J. Farrell
President

Chapter 9

Formal and Informal Salutations

Below is a review of the forms of address in common use. To determine the complimentary close for these examples, see Chapter 2.

Correspondent	Forms of Address	Salutations
Man	Mr. Huntington J. Smith Peter Campbell Brown, Esq. (A British title [Esquire] of courtesy and respect, becoming less common	My dear Sir (formal), My dear Mr. Smith (formal), Dear Sir (less formal), Dear Mr. Smith (less formal), Dear Hunt (informal)
Woman	Mrs. Fay T. Jones, or Mrs. John L. Jones (legal form of address) Miss or Ms. Fay T. Jones	My dear Madam (formal), My dear Mrs. (Ms. or Miss) Jones (formal), Dear Mrs. (Ms. or Miss) Jones (less formal), Dear Madam (less formal), Dear Fay (informal)
Unknown gender	Jean Fredericks Hua Mei Lai L. C. Stewart	Dear Jean Fredericks Dear Hua Mei Lai Dear L. C. Stewart
Two men addressed jointly	Messrs. John Able and Jay Baker, or Messrs. Able and Baker	My dear Sirs,* Sirs* (formal); Dear Sirs,* Gentlemen* (less formal); Dear John and Jay (informal, when first names are used in address)
Married couple	Mr. and Mrs. John L. Jones, or Mr. and Mrs. J. L. Jones	Dear Mr. and Mrs. Jones (formal), Dear Mary and John (informal)
Two married women or one married, one single	Mmes. Carr and Roth, or Mrs. Carr and Ms. Roth, or Mmes. Amelia Carr and May Roth, or Mrs. A. Carr and Miss M. Roth	Ladies, Mesdames (formal); Dear Ladies, My dear Ladies, (formal); Dear Mmes. Carr and Roth
Two single women	Misses Carr and Roth Miss A. Carr and Ms. M. Roth, or Miss Amelia Carr (two lines) Ms. May Roth	Same as above for formal; Dear Misses Carr and Roth, Dear Amelia and May
Two single women with same surname (give name of older first, if known)	Misses Hortense and Lila Skugs Miss Hortense and Ms. Lila Skugs Ms. Hortense and Lila Skugs, or Miss Hortense Skugs (two lines) Ms. Lila Skugs	Same as above for formal; My dear Misses Skugs, Dear Misses Skugs, Dear Hortense and Lila
Unknown	None	To Whom It May Concern: Dear Sir or Madam

Companies

A business firm (of men or of men and women)	Hyer and Lowre, Inc.	My dear Sirs* (formal) (use only when no women officers); Dear Sirs* (less formal); Gentlemen* (less formal)
A specific person at a business firm	Mr. John L. Jones, title; ABC Company	Same as for individual; see Ch. 2, Salutation, and above.
A firm of two or more women	Carr and Roth, or Mmes. (or Ms.) Carr and Roth	Same salutation as for two or more married women; when in doubt use "Gentlemen"*

Professional people

Any person with a doctor's degree (Ph.D., LL.D., D.V.M., etc.), or (PhD, LLD, DVM, DDS, etc.)	Dr. Leon Goldenberg, or Leon Goldenberg, M.D. or MD† Mr. John and Dr. Jane Hemple*	My dear Doctor, My dear Sir (formal); [My dear Madam (formal)]; My dear Dr. Goldenberg, Dear Doctor (less formal); Dear Sir (less formal), Dear Leon (informal); Dear Mr. and Dr. Hemple
Two people with doctor's degrees not necessarily the same. Address senior person first, if known.	Drs. Leon Goldenberg and Jessie Holland, or Drs. Goldenberg and Holland	My dear Doctors (formal), My dear Drs. Goldenberg and Holland (less formal), Dear Drs. Goldenberg and Holland (less formal), Dear Doctors (less formal), Dear Leon and Jessie (informal)
An assistant, associate, or full professor in a college or university	Henry J. Morrow, M.A., M.Sc., or MA, MSc Professor Henry J. Morrow Professor Pauline J. Morrow	Dear Sir (or Madam) (formal); My dear Sir (or Madam) (formal); My dear Professor Morrow (formal); Dear Professor Morrow (less formal); Dear Professor, Dear Henry (informal); Dear Pauline (informal)
Dean of a college or academy (without doctoral degree)	Dean Fullerton Briggs School of Optometry Columbia University	Dear Dean (formal) Dear Dean Briggs (informal)

* Do not use "Sirs" when a mixed group is addressed. "Gentlemen" is a softer word for this purpose.
† Strong trend to omit periods between letters recently.

Correspondent	Forms of Address	Salutations

Clergy

Correspondent	Forms of Address	Salutations
The Pope	His Holiness, Pope Paul VI	Your Holiness, Most Holy Father
A Roman Catholic cardinal	His Eminence, James Cardinal Montilla Archbishop of New Brunswick	Your Eminence
A Roman Catholic archbishop or bishop	The Most Reverend Gerald T. Bole Archbishop (or Bishop) of Chicago	Excellency, Your Excellency, Most Reverend Sir
A monsignor	The Right Reverend Monsignor James A. O'Leary	Right Reverend and dear Monsignor (formal), or either half (less formal)
A Roman Catholic priest	Rev. Stanislaus V. Bonawicz	Reverend and dear Father, Dear Reverend Father
A brother of an order of monks	Brother Jerome, C.F.X.	Dear Brother, Dear Brother Jerome
A mother superior in an order of nuns	Mother Mary Kathleen, Superior St. Mary's High School	Dear Mother Superior, Dear Reverend Mother
A nun	Sister Muriel Joseph, O.S.J.	Dear Sister, Dear Sister Muriel
A Protestant Episcopal bishop	The Right Reverend Francis Conne Bishop of Denver	Right Reverend and dear Sir, Dear Bishop Conne, My dear Bishop Conne
A minister	The Rev. Harvey W. Noordsy	My dear Reverend Noordsy, Dear Reverend Noordsy, Dear Pastor Noordsy (Lutheran)
A minister, dean, or pastor with a D.D.	Dr. John Henry Browne, or John Henry Browne, D.D. (or DD)	Dear Dr. Browne
A rabbi	Rabbi Aryeh Lev	Dear Rabbi, Dear Rabbi Lev, My dear Rabbi Lev

Government officials

Correspondent	Forms of Address	Salutations
President	The* President of the United States	Dear Mr. President, Sir, Dear Sir, Dear Mr. Carter
A member of the Supreme Court (the chief is referred to as Chief Justice	The* Honorable William O. Douglas Justice of the United States Supreme Court, or Justice William O. Douglas United States Supreme Court	Dear Sir, Dear Mr. Justice, Dear Mr. Douglas, Dear Justice Douglas (Dear Mr. Chief Justice)
An ambassador of the U.S.	The* Honorable John Smith Ambassador to Denmark	Dear Sir, Dear Ambassador, Dear Mr. Ambassador, Dear Madam Ambassador, Dear Mr. Smith
An ambassador of a foreign country	The* Honorable (or title or rank if known) Hector Duval Ambassador to the United States, or His Excellency the French Ambassador (if name unknown)	Honorable Sir, Honorable Ambassador, My dear Ambassador, Dear Ambassador, Dear Mr. Ambassador, Dear Madam Ambassador, Dear Dr. Duval
A member of the President's cabinet	The* Honorable Robert E. Smith, Secretary of State, or The Secretary of State (name omitted)	Dear Sir, Dear Mr. Smith, Dear Mr. Secretary
Wife of the President of the United States	Mrs. Rosalynn Carter White House Washington, DC 20500	Dear Madam (formal), Dear Mrs. Carter (informal)
The Vice President of the United States	The Vice President Senate Office Building Washington, DC 20510	Dear Mr. Vice President (formal); or Dear Sir, Dear Mr. Mondale (less formal)
Secretary General of the United Nations	His Excellency Kurt Waldheim Secretary General of the United Nations New York, NY 10017	Dear Secretary General (formal), Dear Sir (formal), Dear Dr. Waldheim (less formal)
President of a foreign country	(Name), President Republic of France Presidential Palace Paris, France	Your Excellency (formal), Dear Mr. President (formal)
United States Representative to the United Nations (Ambassador-rank position)	The* Honorable (Name) United States Representative Mission to United Nations New York, NY 10017	Dear (Name & title) (not position title)
A U.S. or state senator	The* Honorable Richard Fields, or Senator Richard Fields Senate Office Building Washington, DC 20510	Dear Sir, Dear Mr. Fields, Dear Senator Fields, My dear Senator
A member of Congress	The* Honorable Roberta B. Cedar, or Representative Roberta B. Cedar	Dear Rep. Cedar, Dear Ms. Cedar, My dear Rep. Cedar, My dear Ms. Cedar

* May be dropped entirely. When "The" is omitted, "Honorable" may be abbreviated as "Hon." before the person's name, not the title.

Correspondent	Forms of Address	Salutations
A governor	The* Honorable John F. Jones Governor of Minnesota, or Governor John F. Jones	Dear Sir, Dear Governor, Dear Governor Jones
A mayor of a city or town or any local government official	The* Honorable Robert F. Green Mayor of Binghamton	Dear Sir, Dear Mr. Mayor (or other title), Dear Mr. Green

Military personnel

Except when "Mr." or "Chief" is used, the name may be omitted in all military salutations. In the address, rank is usually abbreviated. To insure good delivery, give all information possible in military addresses.

Navy and Coast Guard enlisted men and officers	rank and name	Dear Mr. Jones (enlisted man), Dear Lieutenant (or other rank) Brown. *Except:* the salutation for an ensign is "Dear Mr. Brown"; for a lieutenant junior grade, "Dear Lieutenant Brown"; for a lieutenant commander, "Dear Commander Brown"; for a rear, vice, or fleet admiral, "Dear Admiral Brown"; for a chief petty officer, "Dear Chief Brown."
Army, Marine Corps, and Air Force enlisted men	rank and name	Dear Private (or other rank) Smith. *Except:* the salutation for all grades of sergeants is "Dear Sergeant Smith."
Army, Marine Corps, and Air Force officers	rank and name	Dear Captain (or other rank) Holmes. *Except:* the salutation for a 1st or 2nd lieutenant is "Dear Lieutenant Holmes"; for lieutenant colonel, "Dear Colonel Holmes"; for a lieutenant, major, or brigadier general, "Dear General Holmes"; for a warrant officer, "Dear Mr. Holmes."

* May be dropped entirely. When "The" is omitted, "Honorable" may be abbreviated as "Hon." before the person's name, not the title.

Chapter 10

Job Application

MOST PEOPLE FIND that a letter of application for a job is one of the most difficult letters they have to write. It is an exercise in soul-searching and horn-blowing. What do you really have to offer? How can you state this simply and clearly? Sometimes lucrative positions go begging because of the poor caliber of the letters of application received.

It is probable that the majority of firms fill vacant positions from their own ranks. About one third, however—and these include beginning employees—must be found elsewhere. Every year, one out of every fifty working people is a beginner. It therefore pays to know where to find jobs and how to apply.

Young beginners can often find jobs through friends or relatives in business, through their school placement office. They may look in newspaper advertisements and register with private or public employment agencies or at a social welfare agency. They may sit for Civil Service examinations. Enterprising beginners may do the rounds of company personnel offices, where a list of vacancies may be posted before they are advertised to the general public.

The most usual method of applying for positions is by letter even though the candidate is already employed by the company in another capacity.

Self-Analysis

Before you can apply for any position in person or by mail, you must ask yourself some searching questions: Are you suitable for the job in both personality and qualifications? The only sensible way to do it is to proceed in a logical manner to the basic areas which go to make up your total being—the impression strangers get of you after short acquaintance. It would be well to review your appearance, your health, and your personality.

Application Forms

Whenever you seek a job, you will be asked to fill out an application form. In a sense, an application is a test of your intelligence. In order to make a favorable impression, it might be wise to remember that in many personnel offices the receptionist will indicate in code on your application form the length of time you required to finish it, the way you did it, or the number of times you requested assistance. Before you enter the personnel office, therefore, you should have certain information quickly available.

You must know the kind of job for which you are applying; don't say, "I'll take anything." Be prepared to state the lowest salary you would accept. Of course, you must know your address, zip code, and telephone number, as well as those of your next of kin in case of emergency. Some people name their physician for this purpose.

On a 3″ × 5″ or 4″ × 6″ card in your pocket or purse, you should have the above information as well as other facts for easy reference:

1 Social security number.
2 Your height and weight.
3 Schools attended with their addresses and the exact dates of attendance.
4 Names, ages, and addresses of dependents.
5 Names, addresses, occupations, and telephone numbers of three (minimum) to five references who are not related to you nor are former employers, and who have given you permission to use their names.
6 Your previous part- or full-time employers' names, addresses, and dates you worked there. You should be prepared to give the name of your immediate superior and the salary you received.
7 Be prepared to give the reason you left any previous employment; it will be checked.
8 Skills, hobbies, or awards received.
9 Volunteer work for hospitals, etc.; names of supervisors.

Letter of Application

A letter of application is often written in response to a newspaper advertisement. These advertisements do not answer all your questions about a job. Rather, they are written to arouse your interest and curiosity.

HELP WANTED	COMMENTS
OFFICE MANAGER & hd bkkpr for furniture mfr, parking avlbl, near Inwood, 5 days, $325 XY791 Courier.	Specific weekly wage; industry and location named. Blind box requires letter of application and resumé.
PERSONNEL MGR, Orange dept store. to $18,-000, exp., progressive co., good opportunity. XG77 EXPRESS	Specific salary; opportunity, different meaning to each person; kind of work and experience clear.
PLACEMENT MANAGER TOP $$ Secretarial, comml exp, salary or draw against comm, good opty. LV482	Salary teaser. Salary base optional. Duties not clear. Experience clear.
PUBLIC RELATIONS, Acc. Exec., good writer, women's prod., publcty, fash. food a/c, national contacts. Y3438	No salary stated. Writing and area specified. Duties specific. Letter must reflect writing ability.
SUPERVISOR, steno pool, start $280, train, teach, screen, test, exp in production, writing ablty; write, don't call. Vestey Productions, Inc. 145 West Street, Mr. Ronson, 10013.	Generous salary stated. Duties sound difficult. Real ability indicated. Unusual letter necessary. Implication of need to write form letters and routine replies.

In replying to the advertisement by letter, you must make your letter distinctive in some way. To prevent the letter from becoming cumbersome, you should attach to it a personal data sheet (Fig. 10.1) giving full name, address, telephone number, social security number, age, height, weight, marital status, dependents or children, references, as well as education, work experience, and interests. A sample letter of application and personal data sheet follow.

2250 Commonwealth Avenue
St. Louis, MO 63143
October 12, 19--

Mr. Ronson
Vestey Products, Inc.
145 West Street
St. Louis, MO 63116

Dear Mr. Ronson,

I have read with interest your advertisement for a supervisor of your stenographers' pool, and believe that my qualifications are suitable.

After two years of college (in which I earned the certificate of Associate in Arts and Science, majoring in executive secretarial training), I began my business career nine years ago. I spent one year with Ward Manufacturing Company. Starting as a stenographer with Ark Metal Products, I soon became secretary to the vice president and personal secretary to Mr. Louis Just, President of the corporation. I still hold that position today.

In the course of these past six years during which time the corporation doubled in size, I assisted Mr. Just, trained secretaries for other executives, composed a company correspondence style manual, took minutes at executive board meetings, and generally performed the duties of an executive secretary. Because of Mr. Just's position, it was necessary for me to meet, screen, and handle many visitors and subordinates of my employer. I have always been praised highly for my management of personal relations.

Since Mr. Just's untimely death in an auto accident two months ago, I have decided to seek employment elsewhere. I would like to undertake the challenge of establishing your stenographers' pool, and shall call you Friday morning at 10:30 to determine a mutually convenient time for an interview.

Yours truly,

Elizabeth Booth

The purpose of every letter of application is to sell your skills and abilities, and to obtain an interview. On occasion, an unusual beginning will make the difference between your letter's being set aside in a pile, or being selected for immediate action. In the last paragraph make it as clear as possible that you want an interview, giving information that will help to secure it.

Gentlemen

My facility with house plants—a green thumb—will not benefit your company in any way. The skill I have developed in personal relations with people, however, is just what you need to fill the position of Receptionist. You advertised for one in this morning's *Times*.

. . . .

You may reach me at 555–4242 any afternoon from 1 to 3. Won't you call to arrange a time for an interview soon?

Yours truly

Gentlemen

I have given up all attempts to become an actress. I do not have the talent. I do have an unusual talent as a stenographer, however. Because you deal in business with the theatrical world, I can still keep in touch with my first love while doing what I can do well and enjoy doing.

. . . .

Your prompt call to arrange for an interview will be appreciated.

Yours truly

```
                         PERSONAL DATA


Name:       Elizabeth M. Booth
Address:    24 Astoria Boulevard
            St. Louis, Mo 63137           Telephone:  INdependence 9-8765


Age:        28 years                      Place of Birth:  Chicago, Illinois
Height:     5 feet 3 inches               Marital Status:  Single
Weight:     121 pounds                     Social Security # 071-02-001
Health:     Excellent                     Dependents:  One; mother


Education

College:          University of Chicago, AAS Degree 19--
                  (Major, Secretarial Studies; Minor, English)
High School:      North Side High School, Chicago, 19---19--
                  (College Entrance Course Diploma received)


Special Interests and Activities

Golf:             Active amateur competition - Illinois Girls Champion 19--
                                               Intercollegiate Champion 19--
Swimming
Volunteer
   Work:          Chief of Volunteer Service for St. Louis Orphan Home.
                  Started as stranger here in 19--, now in charge of staff.


Technical Skills

Stenography:      140 words a minute

Typewriting:      Straight copy - 80 to 85 words a minute
                  Business letters - 50 to 60 words a minute

Office Machines:  Mimeograph              Adding and Calculating
                  Liquid Duplicator       Automatic Calculators
                  Offset Duplicator       Switchboards
                  Photocopy               Filing Systems
                  Bookkeeping (NCR)       Billing (Fischer)
                  Checkwriter             Transcribers


Work Experience

7/19---4/19--     Ward Manufacturing Co.   Mr. Harold Schor    Stenographer,
                  123 Market Street        Office Manager      Secretary
                  Chicago, Il 60649
4/19---6/19--     Family moved to St. Louis after father's
                  death; used period for settling down
7/19---Present    Ark Metal Products       Mr. Robert Frost    Secretary
                  333 Lawrence Avenue      President              to
                  St. Louis, Mo 63135                          President

References

Miss Phyllis Kovanda, Executive Director, St. Louis Orphan Home, 10375 Sparks,
                               St. Louis, 63133, 284-6494
Rev. Charles Spence, Pastor, Church of Epiphany, 200 Ames, St. Louis 63175, 894-5366
Dr. Peter Edwards, Family Physician, 35 Dogwood Avenue, Hill Park 63124, 394-1009
Mrs. Evelyn Borden, Neighbor, 22 Astoria Boulevard, St. Louis 63137, 461-2345
```

Fig. 10.1 Suggested form for personal data sheet.

Chapter 11

Post and Postal Cards

TECHNICALLY SPEAKING, ANY card printed by the postal authorities is a *postal card*. All others are called *post cards*. Since the postal card is already stamped and is a uniform size (3¼″ × 5½″), it has advantages over any others. Post cards, however, may be made in any size or shape to suit your special requirements. This is one advantage of the post card. If it is to be stamped by postage meter, the limitations of the postage meter must be considered. If it is to be hand-stamped, the size is of little importance.

The postal card is useful in business. All spoiled, unused cards are redeemable for 85 percent of their value. A double card is also obtainable, one part being used for the message and the other for a reply. However, the double-stamped card could be wasteful; the reply card not used has postage on it which has been paid for. It is far more economical to obtain the double card with the second card blank. When the message is printed or duplicated on it, the special return address with permission to pay postage upon delivery may be used. Regular post cards, printed on card stock, may be prepared in the same way.

Some of the many uses of post cards in business as substitutes for letters or telephone calls or even visits by a salesman are: (a) in letters for prompt or routine reply and in catalogs for convenience in ordering; (b) in new equipment to qualify for the guarantee period; (c) acknowledge order received, or notification of date and method of shipment; (d) register sale of equipment by a dealer to a manufacturer or to a distributor; (e) inform customers of special offers or free samples requiring immediate or time-limit response; (f) request names of neighbors and friends to subscribe to some cause; (g) authorize a proxy signature for voting rights in a corporation; (h) notify of a change of address; (i) selection from lists by members of book, theater, record, or other clubs; (j) entry blanks for contests; (k) request for supplies for representatives of companies; and many, many others.

The use of punched cards, which coordinate into a data-processing system, is increasing. With improvements in the five-channel perforated tape, some firms are using the perforations along the side of the card with the standard admonition: *Do not fold, bend, spindle, or mutilate this card.* With the use of magnetic ink symbols, many routine duties are becoming automated.

These cards have many uses and can be combined, for instance, with carbon copies, invoice forms, or vouchers. It is possible to have a prepared set which will produce a card for the customer, a shipping label, a packing list, an invoice for the customer, shipping instructions for the warehouse, a copy for the bookkeeper, and a copy for the salesman—all from one operation. By holes punched along the edges with a special machine roller equipped with spikes to fit these holes, the forms can be kept in perfect alignment while in the billing machine.

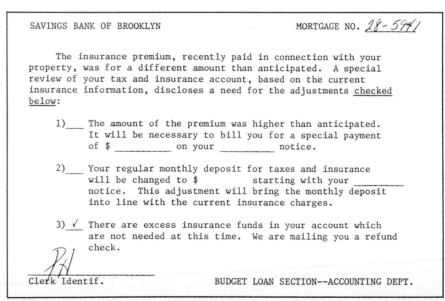

Fig. 11.1 A form post card using a combination of "multiple choice" and "fill-in-the-blanks" saves clerical time. A properly instructed clerk can complete the form.

Fig. 11.2A Example of combination card for reply and temporary membership with registered number on each. (Courtesy of National Trust for Historic Preservation)

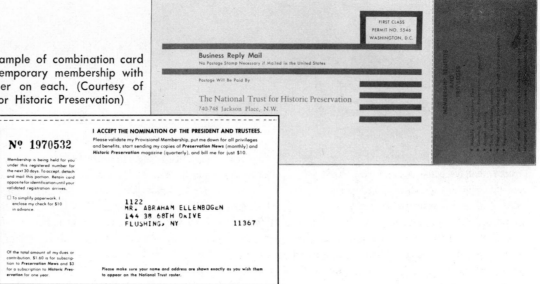

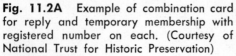

Fig. 11.2B Magazine renewal notice and postcard with removable stub. (Courtesy of *New York Magazine*)

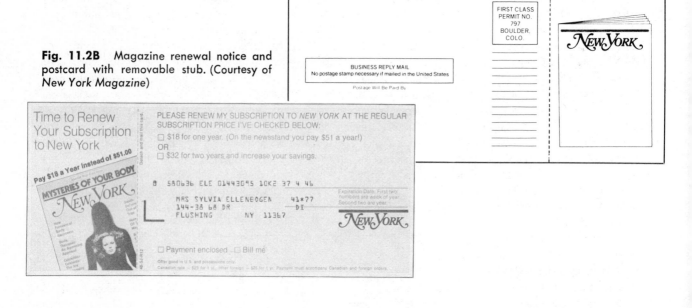

Fig. 11.2C Example of card requiring removal of label from magazine for easy reply. (Courtesy of American Association of Retired Persons)

Chapter 12

Claims, Complaints, Adjustments

THIS IS THE area of the most delicate and skillful correspondence in the business world. It is necessary to answer this type of letter at once because the correspondent is angry, yet it is important to have time to investigate before replying. A writer of such letters should not be ruffled easily, should be logical, sympathetic, understanding, and tactful, as well as efficient and well organized. Just as surely as a business firm employs human beings it can be certain of errors, damage, and angry customers. For this reason, it is necessary to be prepared to deal with each problem promptly and equitably.

Once again it is appropriate to review the ABCD of good letter writing, to remember the necessity for accuracy, brevity, clarity, and dignity. Examine your letter or your response to a letter in this category for dignity and accuracy above all else. Answering or originating, it is important to be firm and sensible. Don't ask for the impossible—or offer it. Follow company policy and request a reasonable solution. Compromise is a stabilizer.

Outgoing Claim

When making a claim against another company, be sure of the accuracy and justice of your request. In this way, you will ensure a favorable response. In composing the letter, try to read it from the other fellow's side. Will it seem just and fair to him?

Gentlemen

Last Wednesday at 7:45 a.m. your truckman dropped off at our rear door seven cases of soap, as ordered. This was a favor to him to save him the delay of waiting until we open for business at 9 o'clock. The cases arrived as expected and were left where we suggested.

It rained quite hard during the night and continued until 8:15 a.m. The alley in front of our rear door was dotted with puddles. The largest one was in front of our rear door. That is exactly where your truckman dropped the cases. Fortunately, the four cases on the bottom protected the three cases on top. So, three cases are in satisfactory condition.

The other four cases are in very sad condition. The corrugated boxes came apart when the boxes were brought in at 9 a.m. The bottom cakes of soap are a total loss. The layer just above is badly soiled. The top layer of soap cakes has soiled wrappers, but the soap is intact.

For the time being, we shall hold the fort with the three cases of soap which are in satisfactory condition. Please advise your truckman that in future he will be required to deliver during store hours to our regular delivery area. Please let us know as soon as possible what we should do with four spoiled cases of soap.

Sincerely

Claret Dyob
Store Manager

vn

The soap-company executive who responded offered immediate action and so was able to reply by wire. Both parties were satisfied.

CLARET DYOB
STORE MANAGER
ROMNEY & SMITH
18 WEST MAIN STREET
BOISE, IDAHO 83707

DISTRESSED TO HEAR OF DAMAGED SOAP. ACCEPT OUR REGRETS. REPLACEMENT SHIPMENT ON WAY TODAY. CAN YOU KEEP DAMAGED CASES AT ONE DOLLAR EACH FOR STORM DAMAGE BARGAIN TABLE AT 5¢ A CAKE? IF NOT, GIVE TO TRUCKMAN DELIVERING NEW CASES.

DEAN BACON
SALES MANAGER

This day letter achieved its objective. The dealer was quite pleased to get fifteen-cent cakes of soap at about two cents each and be authorized to sell them at five cents each. While reaping a handsome profit, he satisfied certain customers who cannot resist a bargain.

Incoming Claim

When claims are received, it is a good idea to verify at once and act upon the findings. As a matter of fact, it is possible by prompt and effective action to convert a basis for complaint into a source of good will. Never belittle the claim or its validity. If a customer claims that the representative who accepted her order for a vacuum cleaner did not give her a receipt for her $10 deposit, the reply could read as follows:

Dear Mrs. Saveth

Your letter received today states that our representative did not leave a receipt for the $10 deposit he accepted with your order. I have checked with him and he informed me that this is a simple misunderstanding. He showed me the duplicate of the sales agreement which he left with you.

Please note that the last paragraph indicates that a $10 deposit is required with all sales agreements. The signature of the sales representative on that form is your receipt for the required deposit. Had you not given him the deposit he would not have given you the sales agreement.

We are very glad that you had the foresight to contract for the SCOOP vacuum cleaner when you did by making the deposit because the price went up only yesterday. You, of course, are guaranteed the same vacuum cleaner at the price specified in the sales agreement, $79.95, less the $10—a balance due of $69.95. Your machine will be delivered to you on Wednesday between 3 and 5 p.m.

I trust that this clears up the matter of deposit, and that you will have many hours of carefree cleaner service.

Yours truly

Other claims are not as simple as the one above, nor can they be settled so easily. A motorist claims that one of your trucks backed into his car, damaged it, and drove off without a word. He has the license number of the truck and the witnesses to prove it. A woman writes to claim that while eating a can of your food she came across a piece of glass or a bug. There will be many claims for accidents or defects in equipment. The person who responds to these claims should keep a very careful file of all correspondence. Legal advice should be sought if the person in charge of such correspondence has no legal background. Many business firms acknowledge receipt of the claim at once in a form letter which avoids accepting or denying responsibility. They are then in a position to take the letter under advisement. Wherever possible, insurance coverage should be utilized. The matter can thus be turned over to people especially trained to evaluate claims.

Complaint Letters

We cannot all be as articulate, humorous, and clear as the distinguished gentleman who wrote this letter of complaint, but it is a good example of tact.

My dear Sir:

Since my hall clock was sent to your establishment to be cleaned, it has gone (as indeed it always has) perfectly well, but has struck the hours with great reluctance, and after enduring internal agonies of a most distressing nature, it has now ceased striking altogether. Though a happy release for the clock, this is not convenient to the household.

If you can send down any confidential person with whom the clock can confer, I think it may have something on its works that it would be glad to make a clean breast of.

Yours very truly,

Charles Dickens

This letter received an immediate response in the form of a repairman who was sent to the house. However, many business houses have a peculiar policy of paying little heed to complaint letters. They hope that the problem will dissolve into thin air and they will hear no more about it. This is a serious error of policy. It must be re-emphasized that every circumstance should be converted into an opportunity for the creation of good will. How many times have you heard people say that they are willing to pay a little more when dealing with a certain firm because they know that they are reliable and will stand behind every sale they make? This is invaluable good will, the rock upon which a sound establishment is based.

It is surprising how many claims can be taken care of easily and satisfactorily. Under the tax laws there are even provisions by which their cost can be turned to the benefit of your company, so that in the long run a claim will not cost you anything and may gain you a great deal. It is likely that there will, however, be a small percentage that are insoluble. It is a good investment to place the claims department of a company in the hands of a person who is not satisfied until a job is completed, who will pride himself on efficiency and promptness.

One of the best methods of elimination of complaints is prevention. Many business-equipment companies have adopted a very intelligent policy which forestalls many complaints. When new equipment is purchased, they send a sales representative and a skilled, experienced repairman to supervise its installation and initial use. They make suggestions as to usage, placement, and handling. It is an excellent antidote to trouble and creates a good impression on the customer. A service contract with the customer may also help minimize causes of complaints.

Strikes, storms, and other calamities can wreak havoc with promises to customers and are unavoidable. In all such cases, rapid explanation to customers will keep tempers from reaching the boiling point.

Gentlemen

We regret to have to inform you of a strike of the truckmen who handle all of our deliveries to your area. This will take place on Sunday at midnight unless the negotiations for this new contract are settled before that time. From our adviser at the contract talks we know that hopes are rather slim. In order not to leave you without the merchandise you need for your special sale we are investigating the following possibility.

A charter plane freight company in this vicinity is not affected by the strike. They inform us that if you can meet their plane at the Kankakee airport with your truck, they will take the shipment for us at the same rate which we would have paid the truckers, just to help us out in this emergency.

Please wire us collect if this arrangement can be made by you. Otherwise, we do not see how we shall be able to keep our commitment to you under the circumstances.

Sincerely

Nathan Freeman, Supervisor
Shipping Department

Adjustment Letters

An adjustment letter is actually the response to a complaint. Many complaints are the result of errors or inaccuracies. Others are the result of misunderstandings. In many business firms elaborate measures are used to prevent errors or misunderstandings. We are all familiar, for example, with packing slips which state "Inspected by #84" or "Packed by G37." Skilled workers check the operation of equipment thoroughly before passing them on for shipment. Where sets consist of several different parts, experienced employees check to see that the complete set, properly wrapped or packaged, is enclosed before sealing.

Most companies go to elaborate extents to compose and print instruction booklets for consumers, especially when self-installation is likely. These booklets are explicit with careful wording and illustrations and diagrams to ensure successful installation and use. Undoubtedly, the booklets reduce the number of letters received by answering inquiries before they can be written. The response to an inquiry may sometimes be effected by sending a booklet with the exact section carefully marked for the writer. These booklets usually contain maintenance suggestions most helpful in avoiding unnecessary inquiries.

It is inevitable that adjustment letters will have to be written. When they are, try to keep these factors in view. Follow this simple formula. Sympathize, advise, and attempt to regain good will. Avoid placing the blame on the customer, make suggestions, and keep the door open to further help or service. Whenever possible, convert the opportunity to an additional sales pitch.

Dear Mr. Coleman

Your recent letter informing me of the many satisfying hours you have had with the MARATHON Sport Fisherman is gratifying. I regret, however, that there were even minor matters to mar your enjoyment of this popular boat.

I am enclosing a copy of the Instruction and Maintenance booklet which should have been supplied to you when you purchased this boat. On pages 77, 84, and 112, you will see sections marked off in red which should help solve the matters about which you write. We want you to have as many trouble-free hours as possible with the Sport Fisherman.

If you should be unable to solve your problems by referring to this booklet, we suggest that you take your boat to the authorized MARATHON dealer in your area, Martin's Boat Yard, 1447 Causeway, Buena Vista. He will be glad to serve you. You are expected. There will be no charge for adjustments about which you wrote as you are entitled to them under the terms of our sales agreement.

Please write to me directly at any time in the future concerning any matter that has not been taken care of to your complete satisfaction.

Sincerely

"Cap" Davie Jones
Sales Manager

ty
cc: Martin's Boat Yard

Dear Mr. Carlin:

It was quite a surprise to receive your cancellation in the same mail as we received many reorders from satisfied dealers in your state. We are certainly comforted that the reason for the cancellation was not dissatisfaction with the new JOHNRUDE outboard motors. As you know, they are the best and latest development in water motoring, having won the medal for the best in their class at the recent Boat Show.

Your letter indicates that you feel that the season at Gold Beach is nearly over and that you do not wish to be left with any stock at the end of the season. Let me assure you, Mr. Carlin, that from our past records your season will go on for another two months at least. You may not know, perhaps, that our regular policy at the end of your season is to redeem all unsold, packed motors at full value, or allow a further 15% discount if they are kept. Floor models which have been unpacked and handled are not redeemable.

All things considered, don't you agree that it might be better to have the motors on hand, so that customers do not have to be turned away or satisfied with inferior motors? Please let us know by Western Union collect today.

Sincerely,

Ward Monroe
Sales Manager

In a computer-dominated society such as ours, and its concomitant consumers' frustrations, the letters below give an example of an attempt to "humanize and defuse" complaints with a touch of humor. Undoubtedly it makes for warmth in a cold business relationship. This fictional complaint has been responded to in the fashion of John P. Finsland of Shell Oil Company, to whom we give thanks.

Dear Mr. Computer Operator:

For seven months I have tried in vain to solve the problem of my very old *paid* bill for which you continue charging me interest for nonpayment and threaten revocation of my credit card. As a matter of fact, at the last gas station where I was using the credit card, I had to call a police officer to get my card back!

In the past I have received computer-produced letters signed by G. Brown, L. Reich, and W. Haynes, assuring me that they would look into the matter. The statement in question is dated January 15, last year, amounting to $37.85. As the months rolled by, finance charges increased the amount to $40.35. My canceled check is dated March 24, last year. This will be my last appeal to summon a live response from someone before I resort to legal processes to clear my credit reputation and restore my sanity.

Please, is there anyone human there to answer my call for help?

Hopefully

Julia Lafayette
#24077688234

Reply sent:

Dear Mrs. Lafayette

> There was a young lady named Lafayette
> Who wrote to us very upset.
> Her complaint involves our computer
> The actions of which did not suit her,
> But a well placed kick on the side of the machine
> Caused its memory to reveal that her account
>   was clean.
> So, dear Mrs. Lafayette, we are cut down to size;
> From the bottom of our heart, we apologize.
> By wire we are notifying our stations one and all
> To honor your credit card spring, summer, winter,
>   and fall.

I hope we're forgiven.

Yours truly

Malcolm A. Weiss
Consumer Relations

bcc: Murdoch's Service Station
        All points bulletin

SOME RULES FOR REPLYING TO COMPLAINTS

1 Keep your letter simple and clear. Don't give unnecessary details.

2 If you have made an error, admit it and offer to rectify it.

3 If an employee is guilty of a blunder, don't blame him unless the aggrieved customer specifically blames one of your staff and you have to agree.

4 Don't be too apologetic. Mature business people understand that people make mistakes. Admit them when they occur. But do everything in your power to avoid repetition.

5 Don't use belligerence or laughter as a cover for a mistake. Solve the problem in the best way for both parties, if possible. If this is not possible, take the loss and gain the good will.

6 Don't indicate that when a faulty article is returned you will see whether the customer's claim is justified. You must trust your customer until he is proved unreliable.

7 Make good your advertised promises of complete satisfaction to each customer. Be positive in your attitude toward the goods you offer and to your customers.

8 Don't overlook any opportunity to build good will and sell your reliability.

9 Don't make the customer do all the work when a shipper is at fault. Put yourself out to do all you can unless, legally, there are actions which the customer must initiate. If so, inform him and explain the situation to him.

10 Be prompt in answering complaints. Whenever possible, answer the same day.

11 Don't blame the customer, even if he is at fault. Instead, offer help at once and suggest that in the future a specific action will probably prevent a similar problem. This will create good will.

12 Follow up installation of equipment by writing to customers to inquire whether it is satisfactory or needs some adjustment. A letter from a customer indicating that all is well can be an important item at a later date. Some firms send a form inquiry at the end of the first thirty days.

13 Don't be hesitant about writing to a customer who has not ordered lately or allowed your salesman to call. You may be able to solve whatever is at fault and obtain re-entry for your representative.

14 When you feel the customer is being unreasonable, don't make an outright refusal. Compromise and show willingness to help.

15 Don't repeat your sales pitch as an answer to a customer's complaint or claim.

16 Don't permit salesmen to oversell or overstate your product. Honesty and conviction can carry you a long way toward success.

Service Industries

For a service industry, which exists almost entirely on good will, it is often desirable to follow up a complaint or claim in a search for new business. Records should be kept scrupulously. Some firms give this task to the same accounts-receivable clerk who is responsible for ensuring that all overdue accounts and unpaid accounts are approached. Policy will dictate how and when accounts are followed up. The person responsible for checking accounts could recognize those where there has been a complaint or claim by a specific marking on the ledger or index card—a red, green, purple, or other tab in plastic. This tab then becomes the signal to learn whether the customer is now completely satisfied and further business could now be done (Fig. 12.1).

These are standard mailings with no signatures or identification. If there is no reply, the sales manager should be informed and he should write a "Won't you kindly tell us what we can do to regain your good faith" letter.

If the customer has purchased since the complaint, a form message may be sent thanking him for his continued patronage (Fig. 12.2). No reply is required to this message. None is expected. It is merely an attempt to chip away at any hard feelings which might remain since the claim or complaint occurred. The fact that these messages were sent should be noted carefully in the account record.

```
Jackson & Perkin--you are missed!

    We want you to know that we are just as anxious as
ever to do business with you.  Our past relationship is too
good to throw away over a little misunderstanding.

    Our new price list and catalog is now available.  May
we send it to you so that you will be up to date on our
latest WHITEHEAD offerings?  Just check off and sign the
enclosed stamped, self-addressed card.  We'll do the rest.

                             Sincerely

S3                                    WHITEHEAD NOVELTY CO.
```

Fig. 12.1 "Quickie" letter attempting to reestablish business with dissatisfied former customers.

```
Thank you, Moore Construction Company

    Your continued patronage is appreciated, and, we hope,
deserved.  We would like to continue our relationship as long
as we merit it.

    At any time you wish us to be of service or assistance
please write directly to me.

    Do not allow the fact that this is a form message fool
you.  Try us for sincerity and helpfulness any time.

                             Sincerely

                             WHITEHEAD NOVELTY CO.
S9                           George Whitehead, Pres.
```

Fig. 12.2 Form post card thanking a customer, who once had a complaint, for his continued patronage.

Chapter 13

Telegraphic Services

THERE WAS A time when "fast" meant "telegraph." But technological advances have given us satellites, microwave towers, direct distance dialing, wide-area telephone service, toll-free calls, mobile telephones, dataphones, automatic dialing, automatic typewriters, automatic telephone-answering service, voice-activated microphones and tape recorders, credit-card calling, and so on. All businesses may now find many of these best suited and within their economic range.

Telegrams are still one way to relay information from one place to another quickly and at a reasonable speed and price. There are three basic types of domestic service available to everyone who has a telephone or a telegraph office nearby. They are: full-rate telegram, overnight telegram, and mailgram.

Domestic Service

The *full-rate telegram* is the most common usage of this service domestically. It is the most expensive of the services but the fastest; it is a first-priority message which the telegraph company tries to deliver within two hours from the time it is filed.* For up to 15 words the charge is a minimum rate. Each additional word is charged beyond that minimum. There is no charge for the addressee's name and address and telephone number; nor is there for the signature and title or firm name of the sender.

The *overnight telegram* will be accepted up to midnight for delivery the next morning or the next business day. It is less expensive than the full-rate telegram and is based on a minimum message of 100 words; there is a charge for each word over 100. Actually this type of communication is excellent for coast-to-coast messages, because time zones create problems. Afternoon messages from the West to the East generally cannot arrive in time before the close of business for the day; they are delivered first thing in the morning. Full-rate telegrams after 3 p.m. Pacific Time are risky. If sent overnight the message will arrive early in the morning Eastern Time. If an answer is required, it can arrive by the opening of business on the West Coast. Remember, morning in the West is afternoon in the East. Tip: Sun rises in Atlantic and sets in Pacific—Atlantic to Pacific.

The most recent addition to the telegraph services is the *mailgram*. It is an example of a combination service: the telegraph company transmits, the Postal Service receives and delivers. A postal clerk places the message directly off the machine in a window envelope for delivery with the morning mail. Mailgrams will not be accepted after 7 p.m. In a mailgram, every word or number counts including the addressee and signature, but the minimum charge is for 100 words. Additional words by the hundred may be added for an extra charge. This is the least expensive of the three services.

Telegraph messages may be filed or received by messenger, telephone, teleprinter, or teletypewriter. Of course, you may go to the telegraph office and file the message in person, but these offices are not as numerous as they used to be because of economy measures by the telegraph company and the improvement in wire and wireless communications.

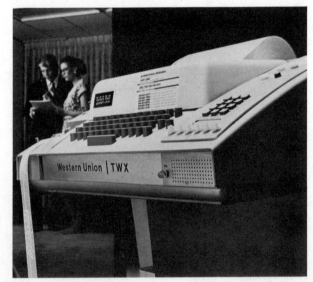

Fig. 13.1 Latest integrated TWX machine. Note 8-channel punched tape. (Courtesy of Western Union)

* The customer *files* a telegram; the telegraph *transmits* or *sends* it.

Word Count

Because telegrams are costly, it is wise to know how to determine word count. Counting words is a special skill and, of course, the last word is with the telegraph company. Below are a few samples of word count for the United States (contiguous states), and others for Canada, Mexico, Alaska, Hawaii, etc. Here are *basic* rules:

1 Dictionary words count as one word each.
2 Place names and proper names count as normally written.
3 All other groups count at five characters per word.
4 Free punctuation: period or decimal, comma, colon, semicolon, dash, hyphen, question mark, apostrophe, quotation marks, and parentheses.
5 Chargeable punctuation: dollar sign, fraction or diagonal, ampersand, number sign; feet, minutes, inches, or seconds signs.

	No. Chargeable Words (5-character count)
Mutilated and Nondictionary Words	
AIREX (5 characters)	1
MAZELTOV (8 characters)	2
URORDER (7 characters)	2
Abbreviations and Letter Groups	
A.M. (if written without space)	1
LB (for pound)	1
WASHDC (6 characters)	2
W N E W (if written with spaces)	4
Trade Names	
DURA-GLO (7 characters, hyphen is punctuation)	2
REDIFORM (8 characters)	2
SWIFTNING (9 characters)	2

Examples of Dictionary Words	No. Chargeable Words
EXCURSION CANCELLED (English)	2
HERZLICHEN GLUECKWUNSCH (German) .	2
NOUS ARRIVERONS DIMANCHE (French) ..	3
DOLCE FAR NIENTE (Italian)	3
UN CABELLO HACE SOMBRA (Spanish) ...	4
(Words in other languages: 5 characters = 1 word)	

Groups of Figures, Combinations of Figures, Letters, and Other Characters	No. Chargeable Words	
	U.S. Alaska Mexico	Canada St. Pierre and Miquelon
B.D/A:C (period and colon are punctuation)	1	3
(WAC) (parentheses are punctuation)	1	1
END/RLA/GTR-1381/ (hyphen is punctuation) ..	4	10
12345	1	5
100% (transmitted 100 0/0)	2	6

Combinations of Dictionary Words	No. Chargeable Words
AIRBILL for AIR BILL	2
AIREXPRESS for AIR EXPRESS	2
ALRIGHT for ALL RIGHT	2
AND/OR (Stroke counts as separate word in this case)	3
CARLOAD (Dictionary word)	1
DON'T (Dictionary contraction— apostrophe is punctuation)	1
ENROUTE for EN ROUTE	2
FIBERGLASS (Dictionary word)	1

Names of Persons and Places	No. Chargeable Words
VAN DORNE	2
VANDORNE (if so written)	1
WMPENN (normally written WM PENN) ..	2
JOHN L. SULLIVAN	3
J.L.R. SMITH (if written without spaces) .	2
UNITED STATES	2
NEWFOUNDLAND	1
NEW YORK CITY	3

Addresses	No. Chargeable Words
JOHN H. BROWN PERSONAL DELIVERY RE-PORT DELIVERY ROOM 1008 DUNBAR BLDG.	2
JOHN DOE PHONE 555–1419 15 HOWARD ST.	NONE
JOHN SMITH OR JAMES BROWN 80 WALL ST.	3
JOHN BROWN FORWARD STATLER HOTEL BUFFALO NY IF UNDELIVERED PENN-SYLVANIA HOTEL NYCITY	7

Signatures

JOHN BROWN PRESIDENT	NONE
SALES DEPARTMENT STANDARD CAN CO. .	NONE
CONTINENTAL BUS SYSTEM 315 CONTINENTAL AVE.	3
DAVID COOPER GEN MGR RADIO STATION WKIN	2
J. W. SMITH BUSINESS MGR LOCAL 533 UMW OF AMERICA NORTH SIDE HOTEL CHICAGO	8

Filing a Telegram in Person

You may go to the telegraph office, file the telegram, and pay for or charge it. It will be sent full rate (immediately), overnight (slightly delayed), or mailgram. You will pay according to the number of words, distance to be transmitted, and the type of service desired.

In addition to the three regular services mentioned, here are some special telegraphic services (available with their appropriate telegram form):

Hotel-motel reservations (service charge)
Commencement wishes
Bon voyage wishes
Get-well wishes
Thank-you messages
Good-luck wishes
Communion, confirmation, Bar Mitzvah wishes
Invitation messages
Anniversary messages
Birth announcements
Condolence messages
Money orders
Wedding wishes
Birthday wishes
Miscellaneous others

For almost all of the services mentioned above, appropriate headings are printed at the top in the position of the standard form for regular messages. They are colorful and have been designed to suit the occasion.

Filing a Telegram by Telephone

You may file any telegram by telephone except a money order. Call the Western Union office nearest you, dictate the message, have it read back for verification, and charge it to your own telephone. You need not be calling from your own telephone to do so. It will appear on your next telephone bill, the same way a long-distance telephone call would. This method is the most expeditious, but the most fallible because it is entirely oral. Spelling names and technical words is recommended. It is advisable to confirm the message by mail at the same time, so that the recipient may have a written record with which to compare the telegram, and a correct copy for the file.

Filing a Telegram Direct

TELEPRINTER-TELETYPEWRITER

A teleprinter is a large electric typewriter with a modified keyboard which operates two machines simultaneously at the receiving end and at the sending end of the line. It has the advantage of being able to conduct two-way typewritten conversations. The machine can turn itself on when called, identify itself, and accept a message. (See *Telex* below.)

Until 1958, if your firm required direct telegraphic contact with branches or other teleprinter subscribers, you signaled an operator at a central office. The operator then made connections similar to those made by a switchboard operator and the message could then proceed to the receiver if someone was on duty to accept it. It was fairly efficient but not instantaneous.

Western Union and the telephone company offer systems of *teletypewriting* which are connected to all of its subscribers who lease the same equipment. Payment is on a toll basis or a monthly basis, depending upon the volume of traffic. These are known as TWX and TWPL (private line). TWX is operated by Western Union.

Both the Western Union teleprinter and the telephone company teletypewriter may be (usually are) connected to a tape-punching device or a punched-card or computer system, thereby incorporating it directly into the data-processing or word-processing system of the company. The inclusion may be all or selected materials. Another variation of this service is a *tie line* which connects directly to the local tele-

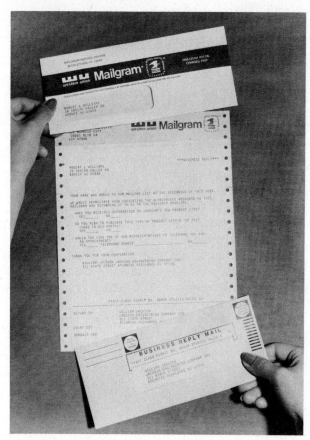

Fig. 13.2 Sample mailgram. (Courtesy of Western Union)

graph office or direct telephone line to another office, warehouse, or installation. The tie line permits direct communication by voice. By the way, it is customary to save up communications on the punched tape for a sufficient run, then send it at the electronic speed of the machine when ready. Many possible combinations of service are available. Consult either company.

TELEMETER

Telemeter is a private wire service available between customers' offices in principal cities of the United States. It is unique, as these services go, because it is furnished on a word-metered basis. Telemeter service provides two-way (sending and receiving) simultaneous teleprinters at each station. It is most practical between points in continuous contact with low word volume. It is not as popular as it used to be.

TELEX

The teleprinter service described above has become streamlined and cheaper since May 1958. Telex is an automatic teleprinter service which covers all cities with direct-dial service in all areas of the world.

In this system a dial or pushbutton grouping is connected to your teleprinter and is used like any telephone dial. However, the receiving machine will automatically answer for you without an operator. As soon as contact is made and the connection is established, the machine, as customary before transmitting, gives its own identification to your operator. The operator then sends the message in the usual way. Your machine automatically produces its copy and the receiving machine has its copy typed even if the machine is unattended.

Imagine what this means to the businessman. He may send his message any time he wishes and he does not have to wait for the machine at the other end to be attended. A twenty-four-hour robot employee?

Other Systems

With the advent of microwave and satellite transmission, there is undoubtedly no limit to the possible communication systems available today. Electronic printed circuits, when coupled with some of the services available, operate on demand unattended. The various branches of the government, especially the military, have such systems in operation at all times. Most of the international corporations have the same type of communications. Domestically, it is possible to receive news, sports, finance, market, currency, weather, commodity, congressional, skiing, and other specialized reports at specific times of the day or week on automatic equipment.

International Messages

International messages (cablegrams) may also be sent or received by all of the methods mentioned above. By choosing the company which serves the part of the world in which your recipient is located, you can get the best service. These companies include French Telegraph Cable Company, ITT World Communications, RCA Global Communications, TRT Telecommunications Corporation, Western Union International, and others. The yellow pages of your telephone directory will give you a more complete listing. If you plan to do frequent international communicating, obtain a simple code book to use. Since international messages charge for *every* word or number, it is wise to use a code to save as many words as possible. Start by choosing and registering with all companies your *cable address*. The cable address is a coded name which saves all who wish to contact you the cost of each word and the address of your company name. Think of the full

name and address of any company you wish. Count
the words. Then compare that with a cable address
which is charged as two words! A standard code
book can do as much as that for you.

Composing Telegraphic Messages

The rules of good letter writing apply equally to the
composition of a good telegram. In addition, extra
care must be taken that the message is clear, because
words are used most economically. No one seems to
mind the removal of nonessentials from a telegram,
yet they do from a business letter. Perhaps some day
the business letter will be pared down to telegram
economy.

In a telegram, date or return address is not
normally needed since every telegram transmitted
begins with the city, state, date, and time it is sent.
The name and address of the addressee must be as
clear and explicit as possible; the telephone number
would be very helpful; furthermore, in domestic
service there is no charge for information that will
assist the telegraph company in delivering.

All normal punctuation is usable. You may give
your name and firm name as a signature in a telegram. If your firm is not well known to the addressee,
it might be well to include the address after the name
and firm name, but keep in mind that you will be
charged for it. The street address is all that is needed
if the city is the same as that of the sending office.

It should be kept in mind that the telegram will
be printed throughout in capital letters. For emphasis
in telegrams, when it is important enough, repetition
is desirable. For example, URGE PROMPT ATTENTION
TO DELAY REPEAT DELAY SHIPMENT FOR THREE DAYS.
DELAY REPEAT DELAY will obtain the necessary attention from the receiver.

While composing a telegram it is possible to project the personality of the sender without sacrificing
clarity or economy. Use positive words as often as
possible. Avoid negatives. Use cordial tone. Employ
words as pleasant as possible. Read and reread for
clarity. If possible, check with another person who
knows nothing about what you wish to say; the message must be intelligible. Always follow the telegram
with a typewritten copy by mail for verification and
clarity.

Chapter 14

Mailing

Mail Service

THE UNITED STATES Postal Service offers a great variety of services, sufficient to fill a tremendous volume for the guidance of those who direct its work daily. Times have changed to some extent, however, and the postal services have had to face competition in the area of package shipping and distribution. In the traditional first, second, and third classes, the Postal Service does not have much competition. Listed below are all of the services of the Postal Service. We shall confine ourselves to the services most affecting correspondence, the subject of this book.

Mail Classifications

Excluding military mail, there can be said to be nine categories of domestic mail to any of the fifty states, or to the territories or possessions of the United States of America. They are:

First class   Airmail
Priority mail   Official or franked mail
Second class   Mail for the blind
Controlled-circulation   Special services
  publications
Third class
Fourth class

Any post office will gladly supply a booklet listing detailed regulations regarding postal services, fees, and charges, called "Domestic Postage Rates, Fees & Information." Fuller information may be found in the U.S. government publication *Postal Service Manual.* In such a vast system, this manual and periodic supplements keep postmasters and all employees up to date. In the following abstracts from this guide, rates are not usually stated, as they are subject to frequent change. As a matter of fact, at the time of this printing there is legislative discussion taking place concerning certain new rates. It is safest at all times to consult your local postmaster for current facts as needed.

FIRST-CLASS MAIL

This class is the most familiar to the layman and the office worker. All first-class mail is sent by air when feasible. The following types of communication may be sent by first-class mail:

1 Any *sealed* mail or packages so marked (otherwise they go by third or fourth class)
2 Handwritten, typewritten, photocopied, carbon-copied, mimeographed, or otherwise duplicated letters in sealed envelopes
3 Any written or typed matter whether written in code, shorthand, hieroglyphics, or other system of writing, except manuscripts (see third and fourth classes)
4 Greeting cards, announcements, acknowledgments, or notifications in sealed envelopes
5 Business-reply envelopes or cards, properly registered at post office for permit number (a small fee over and above regular rate must be paid *on delivery*)
6 Single postal cards (postage imprinted or not) or double postal cards are sent for less than the sealed rate

Before the legislation under discussion results in some changes in rates, the rate for first-class mail is 11¢ an ounce or fraction thereof, plus 2¢. For instance, a letter weighing just over one ounce would cost 11¢ + 11¢ + 2¢ = 24¢ postage. If no postage is placed on the envelope or package, it is returned to the sender. If no return address is given, it is opened to determine a return address. If none is found, it is kept and destroyed or usable objects are auctioned off with all other items of a similar nature. Post(al) cards which have no return address and are undeliverable are kept for a very short period of time and then destroyed.

PRIORITY MAIL

Any package of regular shape may be sent first class at the regular rate, up to 13 ounces. Over 13 ounces, they are sent by *priority mail* (heavy pieces) at a slightly different rate. Priority mail is sent by air to the nearest point, then by surface mail. Priority mail may be insured.

SECOND-CLASS MAIL

This category is a special one primarily reserved for publications and periodicals. If a correct set of forms is filed with the required fee, a permit may be obtained. This mail must be sent in bulk and various procedures must be followed. There are special rates for religious, scientific, fraternal, or philanthropic organizations and another category for classroom publications. All mail should be clearly marked SECOND CLASS.

Periodicals mailed individually, whether by a publisher or private person, in unsealed form, have a new rate structure by weight. No handwritten material may be sent second class.

CONTROLLED-CIRCULATION PUBLICATIONS

This is a special category in the postal regulations for publications of 24 pages or more, circulated free of charge or free to members. For example, this category includes the periodic magazine published by the Associated Hospital Service and sent free to all members, the annual stockholders' report of a corporation, the quarterly publication sent to employees by the telephone company, and so on. When in doubt, consult your postmaster.

THIRD-CLASS MAIL

Third class is not only the category for packages *under* 16 ounces, but it also accommodates all matter not included in first or second class. It is a classification commonly used by most business offices. In this category are:

1 Greeting cards, announcements, form replies, circulars, calendars, samples, and merchandise within the weight restriction. The envelopes are usually marked "Pull Out for Postal Inspection" on one of the rear flaps, which is not sealed. These envelopes are known as "cost savers" because they may go by a cheaper rate up to 2 ounces

2 Proof sheets and corrected proof sheets with the appropriate manuscript copy

3 Books and catalogs of 24 pages or more, with a minimum of 22 printed pages

4 Unsealed letters for the blind in point or raised character printing, or recordings for the blind; *Postal Service Manual* is specific regarding special low rates for the blind

5 Hotel and steamship room keys which are attached to a fixed tag which gives the address of the destination and expressly guarantees postage

6 Seeds, bulbs, roots, plants, cuttings, branches, and some other horticultural and agricultural products

7 Any other mailable matter within the 16-ounce limitation not included in first or second class

8 All mail must be marked THIRD CLASS, and, if a permit has been obtained, must be identified by permit number with "Bulk Rate" or "Nonprofit Organization" above the permit number.

FOURTH-CLASS MAIL

Fourth-class mail (parcel post) includes all mailable matter, 16 ounces or over in weight, but not exceeding a weight of 40 pounds when sent from a post office rated 950 revenue units* or over (first class) or a size of 84 inches in length and girth combined (see Fig. 14.1). At post offices rated up to 949 revenue units the limitation is extended to 70 pounds and 100 inches. The following are some of the regulations governing this class of surface mail:

1 Each piece of mail must weigh 16 ounces or more

2 Rates depend on weight and distance (zone)

3 Printed matter not included under first, second, or third class

4 Merchandise or live animals, but not firearms, explosives, intoxicating beverages, reptiles, and a few other exclusions, not included under first, second, or third class

5 Catalogs weighing one pound or over. These are carried at a special rate

6 Educational materials such as books, films, film catalogs, printed music, printed

* As described in Postal Service Publication 26.

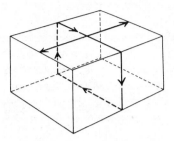

Fig. 14.1 To determine the size of a fourth-class package, measure the length and the girth and add the two figures.

test materials, recordings, and manuscripts, all at a lower rate

7 Library books, films, transparencies, slides, microfilms, recordings, and catalogs of these materials, printed music, bound theses, and other library materials, to certain kinds of libraries, at a lower rate.

AIR PARCEL POST

Since most first-class mail now is sent by air, the only other air service is air parcel post. This category includes:

1 A higher basic rate, depending on weight and distance
2 Weight limit of 70 pounds
3 Size limit of 100 inches in length and girth
4 All packages eligible from 13 ounces up to limit, except items which may be damaged by the hazards of air travel—altitude, cold.

FOREIGN MAIL

See "International Postage Rates and Fees," a publication of the Postal Service, for foreign rates. (See end of chapter for list of free publications.) Inquire of your local postmaster about any questionable matters. Consider the *air letter* if you correspond a great deal with foreign residents or businesses. An air letter is a single sheet, foldable into an envelope inside of which the message rests. It will save approximately one-third of regular cost for foreign air mail.

OFFICIAL OR FRANKED MAIL

Two types of mail do not bear ordinary postage stamps (Fig. 14.2). The first of these is the mail sent out by branches of the federal government. Instead

of paying for stamps they make periodically estimated payments in a lump sum. Government envelopes are marked PENALTY FOR PRIVATE USE TO AVOID PAYMENT OF POSTAGE $300 and are known as "penalty" envelopes. The other type of postageless mail is the franked letter.

The franked letter must have the signature or facsimile and the word FREE in the place normally used for postage. The envelope must show the return address of the person, department, bureau, division, or officer sending the correspondence with the words OFFICIAL BUSINESS under it. The following persons have this franking privilege: Members of Congress; widows of Presidents; the Secretary of Agriculture; the Secretary of the Senate; Delegates to Congress for territories; resident Commissioners of territories; the Vice-President; and the Clerk of the House of Representatives. *Postal Service Manual* gives further details on the use of this privilege.

There are a few other items of free mail most people never hear about. Among them are materials for copyright going to the copyright office in Washington, D.C.; census mail; immigration mail; naturalization bureau mail; absentee ballots for military personnel; mail of senators-elect, representatives-elect, delegates-elect, within the same limitations as those applicable to present officeholders; certain mail to or from the blind.

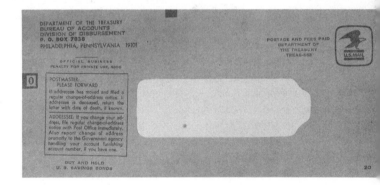

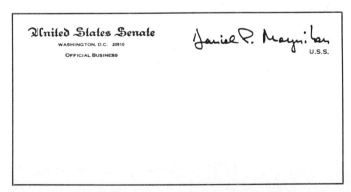

Fig. 14.2 Two kinds of mail which do not bear postage are the "penalty" envelope and the franked letter.

MAIL FOR THE BLIND

All mail to or from the blind is subject to special regulations contained in Part 138 of *Postal Service Manual*. Much of the mail to or from the blind is free or at nominal rates.

BULK MAIL

Large quantities of matter may be mailed by bulk rate. On the stamp area of the envelope is a printed box indicating the permit number, city, state, and the words U.S. Postage Paid. Form 3602 is required for this permit and each bulk mailing must be accompanied by Form 3602-PC.

COMBINATION MAIL

It is becoming increasingly popular to send a letter and package, a letter and catalog, or a letter and samples under one cover. If the package containing the letter is sealed, a statement must be placed on the outside and first-class postage added to the third- or fourth-class charges. If the letter is affixed on the outside with its own postage, then the statement is not necessary. The same is true of large manila envelopes for catalogs or samples. (See illustration in Chapter 16.) It is a highly recommended procedure because it does not depend upon a mail clerk's coordination of the two items at the destination. However, it travels at the rate of the slower class of mail.

SPECIAL SERVICES

In certain businesses *specially constructed containers* must be used for mailing goods. A common type is the mailing tube used for calendars. Another is the fiberboard case for reels of film or tape. This does not alter the postal rate or service.

Occasionally it is necessary to have proof of mailing a letter or package. A *certificate of mailing* may be obtained for a fee which depends upon the number of pieces to be certificated. For further information, see Part 165 of *Postal Service Manual*.

Likewise, a delivery of mail can be certified. The sender receives proof and the post office at the destination keeps a record for six months. A fee is chargeable which varies according to the service required: simple proof, return receipt, or delivery restricted to the addressee. There is no indemnification for loss of *certified mail*. For further information, see Part 168, *Postal Service Manual*.

Special delivery is a service very often misunderstood. Until special delivery mail arrives at the addressee's post office, it is treated as regular mail. Then it is sent out immediately by special carrier. This special service is only available during the hours the local post office is open. Not many post offices are open twenty-four hours a day, and even those which are will only make special deliveries between approximately 7 a.m. and 7 p.m. All classes of mail may avail themselves of this service. Clear marking of mail is urged to prevent oversight. The ideal place for the "Special Delivery" notation is between the name and address and the postage. The fee for special delivery is in addition to the regular fee. For further information, see Part 166, *Postal Service Manual*.

Express mail service, the first new service since the introduction of air mail in 1918, has just completed an experimental run of a few years. It is now a regular service and will be extended to as many post offices as possible over the next few years. This service is more expensive than special delivery but provides same-day or next-day delivery service to about 400 cities. If the letter or package is mailed by the prescribed hour, same-day service is possible. Otherwise next-day service is guaranteed. Unless the delay is caused by a strike or unusually bad weather, the cost of postage will be returned if delivery is delayed. Eventually, 900 cities are expected to have this service. At this time, an 8-pound package to San Francisco from New York would cost about $15 and would be delivered within twenty-four hours, the Postal Service asserts.

Special handling provides for fourth-class mail to be handled with the care of first-class mail. Once it is at its destination, it is delivered in regular service. This service is restricted to fragile packages requiring unusual handling, transportation, and delivery, as in the case of the shipment of baby chicks. The fee is dependent upon weight and is added to the regular fourth-class charges. The words "Special Handling" should appear between the address and the postage. For further information, see Part 167, *Postal Service Manual*.

COD (collect on delivery, or cash on delivery) services permit business firms to ship to unknown customers without risk of loss of goods or payment. Any package may be sent COD by paying the regular postage plus a fee based on the value of the contents. The package, with special tags attached, is delivered as usual except that the letter carrier will not leave it without collecting the total COD charges. The receiver may not examine the contents before accepting the package. The maximum collectible sum for one parcel is limited to $300. For further information, see Part 163, *Postal Service Manual*.

Insurance up to $200 is available on each package sent by third- or fourth-class mail by surface or airmail. This insurance, which can be obtained for a fee over and above the regular postal charges, provides indemnification against loss or damage. The fee is based on the value of the contents up to $200. Packages valued over $10 may have restricted delivery or a return receipt for a small fee for each service. For further information, see Part 162, *Postal Service Manual*.

Registry is a form of insurance for all classes of mail in which the Postal Service is responsible for safe delivery. You may recall some years ago that Harry Winston, a Fifth Avenue jeweler in New York City, sent the Hope Diamond (valued at about $3,500,000!) from Washington, D.C., to his New York store by registered mail. Normally, the Postal Service's responsibility is limited to $10,000, but special arrangements on special occasions are possible. Both restricted delivery and return receipt are available on registered mail for a small additional fee for each. For further information, see Part 161, *Postal Service Manual*.

Money orders are available from the post office for sums not exceeding $300 each. To send more than that amount, multiple money orders would be needed; $310 would require two money orders! Domestic money orders may be cashed at any post office. International money orders, also available, cost a little more. Money orders must be handled quite carefully because the post office clerk does not fill in the name of the payee. It is the duty of the purchaser of the money order to fill in the name immediately, lest someone find it and fill in some other name and cash it. For further information, see Part 171, *Postal Service Manual*.

General Delivery is a special service offered to transients or those who do not know what their address will be or do not wish to divulge it to others. Mail may be addressed to any city care of General Delivery. It will be held for ten days and then returned unless a notation requests holding for a longer period up to thirty days. Many traveling salesmen use this method so that they are free to change accommodation plans at will. Addressees must identify themselves and call for the mail during the post office's normal business hours.

Forwarding mail is free for first-class items or airmail up to eight ounces. All other mail requires additional postage, as explicitly detailed in *Postal Service Manual*.

Change of address forms are available at the post office and may be filed for personal or business mail. The old and the new address must be placed on the form and definite indications of when the new address becomes effective. When a company makes a move, every correspondent should be notified.

Undeliverable mail is returned by the post office with a stamped indication of the reason for nondelivery. Such mail must be sent in a new envelope and readdressed with appropriate postage. Most first-class mail is returned free, but post cards are not. Packages will be returned with postage due. Mail without a return address will be sent to the dead letter office, where it will be opened to determine a possible return address. If none is available, the mail is burned or its contents sold at auction.

Recalling mail is possible, but necessarily made quite difficult. The sender must file a mail recall application (Form 1509), pay all expenses of telephone, telegraph, or return postage relative to the recall. If the letter has already been delivered, the addressee is not informed that the recall was requested, and the sender must still foot the bill for the attempt. For further information, see Part 331.5, .511, .512, *Postal Service Manual*.

Stamps are sold at all local post offices for cash only. They are available in sheets of 100; commemorative stamps are issued in sheets of 50 or so. For business offices, rolls of 100 stamps in a dispenser are easier to handle. For home use, booklets are available. *Damaged stamps* are exchangeable at face value. *Postal cards* are redeemable at 85 percent of face value. Loose stamps are troublesome to organize; they are also a temptation to the most reliable employee to use for personal correspondence. Many mail rooms use large plastic trays with compartments for different denominations of stamps.

The *postage meter* solves this last problem of housekeeping and stops the temptation to pilfer at the same time. The meter is a device for imprinting the amount of postage, date, city, and state directly on the piece to be mailed. (See Fig. 16.2.) Should the piece be too large or bulky for the machine, it imprints the same information on a gummed tape moistened and ready to attach to mail of any shape. There are hand operated and electrically operated models. Some machines not only imprint postage, but seal the envelope as well. More complex machines will fold the letter, insert it into the envelope, seal the envelope, stamp it, and stack it. The imprint may also carry an advertisement to the left of it.

The postage meter has the advantage of providing a built-in check against misuse. It bears a set of dials, showing the amount of postage remaining as well as the amount used up. The post office will set the numbered dials of the machine for the amount of postage paid for, and keeps the key for future adjustments. Used properly, it should pay for itself in a very short time.

Special *post-office boxes* are available to anyone at his local post office. Business houses use them because they can thus control the influx of mail. The incoming mail clerk or messenger can pick up mail from the special post-office box each hour in order to space mail evenly over the day, although the first morning pick-up will probably be the heaviest. This method is superior to waiting for regular delivery and obtaining an unnecessarily heavy load twice a day. There is a small annual fee for a box, depending on size, payable monthly.

Some business houses use special box numbers for special occasions when the mail load is likely to be especially heavy. For instance, a patriotic organization which advertised widely used the special box number P.O. Box 1776, Mount Vernon, New York.

Foreign mail comes under special regulations for such matters as international money orders, international reply postage, international airmail, air letters, letter packages, and even regular letters. Weight and size limitations apply equally to foreign mail, which is subject to national as well as international agreements. Further information can be obtained from your local post office and "International Postage Rates and Fees."

ZIP Code

Originally, ZIP Codes were thought to be a helpful tool for bulk and package mailings. They were. With the advent of sophisticated electronic equipment that could "read" typed or printed letters, it was applied to first-class mail using the official two-letter abbreviations shown in Fig. 14.3. The optical character reader, known as the OCR, can sort letters rather quickly.

ZIP Codes consist of five digits. The first number represents a postal sector of the country. The next two numbers represent a geographic area in that sector. The last two digits are the identification numbers of the specific section in that area in which the actual street address is located. For example, CA 95448 = the postal sector including California; 54 = one of the geographic areas near San Francisco; and 48 = Healdsburg and vicinity.

The National Zip Code Directory will enable mailers to determine the ZIP Code for every mailing address in the nation. ZIP Code listings are arranged alphabetically by state, and within each state a complete listing is given of all post offices, stations, and branches with the appropriate five-digit ZIP Code for each delivery area. An appendix after each state gives the ZIP Code for each address in the larger cities. The directory also has a ZIP Code area map, state abbreviations to be used with ZIP Codes, post offices with multiple-carrier delivery, a numerical list of post offices by ZIP Code, a list of sectional centers and ZIP Code prefixes by states, and a listing of ZIP Code changes since July 1, 1963. Mailers may purchase the new one-volume, 1,668 page *National Zip Code Directory* for $7.50 from the Superintendent of Documents, U.S. Printing Office, Washington, D.C. 20402 or their local post office. For complete information on the new bulk rate second- and third-class ZIP Code regulations and bundling, labeling, and sacking of bulk mail, consult your local post office or *Postal Service Manual.*

In addition to ZIP Codes, there is an electronic printed device for business reply envelopes or cards only. Called *bar coding,* it is explained in the Postal Service leaflet "Speeding Delivery of Business Reply Mail through Bar Coding." The bar code must be printed on the bottom of the business reply card or

Fig. 14.3   Official two-letter state abbreviations suggested by U.S. Postal Service.

Alabama .... AL	Kentucky .... KY	Ohio .... OH
Alaska .... AK	Louisiana .... LA	Oklahoma .... OK
Arizona .... AZ	Maine .... ME	Oregon .... OR
Arkansas .... AR	Maryland .... MD	Pennsylvania .... PA
California .... CA	Massachusetts .... MA	Puerto Rico .... PR
Colorado .... CO	Michigan .... MI	Rhode Island .... RI
Connecticut .... CT	Minnesota .... MN	South Carolina .... SC
Delaware .... DE	Mississippi .... MS	South Dakota .... SD
District of Columbia ...... DC	Missouri .... MO	Tennessee .... TN
Florida .... FL	Montana .... MT	Texas .... TX
Georgia .... GA	Nebraska .... NE	Utah .... UT
Guam .... GU	Nevada .... NV	Vermont .... VT
Hawaii .... HI	New Hampshire .... NH	Virginia .... VA
Idaho .... ID	New Jersey .... NJ	Virgin Islands VI
Illinois IL	New Mexico .... NM	Washington .... WA
Indiana .... IN	New York .... NY	West Virginia .... WV
Iowa .... IA	North Carolina .... NC	Wisconsin .... WI
Kansas .... KS	North Dakota .... ND	Wyoming .... WY

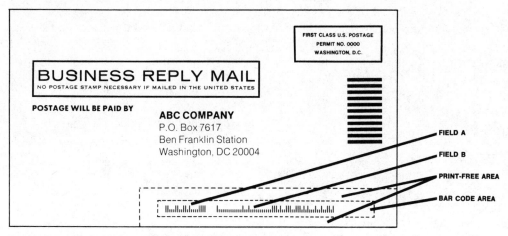

Fig. 14.4 Bar coding for business reply envelopes or cards.

envelope as shown in an excerpt from the Postal Service leaflet, Fig. 14.4. Bar coding has been relatively unsuccessful for the same reason it has been unsuccessful in supermarkets. It is illegible and, therefore, not trusted. The mailing system is not available in all locations as well. People do not like something they cannot read and/or understand.

Postal Service Publications

The following is a selection of post office publications which may be found useful:

USPS Publication 2	—Packaging and Wrapping Parcels for Mailing; free
USPS Publication 3	—Domestic Postage Rates and Fees; free
USPS Publication 13	—Mailing Permits; free
USPS Publication 21	—How to Prepare 2d and 3d Class Mail; free
USPS Publication 23	—Secretarial Addressing; free
USPS Publication 23F	—Speeding Business Reply Mail by Bar Coding
USPS Publication 28	—How to Address Mail; free
USPS Publication 51	—International Mail; free
Many others	—Free and at nominal cost

1 *The Postal Service Manual* contains the regulations and internal instructions governing the operation of the domestic postal service; $33. Distributed to all post offices.

2 *Directory of Post Offices* contains postal delivery zone offices, alphabetical list of post offices by states and counties, as well as military post offices; $5.25. Distributed to all post offices.

3 *Directory of International Mail;* $19 with binder. Distributed to all post offices.

4 *The Postal Bulletin* (weekly) includes information of interest to philatelists, as well as practical information; $18.75 a year. Distributed to all post offices.

5 *National ZIP Code Directory;* $7.50. Can be ordered from the Superintendent of Documents, Government Printing Office, Washington, D.C. 20402.

Chapter 15

Production and Duplication of Letters

DUPLICATING LETTERS IN the modern office has been revolutionized in the last decade because of the appearance of the photocopy machine. At one time in the recent past, copies could be made by a machine which required a technician who was part chemist and part mechanic to operate. Present equipment can be operated by any competent person in an office. By placing a copy in or on a prescribed surface, setting a dial for the number of copies desired, and pushing a button, the exact number of copies are produced in a few seconds each in black and white or color. The latest machines are even faster than that.

Other and older methods still have their place in our offices, however; printing, carbon paper, spirit duplicating, stencil duplicating, offset duplicating, photography, facsimile, automatic typewriter, punched card equipment, addressing duplicators, and others. Below are short descriptions of some of these methods.

Carbon Copies

The most common method of making copies of typewritten material is by means of carbon paper. The copy made directly by the typewriter keys striking against the ribbon onto the paper is known as the "original." Carbon copies are made through carbon paper behind the original. Carbon paper may be reused many times. It is important to buy the exact type suitable to your equipment: manual typewriter, electric typewriter, or typing element or ball machine. The best quality will last longest and make the best copies. If no alterations are made, the carbons are exact copies of the original except for the letterhead and the quality of paper used. The carbon copies are on a cheaper grade of paper than the original, but good enough to withstand handling and storage in the files. Most firms use various colors of paper for the carbon copies with the color signaling the identity of its recipient. The most popular

color for the first carbon copy is yellow. Many business firms, whether they use white or colored paper for the carbon copy, also have the word COPY printed in light but large printing across the face of the paper. A few companies also have the name of the firm printed in small fine letters across the top or bottom of the copy sheet.

The latter precaution is due to the increasing popularity of the letter style that does not repeat the firm name at the end of the letter. (See Chapter 2.) Should such a letter have to be photocopied, the firm name would be missing on a photocopy of the carbon copy, hence the appearance on the copy paper. This is costly because only a very small percentage of letters are photocopied for external use. Instead, the letter to be copied or the copy can be rubber-stamped; or, with the preparation of a simple transparent cellophane strip with the name of the firm imprinted, each photocopy may be properly identified. A notation in the bottom margin of any letter photocopied becomes a permanent record of the fact.

Recently, in place of carbon paper, which can be messy for some typists, some firms are using NCR (no carbon required) paper. This paper produces copies without carbon paper, but it has some disadvantages requiring specially careful handling. More popular are carbon packs, which are prepared sets of copy paper and carbon paper interleaved and attached. The carbon paper is discardable "one-time" carbon. The sets come for one, two, or any number of carbon copies with different paper colors.

However, the availability of low-cost photocopy machines, such as Xerox, requiring minimal maintenance, has begun to change former procedures mentioned above. Now, it is becoming routine to make one original of a letter and photocopy as many copies as are needed once the product has been approved by the dictator. The other school of thought on this topic holds that as long as you are typing the original, you should make a carbon copy or two; it may be all you need. If another copy is unexpectedly needed, *then* make the copy on the photo-copy machine. The author recommends using the judgment of past experience; make that number of carbon copies, even though typing and making carbon copies simultaneously does take a tiny bit longer than typing without carbon copies.

In offices which are understaffed and unusually busy, this is the method being used. When a letter is received from a correspondent, write the answer directly on it wherever there is room; make a photo-copy, mail the copy, and file the original.

SPECIAL NOTATIONS

Should a notation which is no concern of the recipient be desired, the original may be removed and the notation made on the carbon or carbons only. (Use bcc:*) Conversely, when a notation is for the recipient and no one else, the carbon copy may be removed and the notation placed on the original only. If you do not wish to remove the carbon copy, place a piece of scrap paper behind the carbon paper to receive the notation instead of the file copy. When there is more than one carbon copy, it is simpler to remove the carbon copies and type on the original. Or place an index card behind the original to prevent the impression from going through.

As described and illustrated in Chapter 2, when carbon copies of a letter are being sent to persons other than the recipient, the notation *cc:* and the names of the companies or persons to receive copies are indicated under the typist's initials. If these names are not desired on the original copy, one of the methods described above should be used.

SIGNATURE

Normally, carbon copies are not signed. In legal papers, however, as in the various copies of a contract or lease, they *are* signed, since all parties concerned are to receive *complete* copies. As a matter of fact, any alterations of any copies must be initialed by all parties in order to remain a valid legal document.

Spirit or Liquid Duplicator

The forerunner of the spirit duplicator was the gelatin process. In some places the gelatin process is still in use. It is fairly simple and adaptable, involving the use of a bed of gelatin upon which a master copy is placed for absorption. The master is produced by using a special ribbon, carbon, pencil, or ink. By placing the copy so produced on the gelatin for a short period of time, a mirror image is embedded in

the substance. It will reproduce many colors in one application. About thirty to fifty copies can be produced from one impression. This method is used successfully for daily menus, graphs, charts, diagrams, and forms. It is a *very* inexpensive method.

The liquid or spirit process has largely replaced the gelatin process for the duplication of letters, graphs, and charts. Again by means of special ribbons, carbons, pencils, or inks, a master is prepared in one or many colors. It is placed on the drum of the machine and clamped in position. As the drum rotates a wick moistens the master with an alcohol-base fluid, presses it against a blank sheet of paper which in turn is pressed against the carbon master while the paper is still wet, thereby making a copy. The copies are wet when first completed, but dry rapidly. The most common copies are purple, but many colors are available. It is an economical method of producing copies and 50 to 100 *good* copies can be obtained from the master if all the directions of the manufacturer are followed. The master may be used again if it is still capable of producing clear copies when the run is finished. It is a simple matter to block out, correct, or add to the original master at any time. A disadvantage is that long exposure to sunlight will cause the finished copies to fade. Similarly, carbon masters have a tendency to become less effective after storage.

Spirit duplicators are available in manual or electric models. The latter will produce 50 to 75 copies a minute. Models with extra-wide drums are also available for payrolls, inventory, factory work orders, or other requirements. Copies may be produced on almost any surface, but duplicator paper with a long grain and a glossy surface will give the best results and the greatest number of copies. It is also a relatively inexpensive method; no special "operator" is needed.

Dry Stencil Process (Mimeographing)

The most common form of duplication today is the dry stencil process. It is a very simple procedure of placing a typed, printed, or drawn stencil over an inked drum and cranking out copies. It is available in hand or electric models. The electric models produce about 125 copies a minute.

To produce the stencil, any typewriter may be used, a ball point pen, or special styluses (steel pens). If a typewriter is used, the ribbon control is moved to the white (stencil) position. On the new SCM typewriter with the removable ribbon cartridge, merely remove the holder and type. This procedure prevents the ribbon from coming in contact with the key face. Instead, the key face strikes the stencil, a

---

* bcc: stands for blind carbon copy.

wax-coated sheet of paper. In doing so it cuts its shape into the fibers of the paper. You can readily see why the key faces must then be clean for the best results. When this stencil is placed, face down, on the inked drum of the machine, and a sheet of paper is fed into the machine, a roller underneath the paper is activated and presses the paper against the stencil. The ink on the ink pad oozes through the stencil where the letters have cut their impressions and the paper comes out with a copy of the material that is on the stencil. Copies may be produced on any surface, but for the best results, free of smear, mimeograph paper should be used. When it is necessary to produce a copy on a different type of paper, smearing may be prevented by slipping a sheet of absorbent paper between each copy. This is known as "slip-sheeting." It is also effective in preventing offset from appearing on the back of each copy. Some machines are made with an automatic slip-sheeting attachment.

When very complicated material is to be reproduced, a paste-up may be prepared and placed on an electronic device which will prepare a stencil electronically. This machine has an electronic eye and needle which will burn impressions into the stencil surface. In a few minutes the stencil is ready for use. If this is only an occasional need in your office, the stencil will be prepared for you by the manufacturer of your equipment for a nominal fee, so that the machine need not be purchased. It is expensive for occasional use.

Normally the stencil is typed. When printing or drawing have to be incorporated, the stencil is placed over a lighted glass plate on which the work may be observed as it progresses. By placing the copy to be traced under the stencil, the light shining through enables anyone to copy onto the stencil. For forms, for instance, die-impressed perfect stencils may be made up in quantity in advance. The method is quite adaptable; changes may be made at any time as on an ordinary typed stencil.

Colored inks are available, but most work is done in black. Attractive results may be obtained with colored paper. It is possible to turn out copies with more than one color. If the stencil is cleaned after use, it may be re-used until the paper disintegrates, after many thousands of copies have been made. The copies are usually perfectly legible. The dry stencil process is not advised for a small number of copies for reasons of economy. It is best used for runs of hundreds or thousands, and the copies store well. Very commonly this method is used for price lists, advertising flyers, and common forms. Changes are easily effected. It is recommended that either a full-time operator be assigned, or, if there is no need for full-time production, experienced employees be designated to handle the work when it does arise.

Offset Duplicating

The offset duplicator, although a more expensive machine to begin with, does what the other duplicators mentioned do, but does it better. The work produced resembles printing. It may be used to produce letter-heads and any other kind of business forms used in a modern business office. The printing process is based on the knowledge that oil and water do not mix. A master must be prepared, as in the stencil or liquid process. The ink used has an oil or grease base. The master is then moistened. The ink is then transferred by means of rollers, leaving an impression of the copy on a rubber drum or mat. The mat is then pressed against the paper and the copy is deposited on it in a perfect image. The copy produced is similar in appearance to photo-offset lithography.

The master copy or mat may be made of paper, plastic, or very thin metal resembling a thick aluminum foil. The copy is placed on the mat by special typewriter ribbon, pencil, or ink, or by a photographic process. Paper and the plastic mats are cheaper and therefore used the most. Metal foil mats are excellent for long runs and may be used and re-used until copies begin to show signs of deterioration. They are particularly suited to photographic preparation. The paper and plastic mats may also be kept for re-use. They will last well if treated carefully. Any type of material may be reproduced, in color if desired. The offset duplicator can produce between 75 and 150 copies a minute without the smearing that may occur with other processes. A special operator is required.

The equipment necessitates a large quantity of duplicating work for long or repetitive runs to justify the installation. It becomes, in essence, an in-plant printing service.

Electrostatic Process

This process uses the principle that opposite electrical charges attract and like charges repel. A plate, positively charged, has projected on it the copy to be duplicated. The positive charge is neutralized by the projection except where the copy does not permit it to pass through. Negatively charged powder is then put in contact with the plate. It is attracted to the outlines of the copy. A sheet of positively charged paper is then placed against the plate; the powder sticks to the paper, heat is applied and the powder fuses into the surface of the paper in the exact image of the copy. Offset masters or spirit masters may be produced by this process.

Facsimile Process

Facsimile production uses the photoelectric eye as its base. Two drums are rotated side by side. On the first drum is the original copy. On the second is chemically coated paper. As the photoelectric eye "reads" the first copy it activates an electric needle which affects the treated or coated paper, turning it dark wherever an electric impulse has been transmitted. In this way, anything placed on the first drum copy will be produced on the special paper on the second drum copy. This process may even be used over long distances as it is basically the same process as the transmission of wire photos for the daily press. It is a relatively slow process in itself, taking from one to six minutes. Recent adaptations, however, promise great things for the future.

The same type of machine will produce electronically a stencil for the mimeograph process and a master copy or duplimat for the offset process of duplicating.

Heat Transfer Process

A thermal or heat transfer process uses sensitized paper which reacts to heat. Use is made of the fact that dark areas absorb more light so that they become hotter. The material to be copied is bathed in infrared light until the dark areas get hotter than the rest of the surface. These hot spots then burn their impression into the sensitized paper. Carbon-base inks or leads *must* be used for good copy, as other types do not reproduce as well, and some will not appear at all. Typing errors corrected with correction paper *will* show in the copy.

Xerography

Xerography is a process which uses static electricity to fuse a resin to paper. It can be used on both sides of the paper—ordinary paper. Xerography is also capable of producing masters for the offset process or translucent copies for the diazo process. Its distinct advantages are its ability to copy on ordinary paper, and to make up to six or more copies a minute. Some types also reduce or enlarge the size of the copy. It is completely dry, electrical, and clean. It uses ordinary paper, paper offset masters, or other sensitized image-transfer materials. Sophisticated machines can copy in black and white or color, sort, and collate. Set the dial for the number of copies—push the button!

Computer Messages

Generally speaking, computers are not used to produce letters as such. Rather they are used to append notes or notations after other material such as an invoice. Because computers now operate in milliseconds or microseconds through advances in electronics, they are being called on more and more to take over routine notations. Correspondents who attempt to write back to the computer have not yet adjusted to the new problem. In order to avoid the frustration of sending a message to an inanimate object, call the company and talk with someone who can handle the problem. These notations are triggered by a coded stimulus to the machine. An example of a message of this type is in Fig. 3.2. (See also Chapter 12.)

In its truest sense, this method could not be called duplicating since it is the result of a specific stimulus at a given moment and only one copy of a message is produced at a time.

Punched Card Duplicating

When punched card equipment is installed it is sometimes expedient to use it to produce master copies or stencils from which the duplicating may be accomplished. The data on cards can be fed to a tabulator which can type over 120 digits at the rate of over 100 a minute. The disadvantage is that the machine would have to be wired elaborately for this operation. However, the more complex the master copy needed, the more likely this system is to be practical.

Addressing Duplicators

When it is desired to address many envelopes or cards either for an active mailing list or with the same name and address, this machine is the most efficient. There are many types in general use. One is the familiar plate on which the entire name and address are embossed. (The identification tags used in the armed forces are quite similar.) A special machine called a Graphotype is needed to produce these metal plates. If the machine is not needed for regular use, the manufacturer will produce your plates for you for a nominal charge for each. The addressing duplicator may then be used and set to repeat, skip, or duplicate each plate one by one.

A second process employs the stencil method, requiring a small attachment to hold the stencil against the typewriter roller. The stencil has to be treated with water before use. The stencils cost less than the plates used in the first process and are fragile, but this method is also adaptable to the same uses.

The third method involves the use of an automatic typewriter. On the tape or stencil record the names and addresses of all consumers may be kept. When a mailing is desired, rolls of gummed paper can be placed in the machine. When duplication is completed, the gummed paper can be cut to size or torn at perforations, and the outgoing-mail clerk may place the resulting labels on the matter to be mailed. There are machines which will attach the addressed labels for you. No extra equipment is required when the automatic typewriter is used. A variation of this method is to have the names and addresses on a carbon master or stencil sheet. After running off copies, the names and addresses can be cut, pasted on envelopes or cards, and mailed.

The fourth method uses an addressing machine, either with a stencil or metal plates, when it is not possible or desirable to duplicate the name and address directly on the envelope or card.

In certain businesses, where customers purchase on an almost daily or regular basis, the addressing machine is used to preaddress invoices, which should be of a size and design which is easily incorporated in the accounts-receivable system. Statements may be prepared similarly. If a window envelope is used, the addressing of the envelope is eliminated. The addressing machine can also produce the invoice address, the shipping order form, the shipping label, the dispatch form, the bill of lading, or whatever must have the name and address imprinted on it. Peripheral information on the plate or stencil may also signal other necessary data.

A fifth method is the use of properly prepared and spaced master sheets which become the master for Xerox copies on label sheets with self-adhesive backs. The masters are kept on file as a permanent mailing list and the labels are pasted on the mailings.

Last, but not least, is the slowest and oldest method. A typist or receptionist who has some free time types the labels from a list or set of cards, one by one. When a full set is completed, it is set aside for the next mailing.

Automatic Typewriters

An automatic typewriter will produce, with the speed of mass production, business letters which appear individually typed. An efficient operator may be able to keep three to six machines going smoothly, depending on his dexterity and experience. Perforated tapes, magnetic tapes, and electronic cores are used.

An automatic typewriter is able to "read" and follow coded instructions—space up six lines, throw the carriage, start a new paragraph, stop and wait for the operator, and even back-space. It may be used

as a standard machine to personalize a letter by inserting a name, or a date, or other addendum. Normally, the operator types in the date, inside address, and when necessary, the salutation; the typewriter "memory" then proceeds to produce the remainder of the letter. It is even possible to use separate tapes for separate paragraphs in the same letter. The machine types between 100 and 150 words a minute, and an adept operator can change tapes in seconds. The devices are easily filed and are re-usable. They are made of damageable material, however, and must be handled with reasonable care.

Accessory Typewriters

When variety in the finished product is the most important factor, the use of a typewriter that permits varying the size of the type face is invaluable. The VariTyper and the Selectric are suited for this purpose.

The VariTyper is an electric typewriter which permits the operator to remove the entire type font, replace with another set of type face easily, and continue typing. Type faces used may vary from $\frac{1}{16}''$ to $\frac{1}{2}''$ high. This machine has a moving carriage similar to a typewriter. One common attachment will adjust the right margin for a more attractive appearance of the finished product. It may also be used to produce offset masters, which will enable a firm to produce its own letterhead stationery or forms, as well as to add much variety to carbon masters and stencils.

The Selectric is a development of the IBM Corporation. This is an electric typewriter without a moving carriage. The type face, imprinted on a ball-like object, is moved along the paper instead. The ball is removable and replaceable. Each ball contains a different set of type face in various sizes. Moving a lever will change pitch from pica to elite spacing. This typewriter may be used to produce any material for which an ordinary typewriter or the VariTyper is used.

The latest-model Selectric has a correcting feature. When an error occurs, the typist merely backspaces and removes the error. Olivetti and Remington produce this same machine with the ball feature *only*. Of course, it is possible to make any typewriter a "correcting" typewriter. Insert a bichrome ribbon which has the correction material in the same location on the ribbon in which the red coloring normally would be. Such ribbons are available. The same procedure is followed: backspace to the error, switch the ribbon control to the "red," retype the error, re-backspace, switch the control back to black, type the correction. When the correction portion of the ribbon is completely used up, either ignore the fact and use the ribbon until it is used up, or replace the ribbon immediately.

The IBM Selectric typewriter with a memory looks like an oversized typewriter. (See Fig. 15.1.) On one side there is a dial with either 50 or 100 numbered positions. Once the material to be kept on call is typed, refined, and proofread, it is placed in the memory of the machine keyed to a specific number. A copy of this perfect recording is placed in a "procedures book" for easy reference. Whenever one of the recordings in storage is needed, the operator locates the correct number in the procedures book, turns the dial to that number, inserts the proper paper in the machine, and sets the machine in motion. The skill in using the machine becomes merely learning how to place the expected output in the correct position on the inserted paper.

When implanting material in the memory, as with audio tapes, an error or desired change is easily erased by recording over it. The typewriter is quiet and may be operated anywhere in the office, and, of course, may be used as an ordinary typewriter also. In many firms receptionists are assigned to the machine to occupy their time between callers or visitors. The receptionist gets the machine set and goes about the regular duties while it is producing the desired copy.

The IBM Mag Card and Mag Tape machines are more diversified and complex, although they really perform the same functions. The amount of work the Mag Card and Mag Tape will handle is limited only by the efficiency of the operator, the speed of the machine, and the availability of prepared ma-

Fig. 15.2 IBM Mag Card II Typewriter. (Courtesy of International Business Machines Corp.)

terial. These machines are larger than the typewriter with a memory and slightly noisier. The IBM Corporation has decided to allow the Mag Tape machine to phase out, so remarks here will concentrate on the Mag Card.

Fig. 15.1 IBM Memory Typewriter with 50-position storage dial. (Courtesy of International Business Machines Corp.)

Fig. 15.3 IBM Systems/32 with word and data processing functions. (Courtesy of International Business Machines Corp.)

The Mag Card machine (Fig. 15.2) has two newer models which can do more and better things. The Mag Card II is compatible with the Mag Card so that the cards become interchangeable. However, the MC II will accept a set of cards whereas the MC will take only one at a time. All features are automatic on both machines: indent for paragraphs, underscore of word(s), automatic centering, dual pitch for 10-pitch or 12-pitch, fabric or film ribbon, and duplication of any card on the MC II only. The latter can then be used at another location where it is needed or that has idle time to aid in production. The next steps in sophistication are the IBM Word Processor/32 and the IBM Office System 6/430 Information Processor. These have the additional feature of logic, making them mini-computers. The 32 has a continuous paper roll produced and the 6/430 has a viewer on which the information appears. Of course, the more features and capabilities the machine has, the more expensive it is. However, the convenience and efficiency are unbeatable. Choose the right card, insert the paper, press the button, and you have a perfect copy. Some firms, to offset the high cost of purchasing these machines, rent them or choose a rental-purchase plan. Still others buy them and service neighboring firms for a reasonable fee to aid them in meeting the cost.

Word Processing

Word processing, as opposed to data processing, is a coordinated system of producing, recording, and storing worded material manually or automatically. It involves the services of dictation and transcribing equipment, stenographers, typewriters and automatic typewriters, records and records management, and skillful cooperation of all personnel involved. Word processing has divided secretaries into correspondence and administrative types. Correspondence secretaries generally transcribe dictated material at high production rates. Administrative secretaries usually do most clerical duties, accounting, research, and organizing reports. Executive secretaries usually are executives working with a high-ranking officer coordinating his office and business functions and supervising other office personnel.

When properly organized, word processing enhances and expedites the normal handling of typewritten or duplicated matter. Electronic advances of recent years have made it immaterial where the dictator is located at any time as long as instructions can reach the word-processing center by telephone, radio, satellite, telegraph, messenger, or other means.

The original dictation is assigned by the word-processing supervisor to a correspondence secretary, who produces the necessary document(s) in a standardized company style, with the prescribed or requested number of copies. The finished product is sent without delay to the originator for approval, which he indicates by signing. If there are changes to be made, the originator makes them directly on the completed document and it is returned for retyping. When it is approved, the process then continues and the message goes where it was intended without any further loss of time.

The word-processing system uses and develops the high-level skills of these secretaries and other specialists in a central location where their services are not wasted at any time. In essence, it is a pool of services, always in action, ready to roll. Only the highest level of executives have their own executive secretaries.

For instance, when the vice president of a corporation has an important letter to send, this is what occurs *without* word processing. His secretary comes in and both must engage in the dictation process. The executive can go on to other work when it is over, but his secretary must transcribe and produce the finished product for his approval. The secretary cannot do any other work while this is occurring.

In a word-processing system, the executive merely picks up his telephone and (a) dials a number which activates a recording machine which will take his dictation, or, (b) requests a correspondence secretary from the pool to come to take dictation. While this is occurring, his secretary continues with her duties. When the letter is completed, the pool supervisor will give it an expert proofreading and return it to the vice president. The executive secretary now sees the letter for the first time and gives it her expert eye. If it is satisfactory—and her duty is to know what the vice president wants—she has knowledge of it because she was able to read it, and she can pass it on to the vice president for his approval. This entire process can be accomplished in 20 to 40 minutes depending upon the length and priority level of the letter. A doctor making his rounds in a hospital can have notations entered in patients' case records in the same way. An executive traveling in Illinois or France could do the same thing by telephone as well. This is the picture of up-to-date methods which are already becoming commonplace. The system can be operated twenty-four-hours-a-day because of new electronic capabilities which can turn equipment on by a special sound or just the sound of a voice— voice-activated electronic recording devices. It all depends on what the business firm can afford.

Chapter 16

Envelopes and Folding of Letters

MOST OF THE envelopes used by business companies are commonplace and ineffectual. While it is true that the envelope need only serve its purpose as a cover for the message within, there are more subtle advantages to be gained. In many instances, it can be used as a selling device. As the purpose of all business correspondence is to sell or increase good will, no opportunity should be overlooked to present to the public and regular business correspondents your name coupled with that of your product.

Of necessity, the direct mail advertisers have always led the way in the use of envelopes for advertising. Department stores are next in this regard, and magazines and credit cards follow closely after. The latest trend has been to make the message sheet and envelope in one piece, combining the functions of, say, order form and envelope, sales message and order form and envelope, or statement and envelope. It is a good trend, promoting speed and efficiency. If the stigma could be removed from the use of window envelopes for regular business correspondence, a great deal of office work—with its opportunity for errors—would be eliminated.

Correspondence, sales letters, credit, billing, and survey all require different styles of envelope. A good example is a combination metered invoice and envelope used for home oil delivery. The envelope is self-addressed, merely requires separating from the invoice, and is numbered for good recordkeeping. It also saves paper.

Matching the Letter and the Envelope

In keeping with the dignity which, it will be remembered, is one of the principles of good letter writing, the envelope should match the letterhead in quality, size, and color. About seven standard sizes are made:

Standard #6¼ size, Dimensions	3½″ × 6″
6¾	3⅝″ × 6½″
7	3¾″ × 6¾″
7½	3⅞″ × 7½″
8	3⅝″ × 8¾″
9	3⅞″ × 8⅞″
10	4⅛″ × 9½″

If a return envelope is to be enclosed in a #6¾ envelope, it would naturally have to be a #6¼ or slightly smaller. The enclosure of a #9 envelope or equivalent sized card would necessitate the use of a #10 for mailing, and so on.

Postage Meter Imprints

Positions suitable for a message on the envelope of regular letter correspondence are along the top of the envelope, either beside the postage, when a postage meter is used (Fig. 16.2), or near the return address, which should be in the upper left corner of the envelope, identifying the sender. The message, slogan, or motto could be changed daily or weekly in a business with few products, or repeated for a longer time in a larger and more complex business.

The letters referred to above are individual, dictated business letters. Envelopes for sales letters can be designed to suit the needs of the particular product and clientele involved. For instance, an advertisement of a novelty product, such as a plastic desk set, would not be sent in the same kind of envelope as an offer by an investment advisory service.

Other types of external messages can be added to the envelope by offset or other process to enhance the pleasant appearance or give added impact to the sales message. Figs. 16.1 B, D, E, F show ways in which these external messages can be utilized.

Sales Letters

When mass mailing is done, the message must be put across, because the main purpose is to *sell*. Care must be exercised to prevent these letters from appearing to be "junk mail."

Window envelopes are efficient to use, particularly for sales letters. They may be of several kinds: the window may be a cut-out with no cover, or it may have a transparent, cellophane or glassine cover. Their costs vary, but if privacy is essential, the covered window is best.

When a window envelope is used, the name and address of the recipient are printed on the enclosed letter, reply envelope or card, or order form. Many

Fig. 16.1A Business reply envelope, self-addressed, with permit number and city in upper right-hand corner. Most common type in use today. No postage required by sender. (Courtesy of *New York Magazine*)

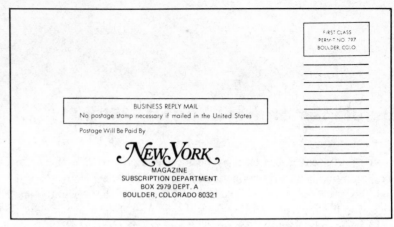

Fig. 16.1B Envelop with imprinted identification of contents, for specialized mailings. Note metered postage imprint at bulk mail rates. (Courtesy of Pacific Gas & Electric Co.)

Fig. 16.1C Back of self-addressed envelope enclosed by vendor with customer's invoice. Note two reminders and space for return address and account number to speed processing.

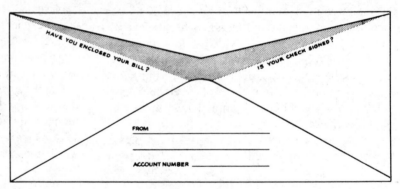

Fig. 16.1D Window envelope with open window and a second window "teaser" to arouse the interest of the recipient. The disk in the round window is to be placed on reply card for immediate action receipt. (Courtesy of The American Museum of Natural History)

Fig. 16.1E Direct-mail attention-getter window envelope. (Courtesy of *New York Magazine*)

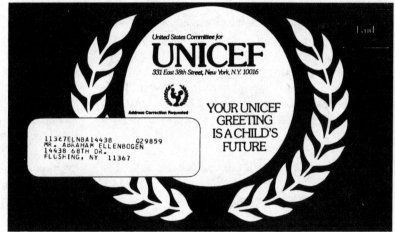

Fig. 16.1F Novel, offsize envelope, transparent, with internal material supplying necessary name and address without hindering message. Note nonprofit organization permit in place of stamp. (Courtesy of U.S. Committee for UNICEF)

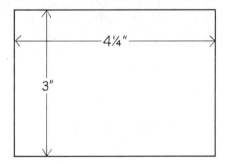

Fig. 16.1G Minimum size. The post office requires a minimum envelope size of 3″ x 4¼″. There are no limitations as to maximum size.

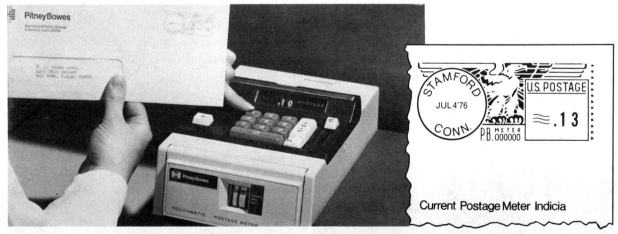

Fig. 16.2 Postage meter and postage meter imprint. (Courtesy of Pitney Bowes)

companies experience the inconvenience of receiving a check from a customer without proper identification; it is a costly affair to identify the sender or the account to be credited with the payment. Imprinted inserts speed up the accounts-receivable process and help provide faster and better service to the customer.

Billing

With the above advantages, many business companies now use statement forms embodying the name and address of the customer, which is imprinted by addressing machine. The lower portion is the statement itself, perforated for easy separation. The top is used as an envelope in which the check or money order is conveniently placed, and when sealed is a self-addressed reply envelope. A sample is shown in Figure 16.3. Whether the envelope requires postage or not is a matter of company policy. We strongly urge paying the postage. Most people are lazy (the self-addressed envelope takes care of that) and appreciate a bargain (even in a postage stamp). Try one cycle of billing with postage-paid business reply envelopes and watch the increased speed of returns.

Ordering

In direct mail advertising especially, the use of a combination price list/order form/envelope is quite good. With the advertising matter in the covering envelope, a form, as illustrated in Figure 16.4, is enclosed. Closed, it is a business reply envelope; open, it is a price list and order form. The only disadvantage is the fact that the customer does not have the price list after mailing this form. This problem is solved by enclosing a replacement with the acknowledgment, notice of shipment, or the shipment itself.

Surveys

In marketing research, accounting surveys by impartial public accountants, or similar work, it is often necessary to reach thousands of customers quickly and accurately. A combination form sent in a window envelope with addressing produced by machine is most effective. A form illustrated in Fig. 16.5 can even be used without an envelope if it is folded properly. One firm which does a great deal of this work reduced its mailing-room staff from five full-time and two part-time personnel to a staff of two full-time, and eliminated overtime to boot with this device.

Business Reply Envelopes and Cards

As shown, prepared forms can take the work out of replying for the customer or prospective customer. Supplying a card or envelope already addressed and with no postage required is a sensible and logical expense of soliciting business, requesting payment, or seeking permission to have a representative call to demonstrate. (See above illustrations and Chapter 11.) According to the law mentioned in Chapter 14 on mailing, a permit is required. Although each item costs a little more than regular mail fees, the business reply envelope is only paid for after it is deposited in the mail.

Dual-Purpose Envelopes

When it is necessary to forward a catalog, booklet or other material too large to fit into the same envelope as the correspondence, the following is now in popular use. The larger envelope required for the catalog is attached to an envelope which is clearly marked and has a window. The correspondence envelope is paid for at first-class rates and the larger

Fig. 16.3 Combination statement and envelope. (Courtesy of The Addis Co.)

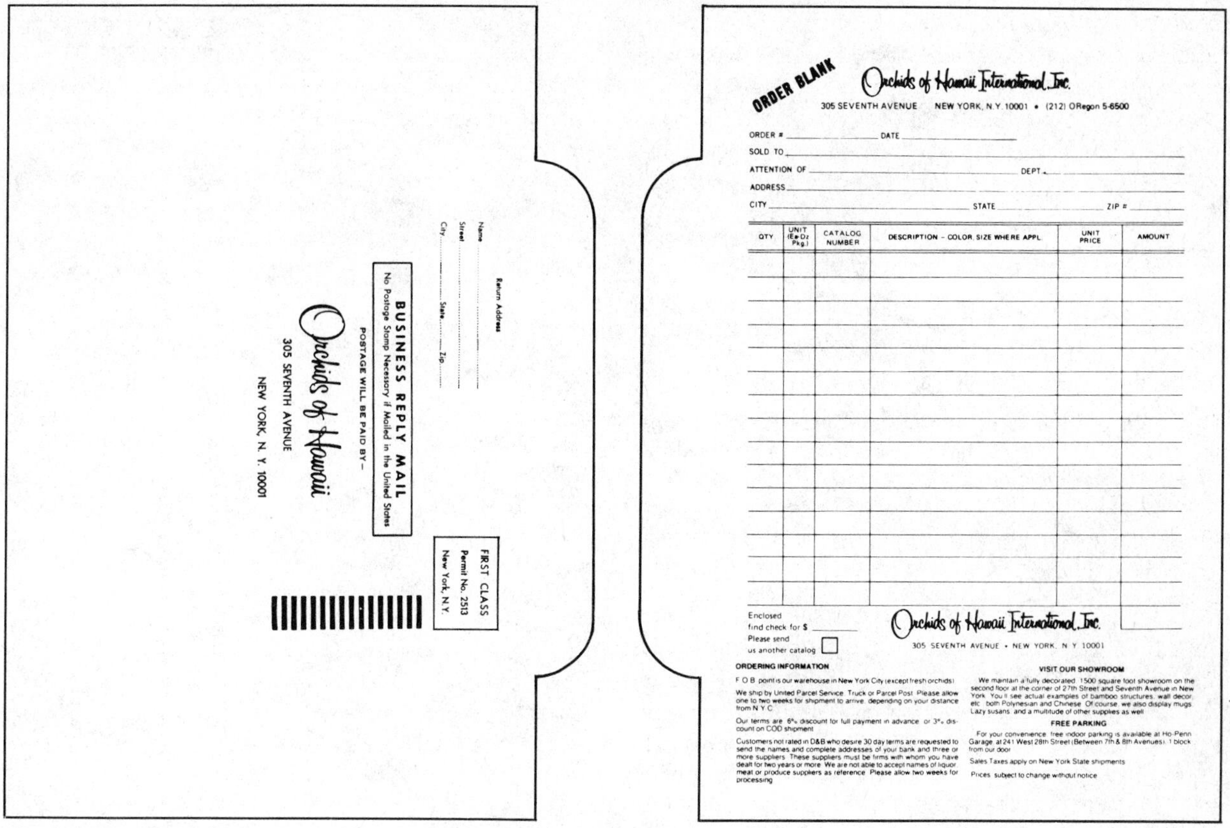

Fig. 16.4 Combination order form and envelope, folds for mailing. (Courtesy of Orchids of Hawaii)

envelope at the rates which apply to its class of mail. The name and address showing through the window from the letter also serve to address the larger envelope. A drawing of this type of envelope is shown in Fig. 16.6.

Addressing the Envelope

Beginning typists are taught in school to type the address on a #6½ envelope 12 lines down from the top and 2½ inches in from the left edge. On the #10 envelope they are advised to move 14 lines down from the top and 4½ inches in from the left edge. Advanced students are taught to make a mark in the center of the envelope with a thumb nail or pencil, place the envelope in the typewriter and locate the mark. Under the mark, 5 spaces to the left, the address should be begun. After some experience, a typist uses her judgment to determine the placement of the address on the envelope.

The United States Postal Service requests that names and addresses be typed double spaced and indented. This is more difficult for the typist. The name and address should be typed blocked, double spaced if it is three lines. If it is over three lines, it should be single spaced and blocked. The Postal Service

THIS IS NOT A
REQUEST FOR PAYMENT

TO ______________________ Account No. ____________

______________________ Sched. No. ____________

____

FOLD HERE

We are sending the records of ______________________

According to their books you owed them on __________

Balance of __________

So that you may receive proper credit, please advise whether this balance is correct. If correct, please sign below. If not correct, explain the difference on the bottom of this letter. Please fold, seal, and return this form to us. No postage required. Your immediate reply will be greatly appreciated.

Very truly yours,

GRAHAM & CO.
Public Accountants

FOLD HERE

___ The above is correct ___ The above is not correct

If not correct, explain why ______________________

Please indicate date of last payment __________

And amount __________

MAKE SURE YOU SIGN HERE
BEFORE RETURNING THIS FORM

____
CUSTOMER'S SIGNATURE

Fig. 16.5 Combination survey questionnaire and envelope.

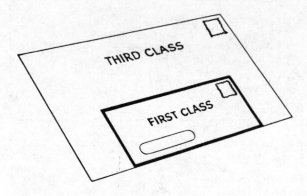

Fig. 16.6 Dual purpose envelope. Note that postage must be placed on both the correspondence envelope and the larger envelope.

requests use of the two-letter designations for the optical character reading machine intended to speed mail sorting. The two letters should be typed in capitals with no punctuation, followed by two or three blank spaces and the ZIP Code. They also ask that *nothing* be typed on the envelope *below* the city, state, ZIP Code line. Other information will only tend to confuse the reading device. See Fig. 16.8 for two examples of properly addressed envelopes.

Folding Letters

For standard business-size envelopes and letterheads reviewed earlier in the text, the folding should be simple, expeditious, and conducive to easy opening. Acceptable folds are shown in Fig. 16.7 with some rules and diagrams.

#6 envelope (or similar small size)
With half sheet (approximately 5½″ × 8½″)

Fold in thirds upward, leaving about a quarter of an inch of the top edge showing. That quarter inch makes it easier for the recipient to open the folded letter.

#6 envelope (or similar small size)
With full-size sheet (approximately 8½″ × 11″)
For single page insertion only

Fold upward bottom to top leaving a quarter of an inch edge at the top. Then fold in thirds similar to a 5½″ × 8½″ sheet, and insert into the envelope with the folded edge first.

#10 envelope (or similar size)
With full sheet (8½″ × 11″)

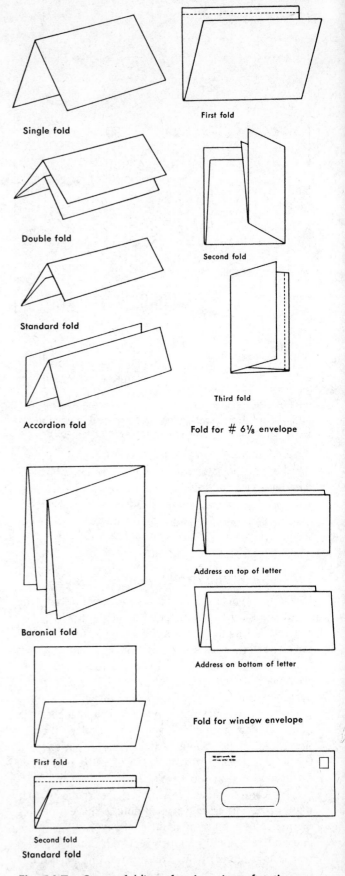

Single fold

Double fold

Standard fold

Accordion fold

First fold

Second fold

Third fold

Fold for # 6⅛ envelope

Baronial fold

First fold

Second fold
Standard fold

Address on top of letter

Address on bottom of letter

Fold for window envelope

Fig. 16.7   Correct folding of various sizes of stationery.

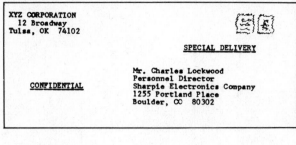

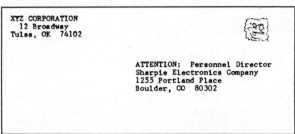

Fig. 16.8 Correctly addressed envelopes. For further suggestions, see the U.S. Postal Service leaflet "Secretarial Addressing."

Fold the same way as the half sheet (5½″ × 8½″) for the #6 envelope, remembering to leave the quarter of an inch at the top.

Some business firms have established the policy of using the #6 envelope for half sheets and the legal or #10 envelope for full sheets. It has the distinct advantage for sender and receiver of less folding and unfolding. The only hitch is the slight increase in cost when using many more legal-size envelopes. We believe it is worth the added expense.

#10 envelope (or similar size)
With a letter of two pages or more

Fold the same as the single sheet above, but see that the sheets are stapled together in the upper left corner before folding with the staple set in *diagonally*. This will permit easy turning of the pages. If the pages are numbered, do not staple.

WINDOW ENVELOPES

Folding the letter for a window envelope may be accomplished in two different ways (Fig. 16.7). In the first method, the letter is typed in standard form; only the method of folding is different. Method 1: the letter is folded as shown at left.

In the second method the name and address of the recipient are typed at the lower left below the identification initials. The last fold of the paper is reversed so that the bottom of the letter comes out on top.

Enclosures

Letters with enclosures should usually be placed in large envelopes unless the enclosures are very small objects. When making enclosures, it is suggested that the object or objects enclosed be stapled to the letter, although recent trends are not to staple because of adverse effects of staples on postage meters when struck during imprinting. If the attachment is intended to be temporary, it should be stapled with the stapler plate in position to spread open the ends of the staple rather than close them in the normal way. (The plate on which the staple presses down moves to an alternate position to produce this temporary stapling.) The Postal Service asks consumers *not* to enclose paper clips.

Envelope Size Restrictions

The Postal Service places a restriction on the size of envelopes. The minimum size limit is 3″ × 4¼″. There is no maximum limit.

Chapter 17

Reference Books

Dictionary

THE BASIC REFERENCE book for all letter writing is the dictionary. It gives spelling, pronunciation, syllabication, derivation, and part of speech for each word, and often abbreviations, foreign phrases, measurements and weights, and proper names. No office should be without several good, reliable ones. The size and quality of the dictionary will depend on the needs of a particular office. Many authentic, easy-to-use dictionaries are available at any fully equipped bookstore or book department. Unwieldy tomes should be avoided. Their very cumbersomeness will make those who need them unhappy about using them.

It may be desirable to have a secretary's reference manual, too; a good manual is the *Reference Manual for Office Employees*. Recommended dictionaries are the *American College Dictionary* and *Webster's New School and Office Dictionary*. If you like a dictionary which gives examples of the usage of each word, try *The New Horizon Ladder Dictionary* (see below).

Grammar

A grammar is only needed in the average office for occasional reference. If the space is available, it should be on hand in the office book case. Kittredge and Farley's *Advanced English Grammar* and Elsbree and Bracher's *College Handbook of Composition* are two reliable grammar books (see below).

Thesaurus

A thesaurus is a reference book in which synonyms and antonyms may be found; it is thus invaluable for the expansion of ideas and vocabulary. It is an essential element in the library of the letter writer or secretary who, by its use, may avoid repetition which makes for monotony. *The New Roget's College Thesaurus* is an example of this vocabulary reference book (see below).

Almanac

An almanac was once a calendar containing astronomical and other statistical data, including meteorology and geography. It has since been expanded to include more information on many and varied topics. Many almanacs now include listings of important events of the year, space age news, world political figures, gazetteer, sports records, population figures, and a thousand and one other items. The *World Almanac* and the *Information Please Almanac* are large, complete examples.

Atlas

An atlas is a volume of maps. It may be an atlas of a country or a section of the world or the entire world. It is not a necessity in the average office. Local businesses may obtain street maps from a gasoline company, chamber of commerce, or local government; these should be mounted on a wall for easy reference. Some good atlases are *Goode's World Atlas* and *Grosset's World Atlas*.

Gazetteer

A gazetteer is a geographical dictionary and a close companion to an atlas. Location in the gazetteer will make the pinpointing of a site on a map a matter of seconds. Most publishers who produce atlases also produce gazetteers which are bound separately or together with the atlas.

Secretarial Handbook

A secretarial handbook is a reference book for the stenographer or typist or other office worker, giving letter mechanics, letter placement, tabulation, letter styles, grammar, punctuation, spelling, and other information related to correspondence and office work.

Encyclopedia

An encyclopedia is a summary of knowledge, arranged alphabetically. Some encyclopedias cover limited areas of knowledge, such as medicine, engineering, agriculture, or chemistry. These are usually contained in a few volumes with provision for additions to be supplied in loose leaf form each year to keep it up to date. There are also encyclopedias which attempt to cover all areas of knowledge. These comprise many volumes, some as many as forty. These comprehensive encyclopedias, such as the *Collier's Encyclopedia*, are sometimes found in an office or, more often, in the office library. Many offices need one or more of the specialized encyclopedias in order to have easy reference for their own field of specialization. For any information that the office bookshelf is unable to supply, it is an easy matter to go to the nearest public library. In many of the larger cities of the country, public libraries provide telephone service during certain hours of the day for any kind of information required.

Who's Who

Who's Who is an English publication containing biographical notes on prominent living people in the British Commonwealth. *Who's Who in America* is an American publication containing biographical sketches of prominent Americans in public life.

Books of Quotations

Books of quotations are compilations of well-known excerpts from history and literature, with cross-references to authors, titles, and words or phrases. The author's name, the title of the source, the location in the original, and any other pertinent information is given. One of the best known is *Bartlett's Familiar Quotations* (see below).

Directories

TELEPHONE DIRECTORY

Telephone directories list the name, address, and telephone number of residents and businesses in each locality. The classified section lists by occupation or profession so that it is simpler to locate a definite or indefinite business firm or individual. In small communities the white pages are the alphabetical directory, and the yellow pages the classified section. These are sometimes bound separately in large cities. The front section usually gives a great deal of telephone service information and local Zip Codes.

CITY DIRECTORY

Many cities publish at intervals of three or five years a directory of all residents of the community, their occupation, their home address, and certain other information. In larger cities these directories are impossible to compile so that only small cities continue to do so today. Some of the latter do so only for city or county employees and elected or appointed officials.

TRADE DIRECTORY

Trade directories are published annually or biennially by trade associations dealing within one business or phase of business; as, wholesale lumbermen's directory, a hotel directory, a laundrymen's association directory, and so on. Some are city-wide or state-wide while others are regional or national. In a city such as Chicago, it would be possible to have a sizable dry cleaner's trade directory for the city alone. Directories are usually available to members or banks, but others may purchase their copies (see below).

BUSINESS DIRECTORY

Business directories are similar to trade directories except that they are generally published expressly for the use of the consumer. Examples are *Moody's Manual of Investments and Security Rating* and *Hotel Red Book and Directory* (see below).

CREDIT DIRECTORY

Dun & Bradstreet's credit service covers all sections of the business community and consequently their credit directory is quite large. In very large credit services, you may pay for each credit report rendered or subscribe at a much lower rate for a certain maximum fee for the year. In most others it is by fee on an individual basis or by membership in the association. There are also some independent associations which cater to anyone who desires information about a business concern in a specific area. Most trade and manufacturing associations have a credit service for members. Computer memory banks store all information for easy access (see below).

Postal and Shipping Guides

The United States Government Printing Office publishes a complete postal guide which will answer any question you might have regarding postal services and charges. It is available from the Superintendent of Documents, Washington, D.C. 20402. There are also several shipping guides giving information on routes, distances, charges, regulations, limitations, and other details about making shipments within and without the country's borders. The most famous of the latter is *Bullinger's Postal, Express, and Freight Guide* (see below).

Government Publications

The publications of the United States Government Printing Office are managed by the Superintendent of Documents, Washington, D.C. 20402. They publish leaflets, booklets, pamphlets, and books on a multitude of topics. Prices range from 5 cents to many dollars for hard covered publications. There are few topics on which they have no literature. On request the Printing Office will send a list of available publications with a synopsis of the contents of each and the price.

Newspapers and Magazines

Many newspapers and magazines are useful sources of information for business concerns. If time is pressing, there are clipping services which will extract information of interest to your business. When the dates are known, old issues of *The New York Times* are available on microfilm in most public libraries. A subject index is also available when the date is unknown.

Miscellaneous Sources of Information

A glance at the reference section of your local library will indicate that there are many other sources of information available. Apart from the many dictionaries and periodicals it stocks, its card catalog is a tremendous directory of sources of information. *The Reader's Guide to Periodical Literature* will supply a list of magazine articles by author or subject for current and less recent sources of information.

If you find the need to refer to the contents of a periodical perhaps more than once a week it pays to subscribe to it, but in general the convenience of the public library cannot be overestimated.

Some Useful Reference Books

Reference Manual for Office Personnel, by House and Koebele; South-Western Publishing Co.
American College Dictionary, ed. by C. L. Barnhart; Random House

Webster's New School and Office Dictionary (paperbound); Fawcett World (Crest)
Advanced English Grammar, by Kittredge and Fairley; Folcroft
College Handbook of Composition, by Elsbree and Bracher; D. C. Heath and Co.
The New Roget's Thesaurus in Dictionary Form; Putnam
Goode's World Atlas, 14th ed., ed. by E. P. Espenshade, Jr.; Rand, McNally & Co.
Grosset's World Atlas; Grosset and Dunlap
Familiar Quotations, by John Bartlett; Little, Brown and Co.
Hotel Red Book and Directory; American Hotel-Motel Association
Bullinger's Postal, Express, and Freight Guide; Bullinger's Monitor Guide, Inc.
Handbook of Modern Office Management & Administrative Service, by Heyel; McGraw-Hill

PERIODICAL INDEXES

Bulletin of the Public Affairs Information Service:
  Sociology, political science, economics
Industrial Arts Index:
  Engineering, trade, and business periodicals
International Index to Periodicals:
  Scholarly and scientific foreign publications
Market Data Book:
  Market conditions in different industries
New York Times Index
  Quarterly listing of daily *New York Times*
The Reader's Guide to Periodical Literature
  Index to title, subject, author of articles in majority of current periodicals, general
Social Science Abstracts
  Social science literature of the world with abstracts of important articles

BOOK LISTINGS

Books in Print
  Annual publication listing all known books available from publishers; two volumes, A-J, K-Z
Cumulative Book Index
  Author, subject, title of books published monthly in the United States
Guide to Reference Books
  Index to reference books of all kinds
Publishers' Trade List Annual
  Annual catalogs of publishers
United States Catalog
  Catalog to which *Cumulative Book Index* is the supplement; reissued about every three to four years

DICTIONARIES

American College Dictionary; Random House
New Standard Dictionary; Funk & Wagnalls
Webster's International Dictionary; Merriam
Winston Simplified Dictionary; Holt, Rinehart and Winston
Dictionary of Art and Artists; Penguin
Dictionary of Science; Dell
Dictionary of World Literature; Littlefield
Dictionary of Quotations; Delacorte
Webster's New School and Office Dictionary; Crest
New Roget's Thesaurus in Dictionary Form; Putnam
Dictionary of Business, Finance and Investment; Drake
Medical Dictionary; Longman
Law Dictionary; Barron
New Horizon Ladder Dictionary; New American Library

BUSINESS ENGLISH AND SECRETARIAL PRACTICES

Effective English for Business Communications, by Aurner and Bortness; South-Western Publishing Co.
Secretarial Procedures and Administration, by Hanna, Popham, Tiltan; South-Western Publishing Co.
Succeeding on the Job, by Rath; Interstate
How to Write Better Business Letters (paperbound), by Buckley; McGraw-Hill
Complete Secretaries' Handbook, by Doris and Miller; Prentice-Hall
Modern English Handbook, by Gorrell and Laird; Prentice-Hall
Standard Handbook for Secretaries, by Hutchinson; McGraw-Hill
Streamlined Letters, by Marra; Retail Credit Association
Modern Business Letter Writer's Manual, by Cloke and Wallace; Doubleday
Modern Business English, by Monro and Wittenberg; McGraw-Hill
Business Letter Writing Made Simple, by Rosenthal and Rudman; Garden City Books
Effective Letters in Business (paperbound), by Shurter; McGraw-Hill
Effective Business Letters, by Morgan; McGraw-Hill
Clerical & Secretarial Systems for the Office, by Dallas and Thompson; Prentice-Hall

Style Manual of the United States Government; U.S. Government Printing Office, Washington, D.C. 20402
The Secretary's Handbook, by Taintor and Monro; Macmillan Publishing Co.
The Secretary's Book of Instant Letters, by Vermes; Prentice-Hall
New Standard Reference for Secretaries & Administrative Assistants, by Janis and Thompson; Macmillan Publishing Co.

BUSINESS AND FINANCIAL DIRECTORIES

Dun & Bradstreet's Commercial Rating of Bankers, Merchants, Manufacturers; Dun & Bradstreet
Standard & Poor's Register of Directors of the United States and Canada; Standard & Poor's Publishing Co.
Fairchild's Financial Manual of Retail Stores; Fairchild Publications
Kelly's Directory of Merchants, Manufacturers, and Shippers of the World; Kelly Publishing Co.
Custom House Guide; North American Publishing Co.
Thomas' Register of American Manufacturers; Thomas Publishing Co.
Moody's Complete Corporate Index; Moody's Investors Service
American Register of Exporters & Importers; American Register of Exporters & Importers Publishing Co.
Commerce Year Book; United States Bureau of Foreign and Domestic Commerce
Lockwood's Directory of Paper & Allied Trades; Lockwood Publishing
Shopping Center Directory; Material Research Bureau, Inc.
Davison's Textile Blue Book; Davison Publishing Co.

These are only a handful of the books available for reference. It would take many pages to list even the more prominent of reference books—encyclopedias, atlases, handbooks, directories, style books, religious handbooks and directories, biographical listings, society registers, travel guides, statistical abstracts, theses, booklets, pamphlets, etc. Your local librarian will give full information on the reference books in any area and supply the more common ones from the reference section of his library.

Chapter 18

Letter Rating

AFTER READING THE preceding chapters you would probably like to have a method of rating your letters.

1 *Was your letter necessary?*

  Do you write letters because you wish to convey a message, sell a product, or build good will?

  Or have you fallen into the habit of answering all mail, whether or not an answer is required, overburdening an already overworked secretary?

  Would a post card have accomplished the same purpose?

  Would a form response have been sufficient?

2 *Was your letter too long or too short?*

  Did you state the case as clearly but concisely as possible?

  Were you considerate of the valuable time of your reader?

  Could you have written your letter in fewer words?

  Did you assume any information your reader may not have had?

  Was the letter too short and stingy with words?

  Do you normally confine your letters to one page?

3 *Did you answer stated or implied questions?*

  Did you place yourself in your reader's position to determine the intelligibility?

  Did you confine yourself only to answering the stated questions without regard to the questions your answers raised?

  Did you refer to a price list, catalog, brochure, statistics, or other technical data without supplying them?

  Will the reader come to the conclusions you wish him to?

4 *Did the letter obey the ABCD set out in this text?*

  Was the letter *accurate?* Have you checked your facts?

  Was it *brief?* Did you become loquacious or repetitious?

  Was the letter *clear?* Would anyone reading this letter be able to understand its message?

  Was the letter *dignified?* Would the reader get the feeling of your sincerity and earnestness?

  Did you stoop to double-talk to get out of a difficult situation?

  Did you treat the reader with respect? Was his name correct? Was his title, if any, correct?

5 *Was the letter conversational?*

  As you read the letter could you hear yourself in conversation with the correspondent? Did it sound like you?

  Were you a little too formal or stiff?

  Was it as warm as you are in your normal conversations?

  Did you "talk" to the reader as to a live human being or merely as to a name and address?

  Would you have said it the same way over the telephone?

6 *Is your style hackneyed or old fashioned?*

  Do you cling to phrases such as "Yours of the 14th inst."?

  Do you express yourself naturally in everyday good taste?

  Do you use slang, clichés, or colloquialisms too often?

  Do you use long phrases in place of simple words, as, "It is undoubtedly apparent that" in place of "Apparently"?

  Do you use legalistic language in place of simpler words when possible, as, "remuneration" instead of "wages," "salary," or "pay"; "inadvertency" instead of "error" or "mistake"; "official records of this organization" instead of "our records"?

7 *What is the proportion of "I" or "We" to "You" in your letters?*

  Do you continually mention what "I" or "We" will or will not do?

  Do you constantly give the reader to understand what he will do for you or what you are able to do for him?

Do you occasionally refer to him by name in the midst of a letter as you would do in conversation?

Do you refer to your own company as "we" or "this company"?

Do you refer to his business firm as "your organization" or "you"?

Do you make the letter seem to be written expressly for the benefit of "you"?

8 *Did your letter begin naturally?*

Do your letters begin with "We are in receipt of your letter of March 18 and beg to inform you that" or "Your letter of March 18 requests"?

Do you realize that "Dear Mr. Brown" is similar to "Hello Mr. Brown"?

Do you keep the first paragraph short as an introduction to the message to follow?

Does your letter begin as though it is a three-minute-long-distance telephone conversation?

Or as though you had started talking to monopolize the conversation?

9 *Was your average sentence under twenty-five words?*

Do your sentences run on so that the reader needs to refresh his memory about the first half after reading the second half?

Do you vary the length of your sentences?

Do you keep them as short as possible?

Do you avoid conjunctions whenever you can?

Do you try to keep each thought complete?

Do you keep your paragraphs under twelve lines?

Do you spatter "however" and "therefore" all over the page?

10 *Did your letter end with a call to action?*

Was there a request to answer?

Was there an enclosed self-addressed envelope?

Was there an order form to be completed and returned?

Was there an application form to fill in?

Was there a request to allow a representative to call?

Was there a catalog or price list to include or indicate as traveling separately?

Was there a special offer with a deadline?

Was there a deadline for payment?

Was the price to be raised soon? Did you tell your correspondent?

Was a new seasonal promotional idea indicated?

Was a telephone number indicated for more rapid response?

Did your letter end indecisively?

11 *Was the tone of the letter suitable?*

Did you begin "Dear Joe" or "Dear Harry" when you could?

Were you talking down to your reader? Was your manner condescending?

Were you "professionally" or sincerely helpful?

Were your words stereotyped?

Were your "teeth" showing? Were you abrupt?

Did you offer an alternative solution to a problem?

Were you stiff-necked and inflexible? Do you know when to "bend" the rules?

12 *Did you close the letter informatively?*

Does the reader know the authority for your remarks?

Was your title clear?

Was the complimentary close fitting?

Do you close "Sincerely" when you've been distant?

Do you close "Cordially" when you have been matter of fact?

Do you close "Yours truly" when you've been evasive?

Do you sign off with "John Smith" without indicating your authority and title by which you make the offer indicated?

Have you considered the more modern letter form with no closing at all, only identification?

Have you considered bolder endings, as "Best regards" or "Good luck" or "Gratefully"?

Have you re-examined your letter style recently to consider its modernization?

13 *Did you check for smooth continuity?*

Did your letter jump around from topic to topic?

Was there a logical flow from one point to another?

Did you suddenly include a *non sequitur?*

Did your letter proceed from introduction to interest to action?

Did you use natural connections between thoughts?

In the case of a very important or involved letter, did you ask a colleague to read it over for accuracy, clarity, and smoothness?

Chapter 19

Filing and Records Management

WHILE THE TERM "filing" is still used freely in business, many medium and large firms really have records management systems now. The extent of it is limited only by funds available. Recently, except for small businesses, the system has been placed under a high-level executive, such as controller or executive vice president for administration. Usually, the system is supervised by a records manager directly responsible to that executive.

Records management is the control of origin, flow, handling, safekeeping, and disposition of all company records. Before World War II, paperwork was usually controlled with a good filing system. Data processing and the growth of federal and state laws and regulations have vastly increased the need for records control. So, records are kept for legal, historical, diagnostic, and policy reasons. The goal of the system is speedy production, storage, and retrieval.

The system must develop from an inventory of the types, ages, and sizes of records which have been analyzed with the cooperation of the auditors and legal advisers. This analysis will determine a retention program and policy. Materials taken from the current files at the prescribed age should go to a shelf filing center which follows the same filing system used in active practice. The papers which do not require the retention of originals can be put on microfilm and stored. The last step requires decisions as to microfilming, destruction, deep storage, or other disposition. Agencies or businesses which must legally keep originals have the greatest problems of space, retrieval, and security.

Mechanized or automated records management systems include the following possibilities. *Microfilm* comes in reels, microfiche, cartridges, or aperture cards. The "reading" machine (the viewer) for these is made in versions which do or do not make copies of the stored document. *Automation*, by computer storage, for those who can afford it, has made records management easier by far, but with occasional giant

headaches, known as malfunction or "down" time. Manufacturers are beginning to produce smaller, less expensive equipment now. It is worth investigating. Materials are kept on cards, tapes, magnetic cores, discs, or other devices which are "searched" electronically for needed data. The data is located in milliseconds and appears on a television-type screen for instant viewing. Some of this equipment also comes with the ability to produce a print-out.

For example, drop in at your local electric company office to discuss your bill. The representative uses an input-output keyboard to retrieve your account from the computer. With the account on the TV screen before him, the representative can answer any of your questions. The entire procedure need not take more than a few minutes. Many other businesses have similar systems.

If you are considering such a system, it is best to determine your needs first. Then, consult different equipment manufacturers to learn what the suggested system and equipment would cost and accomplish for you and your company. The remainder of this chapter will be restricted to the traditional filing system.

The speed with which papers—correspondence, bills, or documents—can be located is the true test of any filing system. The nature and needs of the business will determine whether an alphabetical, numerical, geographic, or subject file is to be kept. Remember that no matter what the system, with the exception of the numerical, the alphabet is the true basis.

The equipment available for filing is varied. There are simple boxes with alphabetical or numerical inserts. There are file drawers in which guides are placed at intervals to divide the alphabet into its component parts. There are vertical files and lateral drawer files (see illustrations in this chapter). Some files are kept in drawers which are labeled on the outside with information on cards. (In effect, this is the same as deep drawers for papers, except that the space is much shallower and narrower.) There is also the visible file, in which cards are placed so that the bottom edge of each is visible below the edge of the card above. The title or topic of each card is printed at the bottom edge so that it is exposed for easy viewing. The cards placed in this fashion are easily accessible for new entries and, since they are hinged in place, stay in their prescribed order. Where quick and easy reference is needed for answering telephone inquiries, for instance, a wheel or circular file with guides and cards is excellent (Fig. 19.7). Whatever the equipment, a filing system must be simple, foolproof, and prevent duplication of effort or waste of time. The importance of the files may be realized if you keep in mind that many papers kept therein are irreplaceable. Whether or not files should be locked each night depends upon how important and confidential are the papers they contain.

One innovation is the use of open-shelf files, in which papers are filed on their sides, top outermost, but with the *guides* sticking out in the front of the open shelf for easy legibility. An obvious advantage is that shelving is much cheaper than sliding drawers and there is no space loss. The essentials of any good filing system may be included in the shelf arrangement.

The most important single element of any filing system is *accuracy*.

Alphabetical Filing

The most common form of filing is alphabetical (Fig. 19.4), and the most common container in which the papers are filed is the vertical file drawer. On the outside of each drawer is space for indicating the letter, letters, or portion of one letter of the alphabet contained therein. Within the drawer, a good filing system will contain guides, folders, and special classifications. Almost everything mentioned here regarding the filing of correspondence in the usual file drawer also applies to card filing.

Inside the drawers, the most prominent items are the guides, which are made of firm hardboard with a metal tab attached at one side; on these is printed the letter, section of a letter, name, or number required to suit the sequence and order used. The drawer will also contain file folders with a tab at the top usually unmarked until insertion into the drawer. Before insertion into the drawer, a label should be typed and pasted over this tab; in some systems the name is printed on with India ink or other permanent writing material. (See Fig. 19.4.)

Every office will have its own standard procedures for releasing material to the files, requisitioning material from the files, and replacing the material in the

Fig. 19.1 Vertical file drawer with suspended file folders. Note rail and hooks at end of folder tops. This is a subject file drawer. (Courtesy of Oxford Pendaflex Corp.)

Fig. 19.2 Lateral-type file drawers. Note that contents of entire drawer are visible when open. (Courtesy of Oxford Pendaflex Corp.)

Fig. 19.3 Eight-tray visible card file. (Courtesy of Acme Visible Records, Inc.)

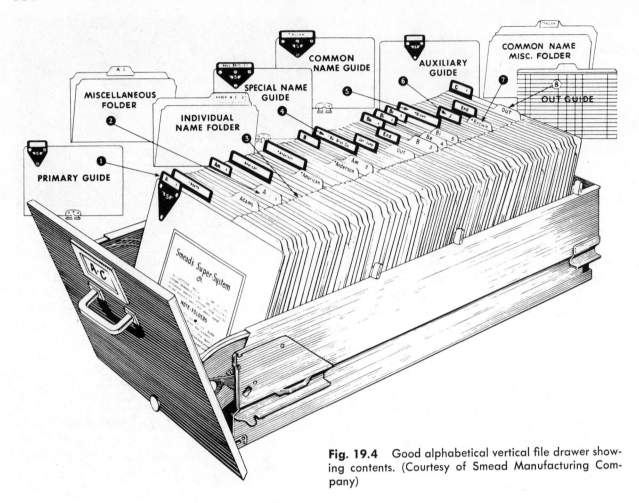

Fig. 19.4 Good alphabetical vertical file drawer showing contents. (Courtesy of Smead Manufacturing Company)

files. It is important to mark letters or memos or other material to be filed in some way so that the filing department knows it is no longer needed and may be filed. Ordinarily, the secretary or writer will initial in the upper-left corner and date the release, but an increasing number of firms are combining the stamp which marks the time of arrival with a last line for release initials. In this way there will be less likelihood of materials getting into the file before they have been acted upon. The released letter must also be marked so that it is filed in the proper place, and, should there be a possibility that the material may be sought under a different name, a cross-reference sheet is filed under the alternate name.

It is also necessary to have a simple, clear system for requesting material from the file. Requisition forms make this task easier for the filing supervisor. The requisitions can be kept in a chronological tickler file on or in the supervisor's desk. If they are stamped with the date and time of arrival, the fairest order of satisfying these requests is assured. In some cases, a folder or material from the file may be requested far in advance by an executive to avoid the last-

minute rush request. The burden is, therefore, on the file supervisor to fill these requests well in order to encourage the habit of submitting requisitions in advance, a process that makes life much simpler for the file clerks.

After the material requisitioned and obtained is no longer needed, the same release procedure is necessary. Many firms use a small rubber stamp to the right of the original, in red, where the release mark may be made. Subsequent requests for the same material may be indicated in the same way. If certain material is requested often and by various people, the filing supervisor might recommend that copies of the material in question be supplied to them to retain in order to reduce the number of requests, wear and tear on the material, and the danger of loss from frequent handling.

Marking a letter, telegram, or memorandum for filing is known as *coding*. When the executive or his secretary fails to code the letter, the filing supervisor must make the decision as to proper indexing of the name for correct storage, even if she is unable to indicate cross-referencing. *Indexing* is the correct placement of the words contained in the name of a person, company, institution, etc., according to the rules of filing in a standardized order by units.

To speed the replacement of materials into the file, sorting should be done before placing in the drawers. Depending upon whether the system is alphabetical, numerical, geographical, or by subject, the material should be placed in the correct order before filing; this prevents inefficiency. For this sorting, some companies use trays with alphabetical or numerical guides into which the papers may quickly be divided. From the tray they are placed into the regular file, one letter or number set at a time. Some companies use a sorting rack with metal or fiberboard pieces with the correct imprint at the top on a tab. By moving the pieces and dropping the paper to be filed into the opening, the materials wind up in the proper order.

In the filing drawer, behind the appropriate letter or section of the alphabet, each company with whom you correspond more than six times a year should have a file folder. Good judgment must be used; there is no fixed rule. For all those with whom you have infrequent communication, a miscellaneous folder is used at the end of the individual folders. Whenever the correspondent's volume increases, an individual folder may be prepared and all of his correspondence from the miscellaneous folder transferred.

When material from the file has been sent to some individual for his use as indicated on the requisition form, the file must show clearly that the material is "out," not missing. When an item has been removed from a folder, a substitution card is usually inserted. The substitution card is attached in some way to an "out" card which is placed in the folder indicating who has it, when he took it, and some idea of what the material was about. When the entire folder is requisitioned, the procedure is handled in much the

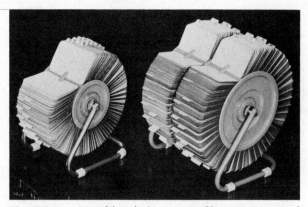

Fig. 19.6 Portable desk rotary file. (Courtesy of Wheeldex Division, LeFebure Banking Equipment Co.)

same way. One system is to leave the original folder in the file, send the material in a transfer folder, and place in the original folder an out card on which the necessary information as to location of the material is given. Another method is to send the complete folder as it stands in the file; in its place in the file an out guide is inserted. On the front of the guide is a small pocket in which is placed a card stating the location of the material. With the increasing use of photocopy machines, the need to send one or two individual papers is diminishing rapidly; the copies are sent instead with no need to return or record.

Subject Filing

In some highly diversified businesses, where dealings with the same correspondents may refer to many different areas of the business, files are kept by subject. For example, if your company manufactures tires, rubber gloves, rubberized gadgets for the kitchen, and hoses and rubberized outdoor-furniture covers, you would be dealing with four different departments of a department store—auto supplies, drugs, house furnishings, and the garden shop. Such a file is very difficult to advise on without knowing the exact needs of the situation. Only someone who knows a great deal about the inner workings of the company can organize a subject file. Captions for each subject section must be natural and meaningful. Because even the best system might leave some areas in doubt, an index is usually set up to aid in determining the correct caption or subject heading. Thus, under the broad heading *Paper* might be a subheading *Offset Duplicating*, just as one might have a main heading in an alphabetical file of *A* and under it the subheading *Ag*. The main advantage of the subject system is that the letters within that section in the file, arranged alphabetically, would all have reference to the topic of *Paper, Offset Duplicating*. The dis-

Fig. 19.5 Mechanized card file with pushbutton controls. (Courtesy of Wheeldex Division, LeFebure Banking Equipment Co.)

advantage is that a letter which refers to several different kinds of paper would have to be cross-referenced under each type mentioned in the correspondence or photocopied and placed in each section.

The file would still contain the usual guides, subguides, and file folders. The filing supervisor would have to be responsible for the coding and placement of correspondence under the proper caption or category. This supervisor would have to know the business better than one who oversees a straight alphabetical system. The index, which is ordinarily kept on a card file, would help standardize the location of all materials.

Numerical Filing

The Dewey decimal system found in all public libraries is an example of the numerical system. In place of subject titles, numbers are used to indicate subject areas which are then broken down further into subareas, and further into sub-subareas, etc. There are ten general areas; 000–099, 100–199, 200–299, 300–399, 400–499, 500–599, 600–699, 700–799, 800–899, 900–999. Each general area is divided into a specific area by tens—800—Literature, 810—American, 820—English, 830—German, etc. These areas are further divisible by ones—801, 811, 821, 834, etc. After the whole numbers, the use of decimals permits still further pinpointing of subject—e.g., 817.28. In this way we can divide the general area of natural sciences, 500, into its various large categories by tens; then, each large category may be broken down into a very specific, small area. Thus a librarian conversant with the decimal system without looking at the card catalog could easily go directly to the right section of the bookshelves if you gave him the specific topic of the text. Variations of this system might be used in a very intricate system —for instance, automobile parts, in which thousands of parts for hundreds of different areas are needed for each make.

In the library card catalog all books are listed by Dewey number in one file, and—for the use of the library users—in another file which lists books by subject, author, and title. As the card catalog is set up, you can look up a book by the subject (nonfiction), title (all), or author's name (all).

For the same reason and in the same way, the office type of numerical filing system, which is much simpler than the Dewey system, requires the same treatment. One card file must be kept which identifies by number the contents of each numbered file folder. One card file must be kept by alphabetical arrangement for any name which might be found in each numbered file folder, and, of course, include the number so it may be located.

Most often, however, requests for a specific file refer to the name of the company or individual whose file folder is desired. The filing department must look in their card index for the number which represents that name. When the numbers are known, this is the fastest filing system of all. By indicating on separate cards the names of all persons or companies referred to in any correspondence, a great deal of cross-referencing is eliminated. For instance, looking up the Morrison Manufacturing Company indicates file folder 345; looking up Morrison, Robert, also indicates file folder 345; there might even be another name or two which would yield the same folder number. This is, in effect, a cross-reference system. In the traditional alphabetical system, if we had looked for a folder for Morrison, Robert, a cross-reference sheet would have instructed us to go to the folder for the Morrison Manufacturing Company.

Geographical Filing

For trucking concerns, railroads, or other endeavors which depend to a great extent on the location of a customer or correspondent, a system of filing by states, counties, cities, towns, or other geographical area might be advisable. A mail-order company uses a ZIP Code system. The geographical filing system of one trucking company was arranged by major trucking routes. On the wall of the filing room was a mural indicating each route in a different color. There were separate file sets for each route in which the geographical system was carried out. For instance, let us assume there is a freeway running through Ohio, Illinois, Indiana, and South Dakota which is used in the business of this trucking company. Let us name it the Four-State Freeway, Route 111. One set of files would be a specific color and the contents would be arranged in alphabetical order—Illinois, Indiana, Ohio, and South Dakota. Within each state the names of all correspondents would be in alphabetical order, first by city or town name, and then by the name of the correspondent. This is in effect a sectional geographical system. The only filing system the author has seen which is truly on a national basis is that of a prominent airline.

Companies which sell on a national scale and which have salesmen assigned by territory will arrange their sales files geographically with a different color or color combination for each territory. The various arrangements may be constructed to suit the needs of each business. It was once rumored that a slick gang had a street-by-street geographical file of about half of Greater London for their petty-thievery ring. The head of the ring must have been a former filing supervisor!

Miscellaneous Filing Systems

When an alphabetical filing system has a very large number of names, a combination system, known as *alpha-numeric filing*, is an ingenious simplification and aid. This system does not interfere with the basic system because correspondence is generally called for by name. Withdrawal from the file is alphabetic, but replacement is numeric. The latter will make filing back six to ten times faster. Of course, color is an integral part of the system too.

In those companies where it is important, a *catalog file* can be very helpful. The folder has a wide, flat bottom to accommodate the thicknesses of filed catalogs or reference manuals.

The *visible-card file* is a file in which cards (from 3″ × 5″ to 5″ × 8″) fit into a cardboard pocket which has a transparent plastic bottom edge. Identifying the contents of the card on the bottom line, the information stays visible when the card fits into the transparent plastic bottom edge; the holders with the cards attached may be placed in alphabetical or numerical order. This type of file system is usually designed for a purpose which combines a definite order with the ability to write information on the cards from time to time. To facilitate handling of these card holders, they are generally fitted into flat trays which in turn slide into narrow slots in a cabinet. Only the front edge of the tray shows; these are identified exactly as the front panels of file drawers are. The method is called a visible-card file because the names are visible as they overlap each other from front to back of the tray with a row of transparent plastic strips. In order to see or use the full card the edge of the plastic strip before it and any other beyond must be flipped over toward the rear of the tray on hinges. The desired card then lies exposed. When the card has been used, the cards are placed flat again and the tray slides back into the opening.

On the transparent plastic strip most companies use small pieces of colored plastic or metal as signals. For instance, a red square marker might mean, in the case of an inventory system, that when the balance on hand reaches fifty the purchasing agent is to be notified of this fact. On others a blue square might mean a balance of a hundred; green, a balance of twenty-five. Round markers might mean other things, triangular still others. In the use of the visible-card file for accounts receivable, a red marker might mean a credit limit of fifty dollars, blue a hundred dollars, and so on, with a double red indicating "cash only." There are as many applications of this file as there are places of business.

A *tickler file* refers to any system of organized reminders kept in a file arrangement. A desk calendar pad will be sufficient for the needs of most; it is a tickler. For more elaborate requirements, a card index could be kept on the desk with guides arranged according to the days of the week, months of the year, or whatever is necessary. In situations in which a more elaborate system than that is called for, a desk drawer or a special insert for a desk drawer might serve best. It is ideally suited to those who are required by law or other compulsions to work by the calendar. A simple example of the use of an elaborate tickler file would be for a magazine which wishes to notify subscribers that they are reaching the end of their subscription and, eventually, to remove their names or indicate the extent of the renewal. A more common example would be an insurance agent who keeps the dates of the expiration of policies in order to warn clients that they are reaching the end of their coverage period, especially

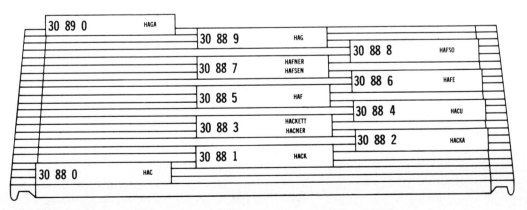

Fig. 19.7 Alpha-numeric filing. (Courtesy of Oxford Pendaflex Corp.)

in types of insurance taken for prescribed periods.

Most office desks may be obtained with one double-depth drawer. It is becoming increasingly popular to insert in this drawer a filing arrangement to contain materials used often, and so save a lot of delay and inconvenience. These drawers may be used in the conventional way with guides and file folders. But it is more advisable to use a filing arrangement in which the guide is a combination guide and folder suspended in the drawer by its left and right edges. Since both sides slide freely on two thin bars, it is easy to reach any folder for any material in as long as it takes to open a drawer, read the correct guide, and find what is needed. It is also quite effective in keeping the desktop as clear of extraneous matter as can be expected in a normal working day. Someone once remarked that one should beware the executive who has an entirely clear desk: he has swept all his problems aside to be solved at some other time. Perhaps not; maybe he has installed this type of hanging file folder system.

Transfer and Disposition

The length of time materials will be kept in the file will depend on need, law, and type. Logically, some business firms keep materials too long, wasting valuable space; others destroy them too soon, causing expenditures to reconstruct the necessary information. Under the increasing number of regulations of federal and state agencies, certain rules and laws must be complied with. In some cases the wonderful expedient of microfilming is not suitable, as the original is the only legal document acceptable.

Federal Agency	Nature of record	Time period
Interstate Commerce Commission	Freight reports	Two years
Civil Aeronautics Board	Flight movements	Six years
Fair Labor Standards Act	Employee earnings	Three years
U.S. Labor Department (Walsh–Healey Act)	Time cards	Four years
Federal Power Commission	Repair reports	Six years

There are many, many more examples which can be given. Obviously, you must suit the method to the legal needs of your business. Whatever the filing system and whatever its equipment, it must be flexible —to be made smaller if oversized or expanded if undersized. Filing is a big, serious job that is vital to the smooth running of the modern office.

Criteria of a Good System

A good filing system skillfully engineered must meet certain basic criteria to be of real and lasting value.

1 It must be easily teachable to newcomers to the filing department without unnecessary loss of time.
2 The equipment and system must be capable of speedy operation so that the cost of locating or replacing each unit is kept at a minimum.
3 The system must be flexible to meet demands for extra space without confusion or extreme changes in procedure.
4 The contents of drawers or shelves must be clearly lighted to prevent loss of time due to poor visibility.
5 Guides and other signposts must be easily discernible and distinguishable.
6 A manual of filing procedures must be available at all times to maintain uniformity of decision in storing materials.
7 Color should be used to advantage to simplify the work of filing and finding.
8 Wherever possible, the bottom drawers should be used for more permanently stored materials, to avoid awkward and uncomfortable bending. If the file drawers are higher than eye level, drawers above that height should likewise be for storage of less frequently used materials.
9 Some responsible, reliable person with supervisory ability should be in full charge of the system agreed upon. Preferably this supervisor should be one fully familiar with the technical rules of filing, the proper use of the equipment, and the needs of the business.
10 Everyone must be made "file conscious" so that all papers around the office are kept moving *to* the files where they belong without delay. The faster they get there, the easier they will be to find when needed, which is obviously to everyone's advantage.

Basic Filing Rules

Since all filing is done by surname or firm name, all rules refer to indexing. (Indexing is the rearranging of names for filing purposes.)

1 Names of individuals are placed in indexed order as last name (surname or family name), first name, middle name or initial, and any known title

other than *Mr.* at the end in parentheses. When the first name is not a common one for a man or is very unusual, Mr. should be indicated also.

Prof. Harold James Doe =	Doe, Unit 1*	Harold Unit 2	James Unit 3	(Prof.) Unit 4

2 Names of companies which contain an individual's full name are similarly indexed for the person's name.

Jane Doe Cosmetic Company =	Doe, Unit 1	Jane, Unit 2	Cosmetic Unit 3	Company Unit 4
Thomas A. Edison, Inc. =	Edison,	Thomas	A.,	Inc.

3 Names of companies which do not contain the full name of an individual are indexed as given except for unimportant words in the name.

The Fullerton Company =	Fullerton Unit 1	Company Unit 2	(The)

Harry the Tailor =	Harry Unit 1	(the) Tailor Unit 2

Smith Container Corporation =	Smith Unit 1	Container Unit 2	Corporation Unit 3

4 Names of companies which contain a number are indexed as though the number were spelled out in letters.

66 Park Avenue Corporation =	Sixty-six Unit 1	Park Unit 2	Avenue Unit 3	Corporation Unit 4

The Unholy 3 Club =	Unholy Unit 1	Three Unit 2	Club Unit 3	(The)

5 Names of companies containing individual letters of the alphabet index each letter as a separate unit.

AAA Collision Works =	A Unit 1	A Unit 2	A Unit 3	Collision Unit 4	Works Unit 5

6 In alphabetizing, follow the principle that a unit with nothing following precedes a unit with something following. (*A* with nothing following precedes *Acme;* see below.)

	1st Unit	2nd Unit	3rd Unit
AAA Collision Works =	A	A	A
Acme Stationery Company =	Acme	Stationery	Company
BO Caterers =	B	O	Caterers
Band Leaders Club =	Band	Leaders	Club
C & L Furniture House =	C (and)	L	Furniture
Chase and Sanborn =	Chase (and)	Sanborn	

(Listed in correct alphabetical order.)

7 Names of individuals containing letters of the alphabet are treated similarly to those in firm names.

	1st Unit	2nd Unit	3rd Unit
J. L. Sullivan =	Sullivan	J.	L.
J. Lee Sullivan =	Sullivan	J.	Lee
John L. Sullivan =	Sullivan	John	L.
John Lee Sullivan =	Sullivan	John	Lee

(These are given in correct alphabetical order.)

8 Persons whose names contain a hyphen are indexed as though the hyphen did not exist; company names with hyphens are treated as separate units on either side of the hyphen unless the word syllabicated represents a hyphenated dictionary word.

	1st Unit	2nd Unit	3rd Unit
Thomas Kent-Smith =	Kentsmith	Thomas	
Antony-Cleopatra Salon =	Antony	Cleopatra	Salon
Co-Operative Dairy League =	Co-Operative	Dairy	League

9 Certain company names begin with two words which might easily be treated as such. It is best, however, to treat these as one word and to train all filing personnel to do likewise.

North West
Airlines   = Northwest Airlines
Northwest Airlines = Northwest Airlines
Air Plane Parts,
   Inc.   = Airplane Parts Inc.
Airplane Parts, Inc. = Airplane Parts Inc.
House Boat
   Supplies Com-
   pany   = Houseboat Supplies Company

10 Names of individuals containing prefixes are considered as one connected word.

L'Adelia	indexed as Ladelia
Da Costa	indexed as Dacosta
O'Brien	indexed as Obrien
MacTavish*	indexed as Mactavish
Von der Ruhe	indexed as Vonderruhe
La Duca	indexed as Laduca
Van Dant	indexed as Vandant
du Clerque	indexed as duclerque

11 Government agencies should be indexed in logical order of branch of government, division, subdivision, and location. Such phrases as *Bureau of* and *Department of* are put in parentheses and ignored.

Department of Parks of New York City *becomes* New York City, Parks (Department of)

Income Tax Bureau of New York State *becomes* New York State, Income Tax (Bureau)

United States Government, Department of Health, Education and Welfare *is* United States Government, Health, Education and Welfare (Department of)

Federal Internal Revenue Service *becomes* United States Government, Treasury (Department of), Internal Revenue (Service)

Public School #137, Manhattan, New York *is* New York City, Education (Board of), Public School #137, Manhattan

Department of Highways, Westchester County, New York State *becomes* Westchester County, Highways (Department of), New York State

12 Married women's names consist of their given name, maiden name, and married name. If the woman is single, her name is indexed as given except that "Miss" is indicated after it in parentheses. Occasionally, a woman prefers her married name to be that of her husband preceded by "Mrs." Legally, the

* Treat all "Mc" and "Mac" names and all names with prefixes strictly alphabetically. These names are correctly alphabetized: MacTavish, M'basa, McGovern, Oates, O'Brien, Vance, Van der Hut.

latter is correct. In regular daily use for business or personal affairs, the choice is the woman's. When "Ms." is given as the title, treat it the same as "Miss."

	1st Unit	2nd Unit	3rd Unit
Miss Madge Evans	Evans	Madge (Miss)	
Mrs. Madge Evans Dale	Dale	Madge	Evans (Mrs.)
Mrs. John Curry Dale	Dale	John	Curry (Mrs.)
Ms. Sherry North	North	Sherry (Ms.)	

13 When a name might be used as is or indexed, it is wise to indicate that fact in both places in the file so that the person seeking the name either way does not feel that it is missing. This is most likely to occur with foreign names or names with titles or religious names. This practice of indicating a name in two places in the file is known as cross-referencing.

Dang Hu	or	Hu, Dang
Yen Shoo		Shoo, Yen
Prince Philip		Philip, Prince
Baron Gold		Gold, Baron
Father Ames		Ames, Father
Sister Muriel Joseph		Muriel Joseph, Sister
Madame Jessica		Jessica, Madame

In all cases given above, the name on the left is properly indexed. The one on the right is only for safety to prevent loss of time and effort in filing. For the name on the right, a dummy folder directs the seeker to the other form of the name where the file folder is actually located.

The above procedure must not be confused with normal cross-reference procedures. When your firm deals with a specific individual directly at a given company, it is always wise to indicate with cross-reference technique that the correspondence sought in the name of Mrs. Marjorie Wurtis will be found under the name of Weiss & Klau. The folder under Wurtis will be a dummy directing the file clerk to the other folder clearly and quickly.

Releasing for Filing

Papers to be filed should be clearly marked so that file clerks know that they have been released for filing. Signals for this purpose are simple. Your own correspondence is signaled by the fact that it is a carbon copy, is a certain color, and has been sent to the file department. Correspondence received from others is marked for filing by most companies by placing initials in the upper-left corner. This indicates to the file clerk without doubt that the letter is released for filing. Some firms use a time and date stamp to indicate when a letter was received. At the bottom of the stamp is a place for noting release for filing or other notation.

At the same time a letter is being initialed for release to the files, it should also be marked for any unusual considerations. For example, a name underscored and marked with an *X* can indicate the manner in which the letter is to be cross-indexed. This will provide for the eventuality that the clerk looks for the letter under the man's name instead of the company name. Either way he looks he will find the letter.

Withdrawing Filed Material

The easiest way to lose filed material is to make no record of its withdrawal. Consequently, there is no check on its return to the proper folder. Regardless of the size of the system, some record must be kept. A form may be prepared for a centralized filing system. By the use of a 3″ × 5″ card file for such a form, a follow-up method may be devised to see that all materials taken are returned to their proper location. When the material requested is on microfilm, copies may be sent and indicated on the card. Ordinarily they need not be returned. If the entire folder is requisitioned, the out guide is inserted in its place in the file as an additional signal to follow up its return. A charge-out guide should show the name of the requester, date of removal, and a description of the items. This also indicates to those searching that the items are not lost. Within a reasonable time it should be requested for return to file, generally three to five days.

In the computer-based retrieval systems, the information may appear on a console screen or as a print-out, depending upon the equipment in use. When required, the input-output operator may indicate on the electronic memory that a copy was supplied to so-and-so and the date. With the availability of smaller, less extensive, and less expensive equipment in this field, more attention will have to be devoted to secure and proper procedures for automated systems.

Appendix A

Punctuation in a Nutshell

Period

Use a period

1 at the end of a declarative or imperative sentence:

> *Tomorrow we're going to get organized.*
>
> *Put these letters in the circular file.*

2 following abbreviations:

> *Mr. Jones, the superintendent of the Highup Bldg., keeps the room temperature at 68° F. (20° C.) between 8:45 and 5:15 p.m.*

3 after an indirect question or a question that is actually a polite request and does not require a reply:

> *I asked him when his office closed.*
>
> *Will you please enclose a check for the amount due.*

4 after numbers or letters in a listing or outline (optional):

> | | |
> |---|---|
> | *1. letterhead paper* | *a president* |
> | *2. envelopes* | *b vice president* |
> | *3. carbon paper*   (or) | *c secretary* |
> | *4. erasers* | *d treasurer* |

Question Mark

Use a question mark (interrogation point)

1 to indicate a direct query:

> *Have we received his order yet?*
>
> *The letter arrived today?*

2 to express a doubt:

> *He has been with the company 23 (?) years.*

Exclamation Point

Use an exclamation point to indicate surprise, disbelief, or other strong emotion:

> *You never answered his letter!*
> *Oh! I'd forgotten all about it.*

Colon

The colon is used

1 to introduce such matter as an amplification, formal statement, list, or long quotation:

> *Take my advice: don't do it.*
>
> *A new policy has been adopted: salesmen are required to send in their expense accounts on the first day of each month.*
>
> *The parts of a letter are: (1) date line; (2) inside address; (3) salutation; . . .*
>
> *I quote from his letter: "I have used your paper clips for many years and have always found them satisfactory. Yesterday, however, as I was . . ."*

2 after the salutation of a letter or of a speaker addressing an audience:

> *Gentlemen:*
>
> *Mr. Chairman, ladies, and gentlemen:*

3 in expressing time, to separate hours from minutes:

> *His flight departs at 6:38 p.m.*

4 in expressing proportion:

> *The compression ratio of this engine is 8:1.*

Semicolon

Use a semicolon

1 to separate clauses of a compound sentence which are not connected by a conjunction:

> *The secretary gave him the letter; he read and signed it.*

2 between clauses joined by a conjunctive adverb (however, therefore, moreover, thus, yet, etc.):

> *In general, I am in favor of doing what you suggest; however, one of your proposals disturbs me.*

3 to separate phrases and clauses containing other punctuation:

> *Miss Doolittle, Mr. Smith's secretary, is intelligent, attractive, and very competent; but she always has a smudge of carbon on her nose.*
>
> *We have offices in San Francisco; Macon, Georgia; Albany, New York; Columbus, Mississippi; and Lansing, Michigan.*

Comma

Use a comma

1 to separate words, phrases, or short clauses in a series:

> *The office manager ordered a new desk, two typewriters, and a supply of erasers.*
>
> *He called Mr. Jones early in the morning, just before noon, and again late in the afternoon.*
>
> *Go into your office, sit down at your desk, and don't come out until you've written that letter!*

2 between coordinate clauses joined by a conjunction:

> *This order must be filled this morning, and it should be delivered by messenger.*

3 to set off nonrestrictive subordinate clauses and nonrestrictive phrases, that is, clauses and phrases not essential to the main thought of the sentence:

> *Mr. Allen, who has been with our firm for forty years, will retire next April.*

BUT: *A man who has been with our firm for forty years will retire next April.*

> *The new letterhead, designed especially for our firm's fiftieth anniversary, will be used beginning May 1.*

4 to set off words or phrases in apposition or in contrast:

> *George Manning, the salesman from Ohio, will visit the home office next week.*
>
> *A personal reply, not a form letter, is called for in this case.*

5 between coordinate adjectives or adverbs in a series:

> *Can you write an interesting, informative letter?*

BUT: *His excellent financial training was a factor in his promotion.*

6 after an introductory modifying phrase or clause:

> *When he walked into the office, everyone stood up to greet him.*

7 to set off words of direct address:

> *The solution, John, is never to give him credit.*

8 to set off the year in dates:

> *On May 14, 1955, Mr. Smith opened a small office on Narrow Street.*

9 to separate the parts of an address:

> *Please send this package to Richard Haynes, 655 Terrace Street, Smithtown, Illinois.*

10 to set off parenthetical words, phrases, or clauses:

> *The message, you know, was not delivered until noon.*
>
> *This book, in my opinion, is the best on the subject.*

11 to set off a short quotation:

> *He said, "Sign those letters for me," and left the office.*

12 to indicate an omission:

> *Jim sold three typewriters this week; Tom, two.*

13 to set off such designations as *Jr., Sr., Esq., Ph.D.*:

> *Thomas Walton, Jr., has taken over as president of his father's firm.*

Quotation Marks

Use quotation marks

1 to enclose words of direct quotation:

> *"What do you think of this approach?" he asked.*

BUT: *He said that the letter was sent.*

2 at the beginning of each paragraph of quotations of two or more consecutive paragraphs, but at the end of the last paragraph only.

Apostrophe

Use an apostrophe

1 to indicate the omission of a letter or letters in a contraction:

> *Don't you think that's a good idea?*

2 before the *s* in forming the possessive of a singu-
lar noun; before the *s* in forming the possessive of a plural noun not ending in *s;* after the *s* in forming the possessive of a plural noun ending in *s:*

> *the man's hat   the ladies' hats*
> *the men's hats*

Dash

A dash is used

1 to indicate a sudden interruption in thought:

> *Miss Agnes Doolittle—her address is in the file—should receive a copy of this letter.*

2 instead of commas, if the meaning is thus made clearer:

> *The parts of a letter—inside address, date, salutation, etc.—are given in Chapter 2 of this book.*

Parentheses

Parentheses are used to set off words, phrases, and clauses which are not essential to the main statement, or to indicate a greater interruption in thought than would be indicated by commas or dashes:

> *The Smithville (Pa.) Variety Store is one of our new customers.*

> *Marian Bartlett (née Moss) has handled this account for years.*

> *I am replying in great haste (your letter arrived only an hour ago) to ask you to reconsider signing a contract with him.*

Words Frequently Misspelled and Misused

Preferred Spellings

abridgment	chancellor	distill	forswear	labeled
accede	changeable	distributor	fulfill	lacquer
accessible	characterize	divisible	furor	legible
accessory	chlorophyll	dossier	gaiety	leveled
accommodate	cigarette	dreamed	gasoline	libeled
accumulate	coconut	dueled	gauge	license
acknowledgment	coerce	dullness	generalize	likable
acoustic	collapsible	durable	glamorous	liquefy
acquire	collectible	ecstasy	glamour	liter
admirable	colossal	edible	good-by	livable
admissible	combustible	eligible	gray	madam
advertise	comfortable	embarrass	grievous	manageable
adviser	committee	emphasize	hemorrhage	maneuver
aging	communicable	employee	heterogeneous	manikin
airplane	compatible	enameled	homogeneity	marketable
align	comprehensible	encase	hypocrisy	marshal
all right	compromise	enclose	idiosyncrasy	marshaled
aluminum	connoisseur	endorsement	idyl	marveled
ambassador	consensus	enforcement	impaneled	marvelous
analyze	consummate	enroll	impel	meager
answerable	contemptible	enterprise	imperceptible	medieval
apologize	controvertible	entrench	imperiled	merchandise
appall	convertible	equaled	imposter	mileage
aquatic	conveyor	exceed	improvise	milieu
aqueduct	corollary	exhaustible	indispensable	millennium
ascendance	corruptible	exhibitor	innocuous	misspell
assassinate	credible	exorbitant	innovation	moccasin
audible	criticize	fallible	innuendo	modeled
battalion	deductible	fantasy	inoculate	modeler
believable	defensible	feasible	inquire	mold
beneficent	deplorable	fiber	insistence	molt
benefited	determinable	flammable	install	monopolize
bloc (combination)	develop	flexible	instill	movable
breakable	diagramed	fluorescent	insure	nearby
burned	diagrammatic	focused	intelligible	negligible
caffeine	dialed	forbade	interceptor	neighbor
caliber	dilettante	forcible	iridescent	occur
canceled	discernible	forego (precede)	jeopardize	occurrence
cancellation	disenfranchise	foresee	judgment	offense
capable	dispatch	forgettable	kerosene	omelet
casualty	dissatisfied	forgo (do without)	knowledgeable	oneself

ostensible	promissory	responsible	subtlety	tranquilizer
paneled	propellent	rivaled	succeed	transatlantic
paraffin	quarreled	sacrilegious	suggestible	transferable
paralleled	questionnaire	salable	supersede	transferred
parceled	queue	satellite	supervise	transship
partisan	rarefy	savable	surprise	traveled
pastime	rarity	savior	surreptitious	tying
peaceable	ratable	savor	surveillance	typify
peddler	rattan	secede	susceptible	understandable
penciled	raveled	seize	synonymous	usable
perishable	recognize	sensible	taboo	vacillate
permissible	reconnaissance	separate	tactician	vicissitude
plaque	reconnoiter	shellacking	tangible	villain
plausible	referable	siege	tattoo	visible
plow	reinforce	siphon	taxied	vying
possible	reliable	skeptic	technique	washable
practice	relieve	skillful	theater	whisky
precede	renaissance	smolder	threshold	willful
pretense	reorganize	soliloquy	tie	withhold
privilege	reparable	stenciled	tied	woolen
proceed	repellent	stratagem	today	workable
proffer	reprehensible	stubbornness	totaled	X-ray
programmatic	respectable	stupefy	trafficking	

Problem Plurals

Because our English (or American) language is an amalgam of many tongues, some plurals may be troublesome. Here are some:

Singular	Plural	Singular	Plural
addendum	addenda	larva	larvae
alumna (fem.)	alumnae	maidservant	maidservants
alumnus (masc.)	alumni (also mixed)	madam	mesdames
analysis	analyses	manservant	menservants
appendix	appendixes, appendices	memorandum	memorandums, memoranda
attorney general	attorneys general		
bacillus	bacilli	moose	moose
bacterium	bacteria	mother-in-law	mothers-in-law
basis	bases	nebula	nebulae
cactus	cacti	oasis	oases
crisis	crises	parenthesis	parentheses
curriculum	curriculums, curricula	phenomenon	phenomena
datum	data	radius	radiuses, radii
deer	deer	secretary general	secretaries general
fish	fish (same kind), fishes	secretary of state	secretaries of state
focus	focuses, foci	stimulus	stimuli
formula	formulas, formulae	stratum	strata
genus	genera	synopsis	synopses
gladiolus	gladioluses, gladioli	terminus	termina
hypothesis	hypotheses	thesis	theses
iris	irises	vortex	vortices

Hyphenated Words

All words beginning with "self" are hyphenated, except "selfish" and "selfless." All "over" and "under" words are *not* hyphenated, as in "overlook." Some words beginning with "ex" are not hyphenated, but most are when it means "no longer." All words containing "in-law" are hyphenated. However, some words require hyphens when combined one way, but do not when combined another. Some examples are:

With	Without
an air-cooled engine	an engine that is air cooled
a cross-country race	the race is cross country
an easy-going fellow (old spelling)	the fellow is easygoing (new spelling)
first-rate performance	a performance that is first rate
first-class mail	send the letter first class
with three-hit pitching	the pitcher allowed three hits
an iron-bound case (old spelling)	the case is ironbound (new spelling)
an up-to-date version	this version is up to date
a well-known actor	the actor is well known
a well-to-do woman	a woman who is well-to-do*
a full-grown plant	a plant that is full grown

Words Often Confused

absorb: take in
adsorb: cause to adhere

accede: yield
exceed: surpass

accept: receive
except: take or leave out

acetic: acid
ascetic: austere

adapt: adjust
adept: skillful
adopt: take as one's own

adverse: unfavorable
averse: unwilling, disinclined

affect: influence
effect: result

affective: emotional
effective: producing a desired result

aid: assist, assistance, assistant
aide: assistant, esp. military or naval

all ready: prepared
already: previously

alternate: every other (time, object, etc.)
alternative: choice (of one of two)

apprise: inform
apprize: appraise

ascent: rise
assent: consent

awhile: for some time
a while: a short time

bazaar: a fair
bizarre: fantastic

biweekly: every two weeks
semiweekly: twice a week

born: brought into existence
borne: carried

bouillon: soup
bullion: metal

callus (noun)
callous (adjective)

canvas: cloth
canvass: solicit

capital: city
capitol: building

carat: weight
caret: insertion mark

caster: roller
castor: oil

casual: accidental, incidental
causal: producing a result

climactic: pertaining to a climax
climatic: pertaining to climate

complacent: satisfied
complaisant: obliging

complement: that which completes
compliment: flattery

comprehensible: intelligible
comprehensive: large in scope

comprise: include
constitute: make up

condole: sympathize
condone: excuse

confidant: one who is confided in
confident: sure

connotation: suggestive meaning
denotation: explicit meaning

contemptible: deserving contempt
contemptuous: showing contempt

continual: lasting, but with interruptions
continuous: lasting, without interruptions

councilor: member of a council
counselor: adviser

decent: respectable
descent: decline
dissent: oppose

depravation: corruption
deprivation: depriving or being deprived

device (noun)
devise (verb)

discreet: prudent
discrete: distinct

disinterested: not influenced by personal considerations
uninterested: indifferent

dyeing: coloring
dying: losing life

elicit: draw out
illicit: unlawful

emigrate: move from one's country
immigrate: move to another country

envelop (verb)
envelope (noun)

dual: twofold
duel: contest between two opponents

equable: uniform, calm
equitable: fair

exposé (noun)
expose (verb)

extant: in existence
extent: range

farther: at a greater distance
further: to a greater degree, in addition

* an exception.

fewer: denoting numbers (*fewer letters*)

less: denoting quantity (*less responsibility*)

forbear: endure
forebear: ancestor

forgo: relinquish
forego: precede

guarantee (verb)
guaranty (noun)

guerrilla: (member of) irregular fighting band
gorilla: ape

healthful: producing health
healthy: having health

homogeneous: consisting of similar parts
homogenous: alike in origin

indict: accuse
indite: compose

inequity: unfairness
iniquity: sin

ingenious: skillful
ingenuous: simple

interment: burial
internment: detention

lath: wooden slat
lathe: machine

liable: exposed to risk of something undesirable
likely: probable

linage: number of written or printed lines
lineage: descent

liquor: an alcoholic beverage
liqueur: a particular type of alcoholic beverage

loath: reluctant
loathe: detest

luxuriant: abundant
luxurious: appealing to sense, usually costly

maize: corn
maze: labyrinth

mantel: shelf
mantle: cloak

millenary: pertaining to a thousand
millinery: hats

mucus (noun)
mucous (adjective)

official: authorized
officious: meddlesome

ordinance: regulation
ordnance: military supplies

peremptory: decisive
preemptory: preference

perquisite: privilege
prerequisite: requirement

personal: private
personnel: group of employed persons

perspective: view
prospective: expected

phosphorous (adjective)
phosphorus (noun)

practicable: feasible
practical: suitable for use

precedence: priority
precedents: examples for future action

principal: chief
principle: tenet

prophecy (noun)
prophesy (verb)

scent: odor
cent: coin
sent: shipped

selvage: edging
salvage: save

sensual: indulging the senses
sensuous: appealing to the senses

sewage: waste
sewerage: drain system

sometime: formerly, at some unspecified time
sometimes: occasionally

spacious: roomy
specious: plausible

specie: coin
species: variety

stationary: fixed
stationery: paper

statue: sculpture
stature: height
statute: law

therefor: for it
therefore: for that reason

timber: wood
timbre: tone

tortuous: twisting
torturous: painful

troop: an armed force, group of people
troupe: a company of actors

valance: drapery
valence: chemical combining power

waiver: release
waver: hesitate between choices

Appendix C

Abbreviations*

a. *acre (surface measure)*
A. *acre*
abbr. *abbreviation*
AC, A.C., a-c *alternating current*
A/C, a/c, ac *account*
acc. *acceptance, according, account*
acct. *account, accountant*
acpt. *acceptance able*
actg. *acting*
A.D. *anno Domini*
ad. *add, advertisement*
add *addition, additional, address*
adj. *adjustment*
admin. *administration, administrator*
adv. *advertisement*
agcy. *agency*
agr., agri., agric. *agriculture, agricultural*
agt. *agent, agreement*
Ala. *Alabama*
alt. *altitude, alternate*
A.M., a.m. *ante meridiem*
amp. *ampere(s)*
amt. *amount*
anon. *anonymous*
ans. *answer, answered*
A/Pay. *accounts payable*
approx. *approximately*
apt. *apartment*
A/Rec. *accounts receivable*
arith. *arithmetic, arithmetical*
Ariz. *Arizona*
Ark. *Arkansas*
arr. *arranged, arrival*
asgd. *assigned*
assn. *association*
assoc. *associate, association*
asst. *assistant*
atm. *atmosphere*
att., attn., atten. *attention*
atty. *attorney*

at. wt. *atomic weight*
aux., auxil. *auxiliary*
av., avg. *average*
avdp. *avoirdupois*
Ave. *avenue*
b. *born*
bal. *balance*
bbl. *barrel(s)*
B.C. *before Christ*
bd. *board, bond*
bd. ft. *board foot (feet)*
bdl. *bundle*
bg.(s) *bag(s)*
b.h.p. *brake horsepower*
bkt. *basket*
B/L., b.l. *bill of lading*
bldg. *building*
Blvd. *Boulevard*
b.m. *board measure*
b.o. *buyer's option*
B/P *bills payable*
bro. *brother*
bros. *brothers*
B.S. *balance sheet*
B.T.U. *British thermal units*
bu. *bushel(s)*
bx.(s) *box(es)*
C. *centigrade*
C.A., c.a. *chief accountant, controller of accounts, commercial agent*
C/A *capital account, credit account, current account*
Cal. *large calorie*
cal. *small calorie*
Calif. *California*
canc. *canceled, cancellation*
cap. *capital*
Capt. *Captain*
car. *carat*
c.b.d. *cash before delivery*
cc., c.c. *cubic centimeter*
cf. *compare*
C.F.I., c.f.i. *cost, freight, and insurance*
ch., chap. *chapter*

C.I.F., c.i.f. *cost, insurance, and freight*
circ. *circular*
ck. *check*
cl. *claim, class, clearance*
c.l. *carload, carload lots*
clk. *clerk, clock*
cm. *centimeter*
cml. *commercial*
Co. *Company*
c/o *care of, carried over*
C.O.D., c.o.d. *cash on delivery, collect on delivery*
Colo. *Colorado*
comm. *commerce, commission, committee*
Conn. *Connecticut*
cont. *continued*
contr. *contract*
contrib. *contribution, contributor*
Corp. *Corporation*
corr., corresp. *correspondence*
c.p. *candlepower*
cps. *coupons*
cr. *credit, creditor*
C.S., c.s. *capital stock, civil service*
ct. *court*
cu. *cubic*
cur. *currency, current*
C.W.O., c.w.o. *cash with order*
cwt. *hundredweight*
C.Z. *Canal Zone*
d. *died*
da. *day(s)*
d.b.a. *doing business as*
DC, D.C., d.c. *direct current*
D.C. *District of Columbia*
D.D., D/D *demand draft*
dd. *delivered*
D.D.S. *Doctor of Dental Surgery*
dec. *deceased*

Del. *Delaware*
dept. *department*
diff. *difference*
dir. *director*
disc. *discount*
distr. *distribute, distribution*
div. *dividend, division*
D/L *demand loan*
do. *(ditto) the same*
doz. *dozen*
dr. *debit, debtor, dram(s)*
Dr. *Drive, Doctor*
dup. *duplicate*
dwt. *pennyweight*
ea. *each*
ed. *edited, edition, editor*
e.g. *for example*
E.M.F., e.m.f., emf *electromagnetic force*
enc. *enclosure*
e.o.m. *end of month*
equiv. *equivalent*
est. *established*
et al. *and others*
etc. *and so forth*
exch. *exchange, exchequer*
exp. *expense, export, express*
ext. *extension*
F. *Fahrenheit*
fed. *federal, federation*
ff. *following (pages)*
fig. *figure*
fin. *financial*
f.i.o. *free in and out*
Fla. *Florida*
fn. *footnote*
f.o.b. *free on board*
fol. *following*
for. *foreign*
ft. *foot, feet*
ft-lb, ft.-lb. *foot-pound*
fut. *future*
fwd. *forward*
g., gm. *gram*
Ga. *Georgia*
gal. *gallon(s)*

* For Official U.S. Postal Service two-letter abbreviations for States see Chapter 14.

gds. *goods*
gen. *general*
gr. *grain(s), gross*
guar. *guaranteed*
hhd. *hogshead(s)*
Hon. *Honorable*
hr. *hour(s)*
ht. *height*
I. *Island*
ibid. *in the same place*
i.e. *that is*
ill., illus., illust. *illustrated, illustration*
Ill. *Illinois*
in. *inch(es)*
Inc. *Incorporated*
incl. *inclusive*
incr. *increased, increasing*
Ind. *Indiana*
init. *initial*
insp. *inspector*
inst. *instant, instrument*
instr. *instruments, instructor*
internat. *international*
introd. *introduction*
inv. *invoice*
irreg. *irregular(ly)*
ital. *italic*
Jr. *Junior*
Kans. *Kansas*
kc., kc *kilocycle(s)*
km. *kilometer*
kv *kilovolt(s)*
kw *kilowatt(s)*
K.W.H., kw-h, kw-hr *kilowatt hour(s)*
Ky. *Kentucky*
l. *liter*
La. *Louisiana*
lat. *latitude*
lb. *pound(s)*
L/C, l/c *letter of credit*
L.C.L., l.c.l. *less than carload lot*
leg. *legal*
legis. *legislation, legislature, legislative*
lg., lge. *large*
liq. *liquid*
long. *longitude*
l.t. *long ton*
Ltd. *Limited*
lv. *leave*
m. *meter*
M *thousand*
manuf. *manufacture*

Mass. *Massachusetts*
math. *mathematics*
max. *maximum*
Md. *Maryland*
M.D. *Doctor of Medicine*
memo. *memorandum*
met. *metropolitan*
mfr. *manufacture, manufacturer*
mg. *milligram*
mi. *mile(s)*
Mich. *Michigan*
min. *minute(s), minimum*
Minn. *Minnesota*
Mlle. *Mademoiselle*
mm. *millimeter*
Mme. *Madame*
mo. *month(s)*
Mo. *Missouri*
M.O., m.o. *money order*
Mont. *Montana*
mph, m.p.h. *miles per hour*
Mr. *Mister*
Mrs. *Mistress*
mtg. *meeting, mortgage*
mtge. *mortgage*
mtn. *mountain*
mts. *mountains*
mun. *municipal*
nat. *national, native, natural*
natl. *national*
N.C. *North Carolina*
N.D., n.d. *no date*
N. Dak. *North Dakota*
Nebr. *Nebraska*
neg. *negative*
Nev. *Nevada*
N.H. *New Hampshire*
N. Mex. *New Mexico*
no. *number*
nr. *near*
N.S., n.s. *not specified*
nt. wt. *net weight*
N.Y. *New York*
obs. *observation, obsolete*
o/c *overcharge*
off. *offered, officer, official*
Okla. *Oklahoma*
o.r. *owner's risk*
ord. *order*
Oreg. *Oregon*
oz. *ounce(s)*
p. *page*
Pa. *Pennsylvania*
par. *paragraph, parallel*
paren. *parenthesis*
parens. *parentheses*

pass. *passenger*
pat. *patent, patented*
payt. *payment*
pc. *piece, price(s)*
p.c. *per cent, post card*
P/C, p/c *petty cash, prices current*
P.D., p.d. *per diem*
pd. *paid*
per. *period, person*
perm. *permanent*
pert. *pertaining*
pfd. *preferred*
pk. *pack, park, peak, peck(s)*
pkg. *package*
pkt. *packet*
Pl. *Place*
P.M., p.m. *post meridiem*
pmk. *postmark*
pmkd. *postmarked*
p.n., P/N *promissory note*
p.o.d. *pay on delivery*
pop. *population*
p.o.r. *pay on return*
ppd. *postpaid*
P.R. *Puerto Rico*
prec. *preceding*
pref. *preferred*
prelim. *preliminary*
prep. *prepare, preparation*
prin. *principal*
prob. *probably, problem*
Prof. *Professor*
propr. *proprietor*
prov. *province*
ps. *pieces*
P.S., p.s. *postscript*
pt. *part, payment, pint*
pts. *parts, pints*
pub. *public, published, publisher*
q. *quintal*
qt. *quart(s)*
ques. *question*
quot. *quotation*
rd. *rod*
Rd. *Road*
rec. *receipt, record*
recd. *received*
rec. sec. *recording secretary*
reg. *registered, region, regulation*
req. *required*
res. *reserve, residence, resigned*
resp. *respective(ly), respondent*

ret. *returned, retired*
Rev. *Reverend*
R.I. *Rhode Island*
riv. *river*
rms. *rooms*
rpm, r.p.m. *revolutions per minute*
rt. *right*
Rt. Rev. *Right Reverend*
S, s. *South*
S.C. *South Carolina*
S. Dak. *South Dakota*
sec. *second(s), secretary*
sect. *section*
secy. *secretary*
sel. *selected*
ser. *series*
shpt. *shipment*
shtg. *shortage*
sig. *signature*
soc. *society*
spec. *special*
sp. gr. *specific gravity*
sq. *square*
Sr. *Senior*
St. *Street*
stge. *storage*
stk. *stock*
subs. *substitute*
supt. *superintendent*
t. *tonneau*
T. *ton(s)*
temp. *temperature*
Tenn. *Tennessee*
Terr. *terrace, territory*
Tex. *Texas*
trans. *transactions*
transf. *transferred*
transl. *translation*
transp. *transportation*
ult. *ultimate, ultimately*
v. *volt*
v., vs. *versus*
Va. *Virginia*
v.d. *various dates*
V.I. *Virgin Islands*
vol(s). *volume(s)*
Vt. *Vermont*
Wash. *Washington (state)*
Wis. *Wisconsin*
wk. *week(s)*
W.Va. *West Virginia*
Wyo. *Wyoming*
yd. *yard(s)*
yr. *year(s), your*
z. *zone*

Proofreader's Marks

In every office in which typewritten or printed material is prepared, proofreading must be done. When it is, uniform and recognized symbols should be used to facilitate understanding between the people involved. There are many of these symbols, but a small number of frequently used ones will serve the needs of most:

Mark	*Meaning*	*Example*
^	Insert	It is ^not^ my problem.
ℓ	Delete	most ~~of the~~ people
∽	Transpose	have ⁀ also been
⌒	Close up horizontally	service ⌒ man
#	Add horizontal space	an excellent # point
>	Add vertical space	> A Use of telephone B Taking of messages
<	Close up vertical space	< a Shorthand b Typewriting
/ ℓc	Use lower case	ℓc for the ⌀eneral
≡	Capitalize	East is ≡ east.
⊏	Move to left	⊏ What is the cause
⊐	Move to the right	⊐ of the problem which is
¶	New paragraph or indent to paragraph	has been proven. ¶ Meanwhile,
Ⓐ	Insert; move other copy down, insert copy attached marked Ⓐ	when the time comes. Ⓐ Therefore, it may be more fruitful to
. . . .	Let it stand	It is important ~~that~~ you do (stet)
—	Italics	a necessary evil (ital)
○	Spell in full (circled word)	There are ③ possibilities